Transmitted Wounds

Transmitted Wounds
Media and the Mediation of Trauma

Amit Pinchevski

UNIVERSITY PRESS

Oxford University Press is a department of the University of Oxford. It furthers
the University's objective of excellence in research, scholarship, and education
by publishing worldwide. Oxford is a registered trade mark of Oxford University
Press in the UK and certain other countries.

Published in the United States of America by Oxford University Press
198 Madison Avenue, New York, NY 10016, United States of America.

© Oxford University Press 2019

First published as an Oxford University Press paperback 2021

All rights reserved. No part of this publication may be reproduced, stored in
a retrieval system, or transmitted, in any form or by any means, without the
prior permission in writing of Oxford University Press, or as expressly permitted
by law, by license, or under terms agreed with the appropriate reproduction
rights organization. Inquiries concerning reproduction outside the scope of the
above should be sent to the Rights Department, Oxford University Press, at the
address above.

You must not circulate this work in any other form
and you must impose this same condition on any acquirer.

CIP data is on file at the Library of Congress
ISBN 978-0-19-062558-0 (hardback)
ISBN 978-0-19-760079-5 (paperback)

CONTENTS

Acknowledgments   vii

Introduction: The Mediation of Failed Mediation   1

1. Radiocasting Trauma   22

2. Videography and Testimony   43

3. Screen Trauma   65

4. Virtual Testimony and the Digital Future of Traumatic Past   87

5. Virtual Therapy and the Digital Future of Traumatic Past   112

Conclusion: Wounding Transmissions   139

Notes   147
Index   175

ACKNOWLEDGMENTS

I am grateful to Paul Frosh, Sharrona Pearl, John Durham Peters, Anna Reading, and Katie Trumpener who read advanced drafts and versions. The book is better thanks to their generosity and invaluable suggestions. To Dori Laub, Shoshana Felman, and the late Geoffrey Hartman for tolerating my take on their work. At the Fortunoff Archive of Yale University I thank Joanne Rudoff and Stephen Naron. Others offered advice, assistance, and free association: Tamar Ashuri, Roy Brand, Lilie Chouliaraki, Daniel Dayan, Isabel Capeloa Gil, Wolfgang Ernst, Bernhard Dionysus Geoghegan, Ruth HaCohen, Andreas Huyssen, Zohar Kampf, Amanda Lagerkvist, Hadar Levy, Benjamin Peters, Ido Ramati, Margaret Schwartz, Ohad Ufaz, Claudia Welz, and Barbie Zelizer. Writing the book was completed with the support of the Templeton Foundation through a grant from the Enhancing Life Project, a joint venture of the University of Chicago and Ruhr University Bochum. I am indebted to Günter Thomas, William Schweiker, Sara Bigger, and Markus Höfner. All the views expressed are entirely my own, and I am solely responsible for any shortcomings. At Oxford University Press I thank Hallie Stebbins and Hannah Doyle. Finally, to Iris and the kids, Ilai, Elli, and Uri for amply supplying everything else.

An earlier version of Chapter 1 appeared as "Severed Voices: Radio and the Mediation of Trauma in the Eichmann Trial," *Public Culture* 22(2), 2010, 265–291; Chapter 2 is an extended and updated version of "The Audiovisual Unconscious: Media and Trauma in the Video Archive for Holocaust Testimonies," *Critical Inquiry* 39(1), 2012, 142–166; and parts from Chapter 3 appeared in "Screen Trauma: Visual Media and Post-traumatic Stress Disorders," *Theory, Culture and Society* 33(4), 2016, 51–75.

Transmitted Wounds

Introduction

The Mediation of Failed Mediation

In 1995 Binjamin Wilkomirski published a book that was to become a source of fierce controversy. *Fragments: Memories of a Wartime Childhood* recounts Wilkomirski's experiences of surviving alone two concentration camps as a small Jewish child from Poland. Having lived most of his life as Bruno Dössekker, the adopted son of a Swiss couple, Wilkomirski claimed to have discovered his true identity through a long psychoanalytic process, which led to writing his story. The book quickly received popular and critical acclaim and won a number of literary prizes, including the National Jewish Book Award. What happened next is fairly well known: a 1998 newspaper article cast doubt as to the authenticity of Wilkomirski's account, revealing instead the story of a Bruno Grosjean, the illegitimate son of an unmarried woman who had given him away for adoption in Switzerland. The book's publisher then commissioned a historian to look into the allegations, which were consequently found to be correct. The book previously described as "achingly beautiful" and "morally important" was now declared as fake and its author a fraud.[1] The Wilkomirski case has since figured in debates on Holocaust memory as a cautionary tale about the facility with which one can pass as a survivor—and convince a worldwide audience. The book was discontinued as memoir only later to be released in tandem with the historical study finding it false.

While Wilkomirski's memories may have been fabricated, the way they were depicted in the book is a fairly accurate description of traumatic memory. Even if the content of these memories is made-up their structure very much conforms to a psychology textbook entry on post-trauma. Evidently Wilkomirski was aware of this fact, as in the afterword to the book, he urges others in a similar situation to "cry out their own traumatic childhood memories."[2] Curiously, his so-called traumatic memories seem to be of a very specific nature: "My early childhood memories are planted, first and foremost, in exact snapshots of my photographic memory and in the feelings imprinted in them"; they are "a rubble field of isolated images and events . . . shards that keep surfacing against the orderly grain of grown-up life and escaping the laws of logic"; and when recollected "The first pictures surface one by one, like upbeats, flashes of light, with no discernable connection, but sharp and clear. Just pictures, almost no thoughts attached."[3] What Wilkomirski describes here is quite telling: his painful memories bear a certain technical nature—snapshots, imprints, images, flashes—that defy rational recounting. These metaphors—all draw from media technology—suggest a kind of corporeal memory emerging involuntarily from the depths of the psyche.

In investigating the case, novelist Elena Lappin discovered that during his long identity quest, Wilkomirski had been a voracious consumer of documents, books, and particularly films about the Holocaust. As she affirms, "Wilkomirski often refers to his memories as being film-like. They are, I believe, more than that: they are, I believe, derived from films."[4] The film-like quality of his memories may therefore explain not only the source of the fakery but moreover its media technological structure. There is a media story behind Wilkomirski's story: not only did the content of his memories come from film but also presumably the form, that is, the way traumatic memories are supposed to appear in the mind, which happens to correspond closely with the prevailing clinical understating of the post-traumatic condition. If Wilkomirski recycled details about the Holocaust from the media, he likewise recycled the traumatic conjuring up of such details as evoked by media depictions. In a way, Wilkomirski short-circuited mind and media in accounting for trauma. And it is arguably the media logic of his traumatic memory that contributed to the authenticity of the purported recollection. What if such transferences between media and trauma as demonstrated by the Wilkomirski case are more than incidental? What if the media connections and connotations of trauma are telling of deeper epistemological and ontological formations? What if they bespeak something essential about the traumatic condition itself? This book takes these possibilities seriously and sets out to explore their implications.

FROM REPRESENTATION TO MEDIATION

The proliferation of trauma theory in various fields of the humanities and social sciences has created a crowded academic discourse with numerous discussions on the figurations of trauma and traumatic memory in literature, art, mass media, and popular culture. An enduring preoccupation in these discussions is the representation of trauma, that is, the ways in which trauma is represented, signified, and performed in literary, filmic, artistic, or popular cultural texts. Janet Walker exemplifies this approach when speaking of "the ability of certain films and videos to externalize, publicize, and historicize traumatic material that would otherwise remain at the level of internal, individual psychology."[5] Walker's view seems to presuppose two interconnected notions: first, that the traumatic material that certain films and videos supposedly make manifest draws from a preexisting, strictly interior, traumatic mentality that is subsequently externalized; second, that such traumatic material is a type of representational content that can be transferred through media, specifically of the visual kind. Similarly, Ann Kaplan comments on the match between "the visuality common to traumatic symptoms (flashbacks, hallucinations, dreams) and the ways in which visual media like cinema become the mechanisms through which a culture can unconsciously address its traumatic hauntings."[6] Here, too, media are seen as conveyers of traumatic content, re-enacting on a grand scale the inner experience of the private mind.

This book proposes to approach the relation between media and trauma from a different perspective: as a question of mediation rather than of representation. Under consideration is not the way trauma and traumatic memory, as specific identifiable contents, figure in the media (film, television, photography, and other popular culture portrayals of traumatic experience), but rather media as partaking in the very construction of the traumatic itself. Rather than probing the ways the traumatic shows up in the media, this study seeks to understand the traumatic as something that is made manifest through media technological rendering. In this I follow a recent trend in media theory that considers media not simply as technical carriers of preformulated meanings but as systems that give rise to and shape meanings. More than message circulation, media encompass the platforms enabling message circulation. Media constitute the "materialities of communication," to use Hans Ulrich Gumbrecht's phrase,[7] the systems that underlie and make possible the production of meaning; or as John Durham Peters puts it: "media are our infrastructures of being, the habitats and materials through which we act and are."[8] What this means in the present context is shifting the focus away from investigating the representation of trauma in the media and refocusing instead on media as setting the conditions of possibility for traumatic representations. If, as Walker suggests, certain films and videos are capable of delivering traumatic materials, it is arguably because such materials (like Wilkomirski's snapshots, images, and flashes) are already shaped in accordance with technological principles akin to film and video. Or if, as Kaplan suggests, visual media can enact traumatic symptoms on a cultural level, it is possibly because visual media, more than merely circulating preexisting traumatic contents, fundamentally suffuse contents reckoned to be traumatic.

This book, then, is about the ways media predicate the conception and experience of mental wounds. Bringing media theory to bear on trauma theory, this book sets out to reveal the technical operations that inform the understanding of traumatic impact on bodies and minds. At issue are the ways trauma is called into being through the affinities between mind and media, which in turn serve to explicate the traumatic through a set of threshold operations between inside and outside, sense and non-sense, private and public, self and other, experience and articulation. Taking up a number of case studies, the book addresses the question of how changing media—with their associated notions, techniques, and artifacts—change the understanding of trauma itself. With this perspective, I hope to bring new insight into ongoing debates about trauma and traumatic memory across the fields of media studies, memory studies, and trauma studies. The main claim I wish to advance has to do with the ways media logic and technology bear upon trauma both clinical and cultural. It is not by chance that the elusive nature of trauma, its teetering between past and present, presence and absence, proximate and distant, is often made manifest by means of media technology. Media constitute the material conditions for trauma to appear as something that cannot be fully approached and yet somehow must be. If the traumatic condition is such that it escapes ordinary cognizance, media provide alternative channels to encompass it precisely as such. Media bear witness to the human failure to bear witness, and in so doing render the traumatic tangible by means of technological reproduction. This operation of media with respect to trauma may therefore be summarized as follows: the mediation of failed mediation. The remaining pages of this Introduction further develop this claim while each of the ensuing chapters presents a different insanitation thereof.

In her influential book *Unclaimed Experience*, Cathy Caruth describes trauma as follows: "In trauma . . . the outside has gone inside without mediation."[9] According to this description, trauma is a violent intrusion of the outside into the inside; it is what happens when the medium between interior and exterior does not hold. If mediation is taken to be the mental processes whose task is to mediate between the outer and the inner, then trauma is the result of failed mediation. This view draws directly from Sigmund Freud's analysis in *Beyond the Pleasure Principle*, where he introduces the concept of the "protective shield" (*Reizschutz*), the psychic mechanism that, so he speculates, regulates the reception of stimuli from the environment. "*Protection against* stimuli is an almost more important function for the living organism than *reception of* stimuli," a task that Freud assigns to consciousness itself. Trauma is the breaking of the protective shield, "a breach in the otherwise efficacious barrier against stimuli."[10] Such a sudden, unexpected breach defies conscious knowledge of it while happening, only to later return and impose itself through repeated re-experiencing and symptomatic behavior—repeated attempts to come to grips with the event of losing grip. Caruth's literary reading of Freud sees here a paradigmatic case of the failure of narrative to recount history, the crisis of giving an account of an event not fully assimilated as it occurred, and returns to haunt belatedly precisely because not properly known. Trauma is the painful experience of the mind's inability to remediate failed mediation.

Yet further to a literary reading, Freud's "protective shield" affords a media reading, especially with reference to his later essay on the "Mystic Writing-Pad." In it, Freud likens the psychic apparatus to a writing device that allows repeated writing and erasing. The device consisted of a wax slab covered by a transparent sheet made of two layers: a lower waxed paper and an upper celluloid paper; separating the two layers cleared the slate for renewed writing. In this analogy, the wax slab is the unconscious, the lower layer is the system receiving the stimuli, and the upper cover is "an external protective shield against stimuli."[11] The device exemplified for Freud two mutually exclusive functions of the mind: reception and memory. The perception-consciousness system receives and passes excitations without retaining any permanent traces while the impressions that form the foundation of memory are produced in the "unconscious mnemic systems."[12] If the former is receptive but not retentive, the latter is retentive but not receptive; the one has the function of transmission and processing, the other of storage.[13] As the original trauma context of the "protective shield" remains implicit here, let us venture a speculative analogy of trauma as a tear in the protective cover that causes damage to the delicate waxed paper, consequently sending direct impact to the wax slate. With the protective and perceptive mechanisms incapacitated, the lower level is left exposed to excessive excitations, to pressures that can no longer be processed as writing. What this media parable illustrates, however reductively, is the incommensurability between the tear in the surface of writing and the act of writing itself. Trauma as the collapse of the medium as barrier prevents the functioning of the medium as a writing surface.[14] It would take alternative, external means to account for the tear.

The imagery of a violent clash between outside and inside is already captured in the word "trauma" itself, which transposes the Greek meaning of a physical wound to designate a mental wound. "Trauma" is literally a transferred wound (from body to mind, from physiology to psychology), and as such constitutes the inaugural gesture of a long metaphorical legacy of interstitial collapse. Ian Hacking has traced the leap of trauma from body to mind to late nineteenth century rise of "sciences of memory" such as psychology, psychiatry, and neurology, which together redefined the perimeters of the human soul.[15] Early designations such as "railway spine" (a term popularized by British surgeon John Eric Erichsen in the context of train accidents), "shell-shock," and "traumatic neurosis" (both post–World War I designations, British and German, respectively) present variations of the wounding theme, together forming an account on the impact of mechanized modernity on unprepared minds and bodies.[16] While the understanding of trauma has changed considerably over the years, versions of the wounding imagery have persisted throughout. The condition now commonly known as Post-traumatic Stress Disorder (PTSD) first appeared in the Diagnostic and Statistical Manual of Mental Disorders (DSM) in 1980, where the traumatic event was described as "generally outside the range of usual human experience."[17] Later editions of the DSM expanded the description to include seeing, witnessing, or being exposed to threatening events happening to others. The most recent DSM-V (published in 2013) accepts, for the first time, the possibility of mediated trauma (although narrowly and only when work-related). While media figure explicitly only in recent PTSD clinical definitions, media logic and technology, so I suggest, have long been fundamental to the making and performing of trauma as a psychic wound. The plausibility of trauma through media (the paradigm of which, as I claim in Chapter 3, is the September 11 attacks in New York) is therefore the culmination of a lengthier historical conjunction of mental pathology and media technology.

OF TRAUMATOGRAPHY

As many have noted since Freud, trauma is undergone belatedly as a traumatic memory. The failure of mediation is not experienced as it happens, in the present, but only later, and often after latency. Allan Young in his critical history of PTSD designates it as a pathology of time: "it permits the past (memory) to relieve itself in the present, in the form of intrusive images and thoughts and in the patient's compulsion to replay old events."[18] The traumatic event is experienced as an unresolved past, as an event that, since not completely lived through when it happened, somehow continues to take place, and is still relived, compulsively, in the present as involuntary memory. The nineteenth century French psychologist Pierre Janet, who was one of the first to study the phenomenon, noted that traumatic memory, unlike ordinary memories, resists narration. It remains fixed, he argued, unassimilable to linguistic recounting, and therefore undisposed to "mental liquidation."[19] The two types of memory, narrative and non-narrative, adhere to two distinct temporal orders, each suggesting a different logic of memory storage and retrieval. That the traumatic, or non-narrative type is often described in technological media terms is a point that has prompted far less curiosity than it deserves.

Further to Wilkomirski's "snapshots," "images," and "flashes" other metaphors that circulate both professionally and publicly include "imprint," "etching," a memory that is "burnt-in," "engraved," "encoded," "registered," experienced by intrusive "flashbacks," sometimes with "cinematic" or "iconic" quality. These metaphors are more than just figures of speech; they are epistemological scaffoldings. As Hans Blumenberg argued, metaphors are precursors of thought insofar as they fashion in advance the basis from which concepts and theories are to emerge.[20] In the present context, I propose that technological metaphorology is not supplemental to the theorization of trauma but in fact fundamental to it. I will have more to say about this later on, but for now it should be noted that all the metaphors above fall under the definition of what Charles Sanders Peirce called an index: markers of direct physical relation of cause and effect, and more specifically, markings whose reference is the event of their marking. What is implied thereby is a direct and causal relation between the event and its impression, a direct imprint of the event, which is made tangible through technical terminology precisely because evoking alternative channels to ordinary human cognition and perception. Hence technological metaphors of trauma are used to designate what is assumed to be indexical—that is, non-metaphorical—relation. Indeed, debates about the accuracy of traumatic memory demonstrate continuous negotiation with the technical status of that memory, a most poignant example being the recovered memory/false memory debate revolving around cases of repressed and later recovered memories of child abuse.[21] Whether clinically accurate or not, such metaphors can only make sense given the preexisting technological context of indexical media.

Trauma presents a perennial problem of communication: how to make sense, and consequently narrate and give an account of, an experience that, strictly speaking, resists and is incompatible with narrative account. If failed mediation is the ontology of trauma, the mediation of failed mediation is its epistemology. Such mediation may proceed by symbolic means, a challenge undertaken by anyone attempting to relate traumatic memory in historical or literary formats.[22] The paradigmatic model of such symbolic mediation of trauma is arguably psychoanalysis, which essentially deems symbolization as part of the therapy itself. Yet the mediation of failed mediation is not restricted to symbolic channels, to words, meanings, and narratives, written or spoken; rather, it involves, and I would even go as far as claiming is conditioned by, non-symbolic channels provided by technological media. The chapters to follow consider media technological operations of transmission, recording, and processing as constitutive of such mediations of the traumatic, at times while complementing the narrative channel, other times while directly competing with it. As I argue below, media and trauma extend to the Real—the realm that media theorist Friedrich Kittler reappropriates from Jacques Lacan so as to recast the relation between technology and corporeality.

The emergence of trauma as a distinctively modern malaise has been the subject of a number of critical histories. Allan Young claims that PTSD is a historically specific pathology that is "glued together by the practices, technologies, and narratives with which it is diagnosed, studied, treated, and represented."[23] This does not mean the condition is not real—rather that such discursive mechanisms are what produce it as real. Ian Hacking reconstructs the history of the condition in conjunction with other mental pathologies that together demonstrate late modern preoccupation with the science of memory.[24] And in her genealogy of trauma, Ruth Leys takes issue with the notion of literal impact—the idea that trauma is an external event that befalls an unsuspecting subject, leaving in its wake a factual imprint in the form of traumatic memory.[25] She proposes instead a more complex view that involves subjective suggestive processes of symbolization and identification: what she names the mimetic model as opposed to the literal, antimimetic model, which she criticizes. Taken together, these accounts reconstruct the processes that led to the discovery of the psyche as prone to mental injury by external pressures.

This study cannot claim to match the breath of any of the above, devised as it is as a constellation of cases more than a comprehensive history or genealogy. Nevertheless, what it might contribute to ongoing critical debates about trauma is a keen attention to the particularities of its registration: the ways trauma gets inscribed, leaves its trace, imprints itself; the ways it marks, stamps, and makes an impression—and subsequently the particularities of its recollection: the ways it reappears, returns, and shows up, the manners of its retrieval, recall, and reliving. All these particularities (which are also the technicalities) of registration and recollection of trauma can be grouped together under one term: traumatography. Ley's critique of the literal impact thus seems to restrict traumatography to internal processes, insisting that trauma is the result of symbolic mediation by the subject rather than the failure of such mediation. And yet, Ley's own distinction between mimetic and antimimetic, symbolic and literal—the distinction at the basis of her genealogy—can itself be revealed as already underwritten by a traumatographical logic—a logic that governs the threshold operations between inside and outside. Whether mimetic or antimimetic, symbolic or literal, or going back to Janet's distinction of narrative and non-narrative memory, all these traumatic descriptors are conceivable only given a context permitting such differentiations to become evident, and as such, are already subjected to traumatographical mediation. Thus trauma is necessarily mediated, but its mediation, in contradistinction to Leys, is not strictly intra-subjective but encompasses extra-subjective referencing by which the very distinction between literal and symbolic gets selected and activated, and consequently becomes intelligible. From this follows that the mediation of trauma cuts across inside and outside, both inhabiting and exceeding private minds, and in this sense may be said to be collective inasmuch as individual, extensive inasmuch as intensive.

While remaining implicit in the critical history of trauma, the conjunction of media and trauma has been at the forefront of recent debates on cultural memory in contemporary technological societies. Thomas Elsaesser has noted the affinity between media depictions of historical experience and the temporal structure of belatedness associated with trauma. He argues that cinematic dramatizations of the past (especially of the Holocaust) have brought about "new forms of media memory" from which "the contemporary subject will have a necessarily traumatic . . . relation to history and memory: in the first instance to her/his own history, but more generally to all history."[26] Furthermore, trauma has a special function in the time of the collapse of grand narratives: it recovers a sense of referentiality that has been lost to the relativism of endless interpretation. In another influential account, Andreas Huyssen argues that it is impossible to think today of Holocaust memory apart from the media of its dissemination—from museums, through documentaries and photographs, to internet sites—and it is precisely owing to these media disseminations that the Holocaust has become a universal trope of traumatic memory that repeatedly migrates to other historical contexts. The cultural obsession with memory, especially traumatic, expresses a growing need for anchoring "in a world of increasing flux in ever denser networks of compressed time and space."[27] More recently Allen Meek has offered a critique of the long litany of trauma theory that links the indexical power of the media image to the historical real, calling instead for an understanding of trauma as "an attempt to articulate the crisis of the political subject" with the media playing a key role in the process.[28] Compelling as they are, these accounts still tend to approach the question of media and trauma against the horizon of cultural meanings, regarding media as mimetic platforms for contemporary culture's traumatic impulses and fantasies. What they underplay are the non-hermeneutical affordances of audiovisual media, their technologically enabled non-discursive capabilities, which are nevertheless presupposed by, and indeed anchor, each of the above accounts.[29]

Nowhere are the stakes in the mediation of traumatic memory higher than in discussions about Holocaust remembrance. Consider Marianne Hirsch's explorations of "postmemory," the intergenerational transmission of trauma in which visual media, photography in particular, play a vital role. "More than oral or written narratives," so Hirsch contends, "photographic images that survive massive devastation and outlive their subjects and owners function as ghostly revenants from an irretrievably lost past world."[30] Rehearsing Roland Barthes's notion of the punctum, Hirsch regards photographs as bearing material and affective connection to the past; so much so that they allow later viewers to "produce in themselves the effects of traumatic repetition that plague the victims of trauma."[31] Yet here, too, a more radical conclusion should be drawn: namely, that the transmitting power of photography does not stop at conditioning postmemory but further encompasses the conditioning of the traumatic quality attributed to that memory. Recall Wilkomirski's childhood memories as snapshots and flashes: photography shapes the very structure of traumatic memory and consequently its potential transmissibility. It becomes almost impossible to think of traumatic memory—let alone of postmemory—apart from photographic traumatography.

Similar claims about traumatic transmissibility have been made with reference to cinema. Alison Landsberg posits cinematic experience as key to what she designates as "prosthetic memory": the memory derived "from a person's mass-mediated experience of a traumatic event of the past."[32] According to her, mass cultural technologies allow for affective undergoing of traumatic past events not lived through, sometimes with favorable moral outcomes. But here again arises the question of the status of the traumatic: If media can impart something of the traumatic effect of past events, is it not because what they impart, more than the depiction of the past, is the fact of it being traumatic, the sensation of what traumatic memory must feel like? Similarly, but more cautiously, Joshua Hirsch considers the potential of cinema "to represent the Holocaust *as* a rupture, to embody that rupture for the audience, perhaps even to assist in mourning that rupture."[33] At the same time, he warns against reductive speculations of traumatic relay and against facile endorsement of vicarious trauma through media. But what if the situation cautioned against is actually telling of something more fundamental about the transmitting potential of trauma: namely, that cinematic and photographic principles are already somehow at work in the conception of trauma as rupture in experience? It is not coincidental that a notion such as flashback circulates in both clinical and cultural contexts, for what it captures is the function of media in mediating trauma across and between the two discourses. Wilkomirski may well be an extreme case of prosthetic memory turned real, or of vicarious trauma turned firsthand, but when resisting the urge to reduce it to a mere aberration, the case of Wilkomirski may nonetheless provide a lesson of the degree to which traumatic processes are coextensive with mediatic operations.

In sum, the focus on mediation of trauma motivates an exploration into the conditions of possibility of traumatic representational operation. What concerns me here are the material and technical conditions that afford the enacting of trauma and traumatic memory across clinical, literary, and cultural contexts. Media (re)produce the traumatic by effecting its ungraspability affectively, by imparting impact in excess of content, sensation in excess of sense. To use Bernhard Siegert's formalization, if media partake in operationalizing the distinction between sense and non-sense, signal and noise, inside and outside, here media further operationalize the effect of non-sense upon sense, of noise upon signal, and of the outside upon the inside.[34] The mediation of failed mediation bears out media's ability to mobilize the traumatic as non-discursive, non-hermeneutic effects—to generate traumatographical impressions. As such, traumatography follows the laws of grammatology: the traumatic origin, the original moment of trauma, is always already deferred; moreover, it acquires the status of origin and original by virtue of its deferral. All the more so when trauma is taken up discursively, as part of an attempt to account for it and render it meaningful. In this recursive process, what exceeds meaning is absorbed within discourse (under designations such as the "unrepresentability of trauma" or trauma as "the crisis of representation"), and once absorbed, proceeds to operate as a representation (of the unrepresentable). Yet it should be remembered that such discursive reappropriation presupposes and is premised on media technological capabilities without which the very invocation of the traumatic as unrepresentable would be meaningless.

TECHNOLOGY AND TRAUMATOLOGY

Trauma is a central theme in the grand narrative of the shock of modernity with media acting as primary shock agents. It is possible to trace a trauma thread running throughout media theory, but for the purposes of this discussion, I attempt a partial reconstruction of that thread by considering the work of three principal representatives: Walter Benjamin, Marshall McLuhan, and Friedrich Kittler. Covering together more than half of the twentieth century, the three jointly form an extended report on the psychopathology of modern media as caused by the displacing and replacing of human sensoria by technological apparatuses. Whereas Benjamin and McLuhan see media as besieging the mind by exerting sensory overload whose mitigation calls for further media, Kittler sees media as infiltrating the mind only to reveal it as already technological in nature. On the one hand media as overwhelming the integrity of the mind (a Freudian theme), on the other hand media as providing channels into the mind (a Lacanian theme). This shifting of media from outside to inside the mind will prove critical for exploring the technological mediation of trauma.

Benjamin famously described modern life as a continuous experience of duress that cuts across the metropolis, the factory, and the battlefield. Borrowing Freud's notion of the protective shield, Benjamin proceeded to speculate on the way that media technologies, such as photography and film, participate in training the human sensorium to cope with the assault of external stimuli. "Perhaps the special achievement of shock defense," he writes, "may be in its function of assigning to an incident a precise point in time in consciousness at the cost of the integrity of its contents."[35] The same logic applies to media in the sense that technical recording and reproduction of experience comes at the expense of the integrity of the experience. Hence the loss of aura due to mechanical reproduction assumes traumatic proportions: the camera is a device that transforms the haptic into optic, and the event into frame, thereby "giving the moment a posthumous shock, as it were."[36] Film is an apparatus that is "in keeping with the increased threat to his life which modern man has to face. Man's need to expose himself to shock effects contributes to his adjustment to the dangers threatening him."[37] Media function as habituation instruments to the besieged consciousness, and the more effective the shock defense the more processed the sensation.

Yet the deep effects of shock are to be found elsewhere, in the blockage of another channel: the loss of the ability to relate and narrate experience. In an essay on the passing of the storyteller, Benjamin asks ominously: "Was it not noticeable at the end of the war that men returned from the battlefield grown silent—not richer, but poorer in communicable experience?" The impact of mechanized warfare far exceeds its casualties, claiming the ability of survivors to bear witness. Modern war casts humanity against technology in extreme disproportion: "A generation that had gone to school on a horse-drawn streetcar now stood under the open sky in which nothing remained unchanged but the clouds, and beneath these clouds, in a field of force of destructive torrents and explosions, was the tiny, fragile human body."[38] The overwhelming power of machine-driven violence makes experience dwindle, and with it the ability to communicate that experience. Benjamin documents the historical moment when trauma became associated with a systemic crisis of human perception, which extends from art through industry to combat, and whose impact on narrative as a medium of experience incapacitates the narration of history itself.

Marshall McLuhan's conception of media as the extensions of man is another example of the elective affinity between media and trauma. Like Benjamin, McLuhan sees media as protective barriers against extensive stimuli, "counter-irritants" to use his term, which through their operation further isolate, even numb, the function they so extend. McLuhan's understating of media is notoriously broad, ranging from print, photograph, phonograph, and television to money, transportation, and weaponry. In each case the stepping up of outside pressures demanded the exteriorization of operation in order to protect the organism from damage. It is in this sense that for McLuhan all media are post-traumatic: they are frantic technological attempts to attain equilibrium in the wake of former technological traumas. Hence the vicious cycle whereby today's protective media are the cause of future irritations, consequently creating the need for further extensions. Electric media mark the latest, most severe stage in the process wherein the extension is of the entire nervous system, "a development that suggests a desperate and suicidal autoamputation, as if the central nervous system could no longer depend on the physical organs to be protective buffers against the slings and arrows of outrageous mechanism."[39] Media have the risk of physical and psychic trauma as their raison d'être, a risk becoming evermore fatal in late modernity. McLuhan seems to be on a par with Freud insofar as accounting for the consequences of the collapse of inside-outside barrier, which in his reasoning is technologically wrought.

While operating as buffers, media induce a generalized numbness that prevents recognition as to their operation. As per McLuhan, we are always late in realizing our situation, compelled to look at the present through a rearview mirror, and likely to misunderstand a new medium in terms of the old. In this respect, approaching media as a question of content—the traditional priority of message over medium—is symptomatic of the difficulty of reaching down into the technological conditions of possibility of message production. Latency is therefore built into our understating of media. Like Freud before him, McLuhan recognizes the danger in belated awakening to emergency: "a technological extension of our bodies designed to alleviate physical stress can bring on psychic stress that may be much worse."[40] *Understanding Media* can be read as a therapeutic project of making sense of, and coming to terms with, the structural gap in our dealings with technology, one that is badly needed given the surmounting pressures of the electric age. To the extent that McLuhan offers an account on the relation between media and trauma, it is tempting to consider his logic also in reverse: not only do we externalize ourselves through media as a protective measure against trauma, we simultaneously internalize media in trying to attest to trauma as a crisis of communication and representation. Media concepts and logic—the various imprints, flashbacks, and unprocessed memories—are adopted in a desperate attempt to account for the inability of giving full account. Trauma entails media inasmuch as media entail trauma.

Common to these two accounts by Benjamin and McLuhan on the crushing impact of technology on body and mind in late modernity is the conception of the human as a vestige of earlier, less taxing times: a maladapted being whose technological dependency only further exacerbates the maladaptation. The human is always out of synch with technology, hence the reality of shock. Yet a more radical line of thought considers the human itself as transformed by technology, which might translate into a completely different understanding of the relation between media and trauma. According to Friedrich Kittler, the advent of electric media of the late nineteenth and early twentieth centuries radically transformed what he called *Aufschreibesysteme* (translated as "discourse networks" but literally means writing-down or inscription systems): "the network of technologies and institutions that allow a given culture to select, store and process relevant data."[41] The introduction of the photograph, the phonograph, and the cinematograph enabled recording and storing the physical effects of light and sound without human intervention and interpretation. No longer did human data transfer have to pass through "the bottleneck of the signifier,"[42] that is, undergo symbolic mediation by means of the Ur-medium of writing. With analog media of image and sound there came about two channels of mechanical inscription—the photographic and the phonographic—which ended the monopoly of alphabetization.

It should be noted parenthetically, but not without relevance to the present study, that the notion of *Aufschreibesystem* itself emerged from the conjunction of media technology and psychopathology. German jurist

Daniel Paul Schreber coined it in his 1903 book *Memoirs of My Nervous Illness* as part of his attempts to recount his delusions during hospitalization. He described mysterious rays, apparently coming from God or some other otherworldly entity, which invade his mind and have the ability to read his pre-inscribed thoughts: "*Books and other notes* are kept in which for years have been *written-down* all my thoughts, all my phrases, all my necessaries . . . I presume that the writing-down is done by creatures given human shape on distant celestial bodies . . . their hands are led automatically, as it were, by passing rays for the purpose of making them write-down, so that later rays can again look at what has been written."[43] According to Kittler, Schreber's paranoia is the byproduct of the interfusion of nervous system and information system anchored in the discourse network of 1900, and whose combined effect is the liquidation of the subject as author and owner of self-discourse. Schreber the writer discloses the psyche as already underwritten through the inscription and storage mechanisms of his time.[44] Psychopathology reveals technology all the way down to the very origin of Kittler's "discourse networks."

Kittler conceptualized the shift of the discourse network of 1900 by utilizing Jacques Lacan's triad of the Symbolic, Imaginary, and Real. In Kittler's rendering the Symbolic refers to the technological processing of data in terms of symbols and representation, the "linguistic signs in their materiality and technicity" from print to typewriter to computer. The Imaginary refers to the Lacanian mirror stage with film as the technology producing for the viewer the optical illusion of continuity and integration, "the mobile doubles that humans, unlike other primates, were able to (mis) perceive as their own body." And the Real constitutes that which escapes both representation by symbols and figuration by images, "the waist or residue that neither the mirror of the imaginary nor the grid of the symbolic can catch: the physiological accidents and stochastic disorder of bodies."[45] To Kittler, the attendant technology of the Real is phonography owing to its unselective registration of vocal and acoustic events as they happen—the materiality of voice (inflection, accent, mispronunciations) as well as the materiality of the medium (statics, hiss, noise). The mediatic instantiations of the Real are therefore of pre-symbolic and non-symbolic enunciations of physical reality as captured through the open channels of mechanical inscription. Yet, important for this discussion, the Real, according to Lacan, presents itself in the form of trauma insofar as indicating corporeality that is unassimilable within, and in fact ruptures, the symbolic framework.[46] Kittler comes close to this point when stating: "in the real everything begins with coldness, dizziness and shortness of breath."[47] The Real is thus both mediatic and traumatic, but here I would go further to claim—and this claim is the crux of this study—that the Real is traumatic *because* mediatic. The story of trauma as told through media is the story of how the Real has become tantamount with the traumatic itself.

Kittler's incorporation of Lacan into media theory goes beyond heuristic purposes, for what it ultimately implies is that Lacan's three registers are themselves technologically determined—namely, that the differentiation among Symbolic, Imaginary, and Real is constituted upon the discourse network of 1900 and its representative media trio: typewriter, film, gramophone. Lacanian psychoanalysis was conditioned by its attendant media regime. Lacan's later interest in cybernetics is suggestive of the subsequent media regime of computerization and digitization—what might be called the discourse network of 2000—which, to further pursue the mind-media affinity, could be seen as forming the material background for present-day cognitive sciences. According to Kittler, there is nothing coincidental in the employment of technical media "as models or metaphors for imagining the human or the soul."[48] The way we understand ourselves and our mind is always historical and therefore crucially informed by the media regime we are at. This might explain the elaborate traumatographical metaphors in the form of flashback, imprint, unconscious registration, trace, mark, and the like. For what these metaphors evoke is a direct link to the originating traumatic event, a link that is made tangible through technological mediation: as though what light and sound are to analog media, the originating event is to traumatic memory. In both cases what is supposedly at work is a form of direct registration without recourse to symbolic mediation (the target of Leys's critique of literal impact). Media technology thus serves to explicate trauma as a mental wound—a wound that renders the mind incapable of accounting for its own wounding, and consequently calls for workarounds to approach the incapacity. It is as though the mind's failure to make sense of the event—the failure of mental mediation—calls for technical mediation in order to make it knowable.

Yet again flashback is a case in point. The history of the term cannot be summarized here, but as others have already noted, its double meaning as a filmic device for cutting back in time and a recurring post-traumatic memory is the product of mutual transferences between cinematography and psychopathology.[49] Its roots go back to the 1916 psychological analysis of film by the German-American psychologist Hugo Münsterberg, who spoke of the "cutback" as "an objectification of our memory function."[50] Also prior to its clinical rendition, the term appeared in a 1948 letter from McLuhan to Ezra Pound, where he likens the poet's imagistic style to the influence of cinematography, as "Flash-backs providing perceptions of simultaneities."[51] It was only in the late 1960s that "flashback" became associated with psychic trauma through the work of American psychiatrist Mardi Horowitz, who was probably the first to use the term clinically. And film also played a key role here: Horowitz had been previously involved in a research program called "trauma film paradigm," which employed distressing films to produce measurable stress effects on viewers in order to study psychic trauma (more on this in Chapter 3). From the late 1980s the term began circulating in psychiatric clinical discourse, where its status as veridical memory has been a source of continuous dispute. As Hacking notes, the tendency to regard flashback as a privileged form of recollection has to do with the problematic construction that sets it in opposition to so-called conventional or narrative memory.[52] Accounting for the role of film in the continuous interchange between mind and media from which flashback evolved provides the material context for understanding this apparent dichotomization of memory. Film accounts for the mind's flashback mode of operation.[53] Designating a distinctively non-narrative form of posttraumatic memory, flashback has the discourse network of 1900 as its media a priori.

All this leads to the following realization: with the introduction of the two technical channels of image and sound it became possible to witness the collapse of the symbolic channel as though from the outside, through alternative channels. Bypassing the bottleneck of the signifier opened up new ways to convey impact, especially when it comes to the failure of narrative to do so. What literary scholar Shoshana Felman identifies as the crisis of narrative in the context of Holocaust testimony (a theme running through Chapters 1, 2, and 4) is made available technologically as physical effects of the Real. Media and trauma converge on the Real, and as such point to corporeality that underlies representation but precisely for this reason cannot be represented in itself. If the Real, to use Lacan's famous formula, is that which can be approached but never grasped, Kittler recasts the Real as approachable only through its media traces, as material contingencies that remain beyond discursive certainties.[54] The Real has a technological unconscious in the form of indexical media, making its effects prone to reproduction and manipulation. The Real is therefore thoroughly mediated, which is another way to describe what I earlier designated as traumatography: the writing-down system of trauma. If for Lacan the Real presents itself in the form of trauma, the question that arises following Kittler is of the technical-material conditions allowing for that presentation.

AGENDA AND OUTLINE

Kittler's analysis serves as an inspiration for the following chapters as each takes on a different instantiation of the mediation of the traumatic Real: radiophonic, videographic, televisual, algorithmic-holographic, and digitally immersive. As this lineup shows, I find it relevant to consider the ways in which the media logic of the Real comes into play in different technologies and through distinctive configurations of minds, technologies, and bodies. While each chapter is a standalone discussion, the book as a whole is comprised of two clusters, with the first three chapters focusing on analog media and the last two on digital technology. The fault lines between the discourse network of 1900 and that of 2000 chart accurately the transformation of the Real from indexical to digital, and from the non-symbolized into the re-symbolized. That said, my agenda is not ultimately faithful to Kittler's, for in the final analysis I regard this investigation into the mediation of the traumatic Real as revealing of corporeal fragility and vulnerability. So while subscribing to Kittler's understanding of the mind as mediated by extra-psychic technical processing, I nevertheless insist on considering what Kittler consistently avoided and even deplored—namely, the ethical and political stakes involved in the technological transmission of mental wounds. Recognizing the irreducibility of pain is not necessarily antithetical to a non-anthropocentric approach to media. Indeed, the conjunction of media and trauma affords an opportunity to rethink the ontology of pain while retaining a critical perspective on the consequences of traumatic transmissions.

Chapter 1 is concerned with radio and its role in the mediation of trauma during the 1961 Eichmann trial. While the trial has been the topic of many studies, none have considered the full significance of it being a radiophonic event. The main claim the chapter advances is that radio broadcasts from the courtroom occasioned a transformation in the status of Holocaust survivors in Israel, who had been previously seen as deeply traumatized, unable or unwilling to speak about their experiences. Taking to the airwaves facilitated a shift in the conditions by which survivors' testimonies could find public articulation: from bodies without speech into disembodied speech. For those once deemed speechless, disembodiment meant the opening of new forms of address and the liberation of new modes of expression. Radiophonic transmission elicited a double return of the repressed: on one level, the return of voice away from the body, on another level the return of the body through corporeal markers of vocality. The dialectics of embodiment and disembodiment enabled by radio during the trial invites re-evaluating the status of trauma between private and public and the role of media therein.

Chapter 2 explores the media logic of the project for videotaping the testimonies of Holocaust survivors. Established at Yale University in 1981, the Fortunoff Video Archive for Holocaust Testimonies has provided source material for numerous studies on history and memory in the wake of the Holocaust, from which developed an intensive intellectual preoccupation with trauma and testimony. Many studies have engaged with the audiovisual nature of the archive, and yet the significance of this novel archival formation, and the way it shapes the production and reception of survivors' testimonies, have not yet been fully recognized. The chapter brings together the trauma and testimony discourse as developed by Dori Laub, Shoshana Felman, Lawrence Langer, and others in the context of the Yale archive, and Kittler's analysis of technical media. I argue that the trauma and testimony discourse has a technological unconscious in the form of videography, which crucially conditioned the way traumatic memory is conceived by this discourse. It is only with an audiovisual medium capable of capturing and reproducing evidence of the fleeting unconscious that a discourse concerned with the unarticulated past becomes intelligible. The chapter offers some potentially far-reaching conclusions as to the status of trauma in contemporary debates in the humanities and social sciences.

Chapter 3 deals with the possibility of televisual trauma. Recent studies in psychiatry and psychology reveal a growing acceptance of the risk of trauma through the media, culminating with a qualified inclusion of such a possibility in the latest PTSD criteria as stipulated in the DSM-V. Traditionally restricted to direct and immediate experience, post-trauma is now expanding to include mediated experience, especially witnessing disastrous events on television. Tracing what made this development possible, the chapter considers three key moments in the process: the "trauma film paradigm," a research program introduced in the early 1960s that employed stressful films to simulate traumatic effects on subjects; the psychiatric study into the clinical effects of watching catastrophic events on television, with the September 11 attacks as a transformative event; and recent reports on US Air Force drone operators who purportedly exhibit PTSD symptoms after flying combat missions by remote, constituting thereby a new type of perpetrator trauma. My contention in this chapter is that the possibility of trauma through media reveals a conceptualization of the post-traumatic experience as one that is fundamentally informed by visual media and, as such, already predisposed to televisual trauma.

Chapters 4 and 5 deal with the question of the digital status of traumatic memory by considering two projects currently under development in the Institute for Creative Technologies at the University of Southern California: New Dimensions in Testimony, a computer generated interaction with a hologram of a Holocaust survivor, and BRAVEMIND, a virtual reality exposure therapy program for treating veterans suffering from PTSD. What is common to the two projects goes beyond the shared institutional settings, as both provide apt cases for the changing status of traumatic memory under digitization. Specifically, they each demonstrate, in different ways, the discretization of the traumatic Real, its re-symbolization into calculative computerized routines, and concomitantly, the decoupling of traumatic memory from narrative as its traditional carrier.

In the penultimate chapter I focus on New Dimensions in Testimony, a project that combines human-computer speech interaction capabilities with three-dimensional holographic imaging to create an immersive experience of a live conversation with a Holocaust survivor. Of special importance is the employment of an algorithm to select and project prerecorded clips of the survivor in response to questions presented by an interlocutor. Its high-tech futuristic gloss of testimony notwithstanding, what makes this project worthy of serious consideration is the way it envisages the transmission of painful experiences far into the future, which raises the question of the status of traumatic memory therein. I argue that this project marks a break between testimonial narrative and traumatic memory, for what was a defining feature of bearing witness in the context of the video testimony archive—the acting out of traumatic memory upon testimonial narrative—becomes extraneous in the context of the digital database. In seeking to simulate a live testimony with a survivor for the benefit of generations to come, this project presents a deeply problematic conception of the relation between past and present, and absence and presence, as these come into play in the performing of the algorithmic-holographic testimony.

The final chapter delves into the inner workings of preset-day exposure therapy technique for PTSD and its employment of virtual reality technology. As a cognitive-behavioral approach, exposure therapy advocates direct confrontation with the feared object or situation as a way to achieve habituation. In so doing it positions itself as an alternative to traditional talk therapy by providing direct access to the relevant "fear structure." The chapter considers the use of VR (virtual reality) technology in PTSD treatment as a case of what Kittler, following Münsterberg, calls psychotechnology: the recursive channeling of mind through media and of media through mind. At issue is the status of traumatic memory as enacted and materialized by an immersive VR platform. I argue that through digital-immersive processing traumatic memory is rendered discrete and modular, and consequently made treatable by its division into separately manipulable elements. This development,

I further argue, coincides with the deposing of talk and narrative as therapeutic access channels into the traumatic condition.

One final note on media and trauma: as is patently clear from the rundown of topics above, war is a thread running throughout this book. This is no doubt for essential reasons: war is a principal circumstance of trauma and has been the context of the development of the psychological understanding of trauma—from the First World War, through the Holocaust and Vietnam, to today's drone war. War occasions fateful intersections of media and trauma. Yet war has another concrete significance for this discussion. Kittler famously and provocatively deemed war as the engine of modern history: war drives technological change, which in turn drives historical change. As Geoffrey Winthrop-Young puts it, for Kittler war is motor, model, and motive.[55] Combined with Kittler's anti-humanistic streak, the result is a rather unsettling viewpoint of the reality of war in recent history. Add to that the German context of the twentieth century and the discomfort only intensifies. My adoption of Kittler's theory is therefore not an easy one, nor should it be, as I am fully aware of its implications especially when it comes to a subject so profoundly defined by pain as trauma. It is my hope that, by adopting somewhat unfaithfully Kittler's framework to study the conjunction of media and trauma, the dark underside of the conjunction of media and war may come to light.

CHAPTER 1

Radiocasting Trauma

Two weeks into the Adolf Eichmann trial, toward the end of April 1961, the poet Haim Gouri, who chronicled the proceedings for a local Israeli newspaper, wrote in his column: "The country carries on as usual, day and night, and this trial accompanies it. The one goes on, the other alongside. Away from the courtroom, there is no outward sign of it. But it is in the air and the water, it is like dust on the trees."[1] Writing his impressions from Beit Ha'am, the Jerusalem theater venue converted to host the hearings, Gouri captured something of the sensation that paralleled the trial, that feeling of "something in the air," gripping and haunting the everyday as the proceedings unfolded. What was in the air, or more precisely on the air, remains implicit in Gouri's prose. As is often the case with media, their operation is likely to remain invisible or to be taken for granted, a tendency that sometimes occludes further understanding of certain historical episodes. Such is the case with the Eichmann trial, an event profoundly marked by what was then the principal mass medium in Israel—the radio.

The Eichmann trial has recently received renewed attention from scholars in various fields. Indeed, some mention the role of radio during the time of the trial. To quote a few notable references: "Much of the trial was carried live on the radio; everywhere, people listened—in houses and offices, in cafés and stores and buses and factories."[2] "The trial, the full sessions of which were broadcast

---

Research leading to this study was done in collaboration with the late Tamar Liebes. This chapter is dedicated to her memory.

live on national radio, changed the face of Israel, psychologically binding the pastless young Israelis with their recent history and revolutionizing their self-perception."[3] "Broadcast live over the radio and passionately listened to, the trial was becoming the central event in the country's life."[4] "The Eichmann trial was *the* most important media event in Israel prior to the Six Day War. . . . Young and old could be seen radio in hand everywhere—in constant earshot of the broadcast from Beit Ha'am."[5] Despite the drama with which the experience of radio listening is described, none of these studies further explicate the significance of the radiophonic medium during the trial.[6] Moreover, radio seems to figure in the above only as an auxiliary apparatus, the focus being the social process already underway, with the broadcast medium itself falling largely by the wayside.

A previous study sheds new light on the media strategy behind the Eichmann trial, especially with respect to the role of radio.[7] Its conclusions cast doubt on Hannah Arendt's claims in her famous report on the trial, which she regarded as an elaborate scheme designed by Prime Minister David Ben-Gurion for political ends.[8] At least insofar as the trial's publicity was concerned, there is evidence to suggest that conflicting interests within the government led to an inconsistent, often contradictory, publicity strategy. A case in point is the Kol Yisrael radio station, then a subdivision in the prime minister's office and the only broadcasting medium in Israel at the time (television became available seven years later, in 1968). Although being the primary medium at the disposal of the Israeli government, little attention had been given to radio as a means for influencing public opinion; indeed, Kol Yisrael's officials were not involved in preparations for the trial and were invited to participate only when it became clear that film documentation would be partial. It is therefore safe to assume that had there been an ideological master plan behind this trial—as some critics following Arendt seem to suggest[9]— it most likely would have included a more coherent publicity strategy.

Although carried out spontaneously and irregularly, live radio transmissions from the courtroom had a tremendous impact on the Israeli public, one that genuinely took the Israeli leadership by surprise. Even today, for many Israelis, the most vivid memory associated with the trial is listening to radio broadcasts from the court on a daily basis. For most, the broadcast testimonies of survivors were the first comprehensive encounter with the trauma of the Holocaust. Many a volume, both scholarly and popular, has since reiterated the memory of the trial as an ongoing radiophonic media event. However, as the study cited above reveals, live transmissions from the courtroom were actually quite rare—no more than sixteen broadcasts over a period of four months (April through August 1961)—hardly an everyday occurrence (see Fig. 1.1). What was aired regularly was a daily trial diary, *Yoman Ha'mishpat*, a thirty-minute-long recap of the day's session, edited and narrated by Kol Yisrael's leading presenters and broadcast immediately after the evening news. That radio—particularly live transmissions—became inseparable from the memory of the trial itself, is presumably related to the dynamics of collective memory, that is, to the way the past is socially constructed in the present. Yet it might also be telling of the distinctive role of media in mediating trauma. This is the subject of this chapter.

Drawing on historical material, various personal accounts, and a series of in-depth interviews with Israelis who witnessed the trial through the radio, this chapter proposes that radio played a vital role in the public articulation of Holocaust trauma in Israel during the Eichmann trial. Rather than merely serve an instrumental role in broadcasting the proceedings, radio importantly shaped the way the trial was perceived by the Israeli public. Specifically,

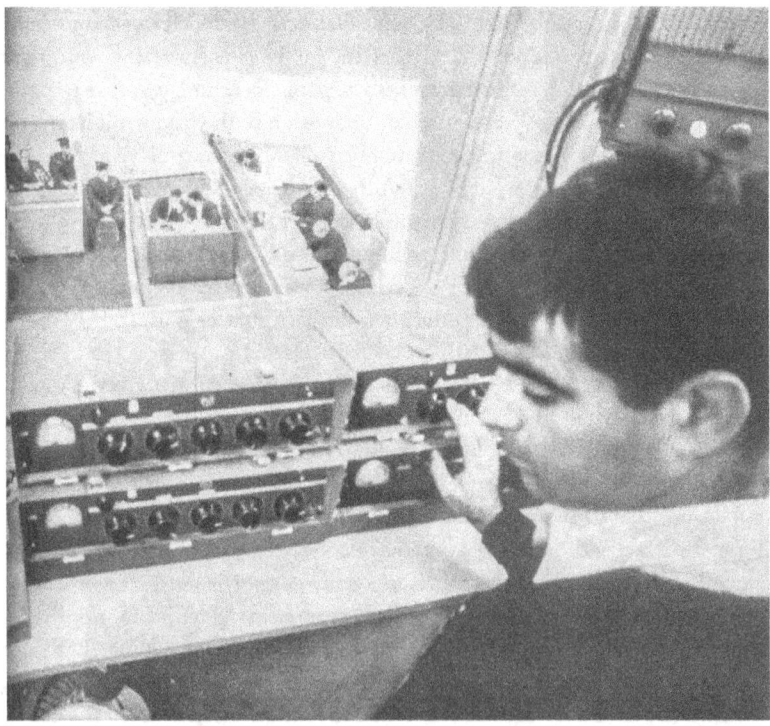

Figure 1.1. Kol Yisrael transmission booth overlooking the judges and Eichmann in the glass cage. Photograph Courtesy of Kol Yisrael Archive.

radio facilitated a fundamental shift in the status of Holocaust survivors in Israel: previously seen as deeply traumatized, unable, or unwilling to speak about what happened "over there," survivors were now invited, for the first time, to publicly bear witness to their stories. Through radio, survivors underwent a profound transformation: from bodies without speech into disembodied speech. For those once deemed speechless, disembodiment meant the opening of new forms of address and the liberation of new modes of expression. The Eichmann trial provides a compelling case of the significance of media in transforming private traumas into a socially shared trauma—in other words, in the mediation of cultural trauma.

TRIAL AND TRAUMA

According to Shoshana Felman, the hidden link between trial and trauma became dramatically apparent during the second half of the twentieth century, the century of unprecedented catastrophes but also, and concurrently, the century of the theory of trauma. Felman identifies the Eichmann trial as a groundbreaking event wherein the instrument of law was called on to cope with the traumatic legacies of the past. However, the introduction of trauma into the court meant the pollution of the legal process by claims that cannot be strictly articulated in legal language. This marked both the crisis of law and its transmutation: it was the failure to translate trauma into legal code that inadvertently performed the "acting out" of trauma. The courtroom became what Felman calls a "theater of justice," a public stage not only for the practice of law but also for the reenactment of trauma through the deficiency of the law.[10]

Notwithstanding the historical conjunction pointed out by Felman, law and the theory of trauma—that is, psychoanalysis—share several structural similarities, drawing on common language and themes. Law and psychoanalysis proceed by soliciting confessions and testimonies, which are then used to construct a narrative of past events under the guidance of authority. Both are concerned with subjective attachment to authority (the father figure) and its power to command, prohibit, punish, and absolve (recall Freud's notion of the superego as the inner judge).[11] Practitioners of both professions—namely, lawyers and analysts—take cases in order to resolve conflicts and ultimately help the individual adapt to social and institutional settings; in so doing, both undertake interpretative readings of narrative, seeking explanations beneath the surface in terms of gaps, repetitions, symptoms, and motivations.[12] Although concerned primarily with individual cases, both law and psychoanalysis are fundamentally social institutions, pervading almost every aspect in the relationship between the individual and the collective. Finally, law and psychoanalysis are distinctively spoken practices that yield to the verbal while discarding the visual: Lady Justice is blindfolded so that she may not be affected by appearance; the "talking cure" works best when the analysand lies on the couch with little eye contact with the psychoanalyst.

Yet law and psychoanalysis nonetheless proceed in two very different—indeed, contradictory—trajectories: whereas the law draws on reason and certainty (its key figure is the "reasonable man"), psychoanalysis attends to the chaotic, irrational, and libidinal drives of subjectivity. Whereas the procedure of law aims at a clear, unequivocal resolution through a public process of preestablished rules, the psychoanalytic process develops haphazardly and confidentially, from one provisional revelation to another, and is in principle open-ended. And while the law attempts to investigate the goals and desires of subjects, it has traditionally avoided delving into the depths of the soul. In this sense, psychoanalysis might be said to represent law's unconscious, its repressed underside, its "other scene."[13]

In Felman's seminal study, she takes issue with Arendt's account of the Eichmann trial, arguing that the trial's impact and ultimate significance are linked precisely with what Arendt declared as most problematic. Specifically, it was the summoning by the prosecution of more than one hundred witnesses to the stand (while it was clear that none would have been necessary for conviction) that effectively transformed the trial from a criminal litigation into a public narration of trauma. Rather than follow the path of the Nuremberg trials in setting legal precedents for crimes against humanity—what the proceedings should have been about, as per Arendt—this trial exceeded jurisprudence to involve personal narratives of survivors for extralegal purposes. It was the public performance of testimonies, suggests Felman, that made the Eichmann trial revolutionary: "Now, for the first time, victims were legitimized and validated, and their newborn discourse was empowered by their roles not as victims but as prosecution witnesses within the trial."[14]

The point where Felman diverges most radically from Arendt concerns the testimony of the writer Ka-tzetnik.[15] For Arendt, Ka-tzetnik, "the author of several books on Auschwitz that dealt with brothels, homosexuals, and other 'human interest stories,'"[16] seemed an overly theatrical witness whose collapse on the stand was very much in line with chief prosecutor Gideon Hausner's flair for the dramatic. For Felman, conversely, Ka-tzetnik's collapse encompassed the very essence of the trial: the interruption of the law by what cannot be expressed by the law—the wordless trauma, which was re-enacted in the court and gained articulation precisely through the failure of the trial's legal framework. It is for this reason, argues Felman, that Ka-tzetnik's testimony, although legally inconsequential, became one of the most memorable moments of the trial, a moment "in which history as injury dramatically, traumatically spoke." The collapse of the witness was a "physical reminder of the real, a physical reminder of a bodily reality that fractured the totality of the facts sought by the law."[17]

Felman ultimately suggests that the Eichmann trial demonstrates the confluence of private trauma and collective trauma. Insofar as the prosecution was concerned, the trial was about a collective crime to be tried on the collective level, which in turn required transforming "an incoherent mass of private traumas (the secret, hidden, silenced, individual traumas of survivors) into one collective, national, and public trauma."[18] Yet in the courtroom, as Felman astutely shows, a more profound process was taking place whereby survivors' private traumas were inadvertently gaining a transmitting power, engaging—unprecedentedly—audiences both inside and outside the courtroom. Felman indirectly attributes the widespread impact of the trial to radio broadcasts, which were "passionately listened to" and made the trial into "the central event in the country's life."[19] However, her analysis does not offer further insight into radio's impact. Moreover, it remains unclear how Felman accounts for the sudden and almost contagious transmissibility of survivors' private traumas, especially given that prior to the trial, as she indicates, "survivors did not talk about their past, and when they did, they were not listened to."[20]

Recent discussions on cultural trauma prove helpful in this respect. According to Jeffrey Alexander, trauma on the collective level does not share the structure of individual trauma: it is not an immediate, unreflexive response to a shattering event; rather, it is a socially constructed process of representation and mediation that renders an event traumatic for a society. Arguing against popular wisdom and psychoanalytic reasoning, Alexander claims that "events do not, in and of themselves, create collective trauma. Events are not inherently traumatic. Trauma is a socially mediated attribution."[21] This attribution may be made before, during, or after the event, but in any case it is always related to social communicative processes. For an event to be collectively traumatic, it must be coded and mediated as such. As opposed to psychological trauma, cultural trauma refers to a dramatic loss of collective identity, which may not be felt by everyone in the community or even experienced directly by all.[22] While some originary event is necessary to instigate cultural trauma, its significance is made fully explicit only over time and in retrospect, after its meaning is established, understood, and accepted collectively. The recognition of trauma on the social level evokes, in turn, the need for an alternative narrative through which collective identity could be reconstituted, "as a way of repairing the tear in the social fabric."[23] Mass media have a vital role both in representing cultural trauma and in recuperating from it, providing the symbolic means for a community to reconnect past and future.

The social construction of trauma proceeds as a process that defines an injury, establishes the victim, attributes responsibility, and elicits transformation.[24] This process involves different agents: on the one hand, carrier groups—the collective agents of the trauma process—which make the claim about the injury suffered, and on the other, the wider audience, which typically had no relation to the victimized group beforehand but might come to symbolically participate in the originating trauma, if successfully represented. In-between, there are the institutions that mediate the representations of trauma, chief among which are the mass media. This model applies accurately to the Eichmann trial: the survivors-witnesses as the once discredited victims who became the carrier group of trauma; the court as the immediate audience and the Israeli public as the wider audience, both coming to terms with the catastrophe during the trial; and radio as the principal medium of mass communication at the time, relaying the process whereby the Holocaust became a collectively shared trauma in Israel.

Although stressing the importance of media in the mediation of cultural trauma, this approach nevertheless lacks a clear understanding of precisely how media are involved in the process. As the following shows, at issue is not only the coincidence of trial and trauma but also their intersection with media technology—the way the trial, the traumatic past, and the broadcast voice converged into a collectively mediated speech act. In this sense, the story of the Eichmann trial could be summarized as the convergence of three endemically blind figures of speech: Lady Justice meets the "talking cure" meets the "theater of the mind."

RADIO, BODY, VOICE

As a broadcasting medium, radio produces a social space riddled with paradoxes: public transmission heard in the most private settings; socially shared experience that triggers individual imagination; solitary reception that breeds a distinctive sense of togetherness; signals from afar that make intimate contact.[25] In line with the above, it could be added that radio, like law and psychoanalysis, simultaneously invokes the most universal and the very particular. While these paradoxes could be said to apply to electronic media in general, radio constitutes a distinctive configuration of presence-at-a-distance through the separation of body and voice and the reconstruction of a disembodied voice.

It is common knowledge that the body cannot endure transmission, whereas the voice can. Through technological extensions, speech gains what is forever denied to the flesh: omnipresence and afterlife. Radiophonic space, to use Gregory Whitehead's words, is a space of nobodies;[26] or, as Allen S. Weiss puts it, "Radio is, *a fortiori*, the site of the loss of face and body."[27] As a veritable acousmatic technology, radio produces voices whose source cannot be identified.[28] Yet as the voice travels away from the body, it nevertheless retains much of the timbre and tone produced by the body's echo chamber. In fact, out of all media the audible provide a better approximation to the original both in quality and scale: the recorded or broadcast voice is a more direct, one-to-one replica of the authentic pronunciation than, say, a written sentence is of the initial thought or a film frame is of the actual figure. Radio voice produces an acoustic space, evanescent yet encircling, which commands the listener's attention while liberating her imagination. And what is heard tends to be gripping, precisely because it is not seen: as Edmund Carpenter and Marshall McLuhan observed, a squeaking door is far more terrifying over the radio than on television because the image evoked by sound comes from the mind's eye.[29]

It is perhaps radio's disembodied nature that led thinkers to speculate about its resonance with the psychic unconscious. Gaston Bachelard understood radio as speaking directly to the unconscious, a powerful tool that "really does hold the key to tremendous daydreams."[30] He identified radio's promise in its ability to evoke collective archetypes and create reveries in the privacy of one's home, thereby effectively relocating the psychoanalytical session to the airwaves. McLuhan also saw radio as addressing the primal levels of the psyche: "The subliminal depths of radio are charged with the resonating echoes of tribal horns and antique drums . . . with its power to turn the psyche and society into a single echo chamber."[31] Hence radio ushers in the return of the atavistic past, as in the case of Adolf Hitler's broadcast speeches, calling the Teutonic tribes to battle. (There is bitter irony in the fact that the medium said by McLuhan to put the Nazi leader in power is also the medium that introduced the scope of Nazi atrocities as heard in the trial to Israel and the world.) And Friedrich Kittler links sonic technologies to the Lacanian register of the Real: "the recording of vibrations that human ears could not count, human eyes could not see, and writing hands could not catch up with."[32] The Real is captured as the residues left by visual and typographic technologies (which correspond to Jacques Lacan's Imaginary and Symbolic, respectively), an entire spectrum of unfiltered acoustic events, including noises, parapraxes, silences, and repetitions—"the physiological accidents and stochastic disorder of bodies."[33] Acoustic media constitute a cultural repository of what remains unseen and unwritten, an indiscriminative record of the audible traces of reality.

With the splitting of body and voice comes the collapse of ontological borders. In bringing sounds from the concert hall, the stadium, and the political rally into the home, radio effectively redefined the boundary between inside and outside, private and public, allowing for a new kind of participation at a distance. Indeed, the impact of radio as a broadcasting medium on the experience of social space has been a major concern for media scholars.[34] Yet in addition to the transformation of the social space, radio is also said to implicate the mental space, inviting a whole range of out-of-body experiences. As Whitehead argues, the bodiless voice of radiophony mimics that of schizophrenia: "a public channel produced by an absent other entering into a private ear."[35] Radio fills the head with more voices than available in corporeal existence, and with the departure of the voice from its originator comes the fear of stolen words and thoughts, as in the paranoiac anxiety.[36] As acoustic technologies become embedded in everyday life, so do the experience of hearing bodiless voices, an experience traditionally exclusive to the insane (or to the visionary, from Moses to Joan of Arc). The logic of broadcasting has made the separation of body and voice a commonplace, normative phenomenon.

Yet the abandoned body is never totally absent from the broadcast or recorded voice, as it leaves its marks on the voice that reiterates, sometimes unwittingly, the anatomical origin of vocality. Antonin Artaud's 1947 radio drama *To Have Done with the Judgment of God* (which was banned at the time and aired only thirty years later) was all about voicing what is intentionally removed from mainstream radio: by reveling in subvocal sounds, bodily noises, cries, and glossolalia, he attempted to render fragmentary the unified body of Western theater. Controversy aside, what Artaud's experiment exposed is the artificiality of the sterilized voice normally heard on radio in its attempt to strip itself of any corporeal references. The vocal presentation on mainstream radio is indeed ever so mindful of any on-air somatic transgression (coughing, sneezing, lapsing, and the like), which are typically exhaled off the air. Yet, as Roland Barthes noted, the body is inevitability inscribed onto its media traces, broadcast or recorded. It is the body's singular mark on the voice that brings out the expressive over the intelligible, the materiality of the body, "The 'grain' is the body in the voice as it sings."[37] The body persists through what Julia Kristeva designates as the semiotic, the anatomical and instinctive drives that infuse language before and beyond the linguistic structure, generating a distinctive acoustic imprint of a specific body in a particular setting.[38] Thus the phantom body is evoked every time the mediated voice is heard; it is as if the body returns to haunt its own vocal reproduction. In this respect, the spectralization of the body corresponds with the structure of psychic repression: in both cases what is repressed keeps coming back, compulsively, in a displaced manner.

FROM SPEECHLESS BODY TO DISEMBODIED SPEECH

To further ascertain the radiophonic effect of the trial, an examination was needed of what Israelis remember of the event. Two types of material were employed: (1) previously published or broadcast personal accounts, both fiction and nonfiction; and (2) a series of in-depth interviews with five groups of Israelis from different cities who were in their youth at the time of the trial.[39] The purpose of this combined approach was to consciously depart from the examination of historical facts and instead delve into the impressions of those who witnessed the trial through the radio. A reception study half a century after the fact inevitably presents problems of accuracy, but the time elapsed and the extent to which certain things are still remembered might serve to affirm the effect of the original event. What is offered, then, is a glimpse into memory as carried and circulated by individual agents—the original sense of collective memory as intended by Maurice Halbwachs.[40] The examination of what people actually remember has attracted much less attention than the more popular focus on social commemoration.[41] Insofar as the Eichmann trial is concerned, an analysis of its living memory may provide insight into social processes that are otherwise inaccessible, particularly with respect to an issue as intricate as the relationship between private traumas and collective consciousness.

Several historians and critics have argued that prior to the Eichmann trial, knowledge about the Holocaust in Israel was limited and awareness of the survivors' plights was minimal.[42] The years before the trial were ones of collective silence: survivors opted not to speak, and native Israelis—including survivors' children—opted not to ask. Even if this claim is overstated (as recent studies suggest[43]), it is clear that survivors' personal experiences were not part of Israel's public sphere at the time. Avoiding survivors' pain complemented Zionist ideology in its construction of a new national Jewish identity: the native Israeli, or Sabra, who was deemed strong, courageous, and masculine—the polar opposite of the old Jew of the Diaspora, who was viewed as servile, weak, and cowardly. In Zionist identity politics, Holocaust victims were cast as the ultimate case of submission, those who had been led "like sheep to the slaughter," and therefore as somehow complicit in their extermination.[44] Moreover, survivors were often met with suspicion as to how they managed to survive, what they had to do or whom they had to sacrifice so as to be spared from the fate of so many others.[45] The public climate in Israel of the 1950s was unsympathetic to survivors' pain, urging them to put the past behind and focus on the future.

The memory of silence and repression is confirmed by the personal accounts of those who were children and young teenagers at the time. A program on Israeli radio titled *When Eichmann Entered My Home*, broadcast in 2002 for Holocaust Memorial Day, featured interviews with a number of Israeli public figures about their memories of the trial. All mentioned the Eichmann trial as marking the end of years of reticence. Israeli singer-songwriter Shlomo Artzi stated that "Back then it was mostly silence. At eleven I didn't know much. I knew that something had happened and thought it was the same in other homes." The historian Nili Keren added, "I was in the eleventh grade, majoring in the humanities with an emphasis in history, and we didn't study anything about the Holocaust." This overall sense of silence and ignorance is affirmed by interviewees, who, unlike in the radio program, were asked to reflect on how they first came to know about the Holocaust without any reference to the Eichmann trial. For many, particularly for survivors' children, restraint and taciturnity were the substance of their childhood. As a woman from Kiryat Haim recalls: "With my mother I never spoke about Auschwitz one-on-one. Some things I knew from others. My mother would only speak about Auschwitz with her friends who were also there, and I would listen through the door." Another recounts her memories of childless neighbors who always greeted her with chocolate: "But that silence, I remember the silence. They would touch you, give to you, but never speak. I can't remember any story, certainly not at home, but also not at the neighbors'. Also as a student, school didn't help either. I don't remember the teachers talking about it."

Against the background of collective silence, with the bulk of survivors remaining tongue-tied, a distinctive figure of the Holocaust survivor came to dominate public perception in Israel. It was the survivor as an eccentric, dumbstruck figure, living on the margins of society, and often on the verge of insanity. Israeli fiction written in the years following the trial is replete with such figures. David Grossman's novel *See Under: Love* features a cast of survivors living in Israel in the late 1950s, who are irrecoverably damaged by what had happened "over there." An old uncle who is brought to the family after years in a mental institution is seen upon arrival as "swimming like maybe a fish in an aquarium . . . talking to himself in a weird voice that went up and down excitedly." Other eccentrics inhabit the background: one of them "always walked around saying Who am I who am I but that's because he lost his memories on account of the Nazis," while another "just smiled at everyone all the time and they said he was empty inside."[46] Another example is Amos Oz's *My Michael*, set in 1950s Jerusalem, where the protagonist's neighbor, a childless Holocaust survivor, suffers from repeated fits of hysteria and agonizing, sleepless nights. She is finally moved to an institution, after which her husband mutters: "My poor Duba, they are giving her electric shock treatments."[47] The mental pathology of survivors is also the main theme of Yoram Kaniuk's *Adam Resurrected*, which takes place in an asylum populated solely by camp survivors and situated in the Israeli desert in the early 1960s.[48] Such disturbed figures inhabit the childhood space of the Israeli generation raised after the war, as clearly reflected in the books and films they produced as adults.[49] The literary depiction is confirmed by personal accounts of Israelis who were young teenagers at the time. Former minister Yossi Beilin shared the following in an interview on *When Eichmann Entered My Home*:

> Our streets were in the shadow of the Holocaust. Some of the people I used to see on the way to school were Holocaust survivors, wandering around, whom we regarded as crazy. There was this tailor who was sitting and sawing at a corner somewhere on Allenby Street. And there was this lady who used to chase us with a stick. And all were people of the Holocaust. For my generation, those who were born with the state of Israel, the Holocaust was seen during the 1950s as something that had produced sad people with numbers on their arms and insane people who wandered around with staring eyes.[50]

Interviews also confirm the pervasiveness of the figure of the mad Holocaust survivor. Many recall someone from their neighborhood whose eccentricity was attributed to what had happened to them in the camps. Referring to an area where survivors used to live in shacks, a man from Binyamina remembers: "As a boy I used to pass by Machlul neighborhood in Tel Aviv by the beach. When I asked what's out there, I was told stay away, these are the crazy people. . . . They were very odd, they used to watch the sun come down, and you couldn't talk to them. They talked to themselves." A woman from Tel Aviv recalls: "When I was five or six we had a neighbor who kept screaming at her son, she had one child, and she was like half-deranged, and I remember my mother telling me, 'Don't judge her, she came from Germany.'" And a woman from Kiryat Haim recounts: "We lived in a little apartment which we shared with a Hungarian couple who both survived Auschwitz. . . . Both had numbers on their arms. She was very ill because of the Holocaust. She was mentally ill and was hospitalized for long periods." The image of the survivors as it arises from the second generation's personal accounts is the combination of a pariah and a freak. Often remembered as ghastly and grief-stricken, these figures are evoked as either screaming or silent, but never as speaking. In Israel of the 1950s, the Holocaust survivor was one with the mad, a figure divested of language, a traumatized, speechless body.

The Eichmann trial is said to have brought a profound transformation to Holocaust memory in Israel. For the first time, survivors were validated and legitimized, summoned to address the court and, through it, the entire world. With the trial, a public space was made available for survivors to bear witness, their experiences gaining the public recognition they had long lacked.[51] And it was precisely at this juncture that radio became crucial: not only by transmitting testimonies and making them public but also, and more crucially, by instigating a fundamental shift in the survivors themselves and in their public perception in Israel. Taking to the airwaves meant an opportunity to speak away from the tattooed, traumatized body, clear of the label of madness and unintelligibility.

For it was precisely the transfiguration induced by radio of the speechless body into disembodied speech that rendered survivors' testimonies universally accessible. It is as if the logic of radio dictated a necessary trade-off: for trauma to gain voice, the body—the locus of trauma—had to be discarded. By removing survivors' voices from their bodies, radio effectively redefined the conditions by which trauma could find public articulation. The radiophonic separation between body and voice invited the return of the socially repressed. It is in this respect that radio afforded survivors passage from silence to speech, from "bare life" to social life. Paradoxically, it was the faceless medium of radio that gave survivors face in the Levinasian sense. Only as disembodied speech did victims become bearers of testimony; only as severed voices could they be heard.

Clearly, these voices were unlike anything heard before. All the interviewees state that listening to court sessions on the radio was for them the unveiling of what had previously been shrouded in silences, whispers, and fragments. For those who are second-generation to Holocaust survivors, the trial gave their parents the public recognition they had been missing, as a woman from Petach Tikva claims:

> My mother tells that when they just came here those who had already been living here did not believe their stories. There was total disbelief. They even disparaged them; they didn't want to hear and dismissed the whole thing. The issue of the Holocaust, with all these stories that came out in the Eichmann trial

and everybody heard it, then they started to believe their story. It started then because, before, nobody had believed anything.

Almost unanimously, the trial is remembered as being broadcast live on a daily basis for months on end: "As long as it went on, the trial was live on radio . . . every day they broadcast it live. It emanated from every house; it was part of our lives" (a woman from Petach Tikva). "The radio was on all the time. . . . As long as the trial was happening, the radio was on" (a couple from B'nei Brak). Three specific radiophonic moments clearly stand out among all interviewees: Prime Minister Ben-Gurion's announcement of Eichmann's capture, the opening speech of chief prosecutor Hausner, and Ka-tzetnik's collapse on the stand. For most, the experience of listening is linked to concrete settings. At school: "I remember in school at noon we had a radio and the teacher let us listen. I remember it clearly . . . we had a radio there and I think it was the opening session of the trial, which everybody was waiting for" (a man from Jerusalem). At home: "I was at home and there was something on the radio and Mom and Dad were very upset, holding each other, and later they told me that it was Eichmann. They were very emotional, and Mom started to cry" (a woman from Petach Tikva). On the street: "I remember the minute and the day where I was when I heard about it [Eichmann's capture]. Tremendous excitement. I was on Nordau Street in Haifa with a friend and we passed by a barber's shop with a radio set on the street, and people were talking about it and there was this big commotion" (a woman from Jerusalem). With one's parents: "The radio was on constantly. It seemed to me like Mom and Dad were not going to work. They had to go and feed the cattle or something—the cattle would wait. It was just obsessive" (a man from a village near Hadera). Or specifically in the absence of parents: "All you wanted was to listen and stay at home from school. I think it was even allowed not to go and stay home to listen. So it wasn't really skipping, otherwise they wouldn't have let me stay" (a man from Tel Aviv).

The intergenerational drama triggered by the trial through the radio is captured most evocatively in a recent column by an Israeli commentator:

> It was in the beginning of April 1961, when I was sitting underneath my mother's chair, one of dozens placed around a big hissing Philips radio, that I discovered I was a part of the Jewish people. It happened when Gideon Hausner opened his speech. . . . This was the first time I saw my parents cry and immediately came out from my hiding to hug and console them. "This is a very important day for us," Mother apologized. "Forgive us for crying."[52]

What seems to have made a particularly poignant impression is the distinctive sound of the trial. Hausner's voice was repeatedly mentioned as most memorable. To quote three of the interviewees: "His dramatic voice that you would hear, kind of a metallic voice, dramatic, awesome, which was overwhelming for us as kids" (a man from Kiryat Haim). "Hausner's voice, it was this kind of voice that, even today if you heard it on the radio, you'd never forget his voice. A very distinctive voice, representing the six million" (a woman from Herzliya). "His voice echoed from everywhere. The radio was on everywhere and his voice echoed. The pathos in which he spoke, you could hear it everywhere" (a woman from Petach Tikva). In contrast to the unequivocal memory of Hausner's piercing voice, survivors' testimonies are mostly remembered en masse, as a clutter of indistinguishable voices rather than individual narratives. In the words of a man from Binyamina, "There were so many testimonies, it's really hard to remember it all. It just went on and on, testimonies all the time. We couldn't tell the facts with so many testimonies." And another woman adds, "I think at some stage, after the Eichmann trial, it seemed there were too many stories in the background, and so we somehow blocked it out . . . we didn't want to hear any more. There was this period when it was too much, you got fed up with it, overload." As opposed to the silence that characterized earlier years, the time of the trial is described as that of incessant talk, an indistinct, ongoing rumbling of testimonies.

Significantly, some recall sounds of disquiet, disturbance, and collapse emanating from the radio, especially coming from the background. As a woman from Kiryat Haim attests: "What I remember from the trial is the screaming. I hear survivors screaming, as if not speaking in a human voice, not in their own voice. I can't remember if I listened to the stories they were telling. . . . Maybe I remember it wrong, but there was an audience inside the hall and the screaming was coming from the audience." A man from Ramat Gan: "As long as the trial was happening, the radio was on. . . . I think there wasn't a day without outbursts from people who came [to watch the trial]. It was clear that Holocaust survivors were sitting there. I remember there were outbursts every day." And this is what a woman from Jerusalem said after listening to a recording of Ka-tzetnik's testimony: "It gives me a stomachache. Funny, it's not only the talking. I just started to hear this rustling sound beyond any speech and story, the noises you hear . . . the noises from the transmission itself, just the noises between the words, it's something already horrifying." Ka-tzetnik's testimony, one of the most unsettling moments in the trial, is remembered by two moments: the phrase "other planet," which he used in his testimony to describe Auschwitz, and his collapse on the stand with the commotion in the courtroom that ensued. The phrase and the breakdown encompass the two poles in the crisis of testimony that typifies this trial: on the one hand, the attempt to express the inexpressible through language, and on the other, the inexpressible as expressed precisely through the failure of language.

The trial therefore seems to have left a distinctive acoustic memory with those who listened to it on the radio. Ultimately, it was not just the testimonial narrative but an entire catalog of sonic moments that stuck with the audience: accents, silences, echoes, cries, whispers—the auditory traces of the trial. To use Kristeva's terminology, the trial's radiophonic effect lies not only in its *phenotext* but in its *genotext*: not simply in giving voice but also in exposing the body in the voice.[53] Though severed from their source, radio voices nevertheless carried the mark of the specific setting and the materiality of their emergence. Radio removed the survivor's wounded body only to reintroduce it as the "grain" in the witnessing voice—the Real of voice as captured and transmitted through the acoustic medium. The radiophonic might now appear as the dialectic, rather than the separation, of body and voice—or, better, the body as displaced and condensed onto the voice. Hence a double return of the repressed: on the one hand, the return of the socially repressed as occasioned by the disembodied voice, and on the other, the return of the repressed traumatic body as effected by the sounds of corporeality teeming within the disembodied voice. The body reappeared as its own specter; it returned, vicariously, as a surrogate for the inexplicable. And so, as the voice took to the airwaves, it did not travel completely discarnate, for within it resounded the pain of the originating body.

THE RADIOPHONIC REAL

Studying the role of radio during the Eichmann trial may have implications beyond the particular historical episode. Indeed, the issues raised here can provide insight into the processes by which private traumas become a collectively shared cultural trauma—namely, the mediation of trauma. Specifically, what this chapter suggests is that technological mediation bears importantly on the ways trauma is rendered public.

As discussed earlier, it is possible to identify two opposing approaches to the mediation of trauma: the psychoanalytic approach, represented by Felman,[54] and the sociological approach, represented by Alexander.[55] However, both approaches are largely oblivious to the technological specificities of the media involved in the process. On the one hand, Felman maintains that the Eichmann trial occasioned the "transmission" of private trauma into collective consciousness, serving not only as a legal tool for establishing facts but also as a means to "transmit truth as event and as the shock of an *encounter* with events, transmit history as experience."[56] Yet her analysis altogether ignores the actual transmission happening on the air, thereby missing the uncanny conjunction of the two kinds of "transmission" conjured up by the trial—the traumatic and the radiophonic. On the other hand, the theory of cultural trauma as introduced by Alexander and others suggests that trauma on the collective level operates differently from that on the individual level: rather than a break in language and consciousness, for trauma to be shared collectively it must be made intelligible, hence undergo representation. While scholars in this approach do refer to media as central to the social construction of trauma, they tend to confuse mediation with representation and narrativization and often treat different media as interchangeable means of propagation.[57]

Like other forms of mediation, the mediation of trauma is predicated on the media technology at work. Yet what is distinctive about this form of mediation, when it occurs, is the way a specific medium figures in the process whereby trauma gains articulation. Consider the case of the television coverage of the Eichmann trial in the United States. According to Jeffrey Shandler, the trial telecasts failed to "become a fixture of American Holocaust memory culture."[58] One main reason was the preoccupation with watching Eichmann: seeing the archvillain on the television screen was so gripping that it overshadowed everything else. The image of Eichmann inspired a range of associations, starting with speculations about the "Nazi character," through the inner monstrosity revealed by his involuntary gestures, and ending with outright fascination with the glass booth, which seemed to some like the glass cage used in American televised quiz shows. As Shandler concludes, "In contrast to Eichmann's corporeal, if inscrutable, presence at the trial, 'the six million' remained elusive."[59]

While any comparison between the United States and Israel on that matter would be somewhat tenuous, the contrast is nevertheless telling. Whereas in the United States, television brought fixation with the spectacle of Eichmann, in Israel, radio yielded concentration on the survivors' testimonies. The two media radicalized the disparity between image and sound with respect to the same event. Obviously, there were other reasons as well for the trial's fundamentally different impact in the two countries. Still, any examination of the social life of trauma would be seriously lacking without taking into account the ways media technologies converge with certain modalities of articulation stemming from the originating event.

This chapter suggests that media do not simply relate trauma but, importantly, participate in *performing* trauma. What was heard on the radio was not only the speaking voices— the process of narrativization involved in the making of cultural trauma, as per Alexander's definition—but also the sounds of mediation itself: the acoustic repercussions of discarding the body and resurrecting the voice—the radiophonic Real. In other words, the mediation of trauma by radio did not simply have to do with narratology but also, and crucially, with traumatography. Radio re-enacted what is fundamental to the traumatic effect: the severance between the somatic and the phonetic, between the corporeal container and its expressive signs. And that effect always implies an uncanny brush with mortality, a touch of death. As Barthes observed, death is the eidos of media both photographic and phonographic: the finitude and transience of the body appear most acutely through its media traces—and most ominously after the body's demise.[60]

It is no coincidence, then, that media technologies have been associated in late modernity with attempts to communicate with the dead. By extending indefinitely the gap between the body and its traces, by exceeding the ontological opposition between presence and absence, media technologies conjure up a "spectral logic."[61] The interrelations between mental and technological energies go back to the second half of the nineteenth century, to spiritualist telecommunication with the dead.[62] Indeed, the two contemporaneous practices of spiritualism and psychoanalysis might be regarded as two comparable attempts to overcome a profound loss: both seek to repair a decisive moment of separation that returns to haunt and possess the present. [63] In this sense, media technologies, in establishing telecommunication lines with the dead, might be conceived as modern-day apparatuses of mourning.[64] As Kittler suggest, "Media always already provide the appearances of specters," and adds that "The realm of the dead is as extensive as the storage and transmission capabilities of a given culture."[65] By constantly reproducing the presence of the departed, modern media technologies perform a collective work of mourning, a publicly mediated process of contending with ghosts.

Herein lies another level of mediation performed in the Eichmann trial. The trial summoned the living to bear witness to the dead in the presence of audiences both near and far and in so doing invoked a spectral dimension that persisted throughout the proceedings. Consider chief prosecutor Hausner's opening speech, which in its first words portends a spiritualistic motif:

> When I stand before you here, judges of Israel, to lead the prosecution of Adolf Eichmann, I am not standing alone. With me are 6 million accusers. But they cannot rise to their feet and point an accusing finger toward him who sits in the dock and cry: "I accuse." For their ashes are piled up on the hills of Auschwitz and the fields of Treblinka, and are strewn in the forests of Poland. Their graves

are scattered throughout the length and breadth of Europe. Their blood cries out, but their voice is not heard. Therefore I will be their spokesman and in their name I will unfold this awesome indictment.[66]

Thus not only judgment and historical reckoning were sought in this trial but also mediating the voices of the murdered, bearing witness for their unspoken accusation. In this sense, the trial introduced another level of justice beyond the judicial: justice as intended by Jacques Derrida, a pledge of hospitality and responsibility for the silent, absent, and bygone, "justice which, beyond right or law, rises up in the very respect owed to whoever *is not*, no longer or not yet, living, presently living."[67] It is significant that this mediation was radiocast, that is, took place both in the courtroom and on the air. For in addition to testifying for the dead, the broadcast voices of survivors, precisely because they were severed from their bodies, also bore witness to a fundamental traumatic effect—the intrusion of absence into presence, the persistence of that which cannot be mediated within mediation, the interruption of narrative by what cannot be narrativized. The Eichmann trial constituted a collective séance, as it were, inviting the inarticulate source of trauma to haunt the ongoing attempts at its articulation (as illustrated figuratively in Fig. 1.2.). As a mass-mediated event, the trial inaugurated a collective process of coming to grips with the catastrophic past through a public re-enactment of trauma.[68] Yet it is still debatable whether this "acting out" of trauma has led to a process of "working through," that is, to a successful work of mourning with respect to Holocaust memory in the Israeli society.[69]

Finally, evaluating the role of radio in the mediation of trauma in the Eichmann trial would be incomplete without considering it as a "media event": a historic event that is experienced as such publicly through the media. The trial seems to fit neatly with Daniel Dayan and Elihu Katz's main criteria: transmissions from the courtroom interrupted broadcasting routine; court sessions were transmitted live, even if infrequently (and are certainly remembered as such); the event itself took place on location outside media, which required elaborate technical preparations; it was partly planned, organized, and advertised in advance; it was presented with reverence and ceremony reserved for historic occasions; and it evidently developed into a transformative event by addressing previously silenced concerns and bringing them to collective awareness.[70] As with most media events, the trial was more about reconciliation than confrontation, which led in this case to a public affirmation of the survivors' misfortune, what Axel Honneth calls "recognition."[71] Yet there is more to the trial as a media event insofar as the mediation of trauma is concerned.[72]

Figure 1.2. "You shall not kill: the testimony of the slayed commandment." A drawing by cartoon artist Arieh Navon, Davar Newspaper, May 19 1961. (Reproduced by permission of David Navon.)

As mentioned before, radio coverage of the trial proceeded in two main formats: daily recaps—an entirely edited and narrated thirty-minute broadcast—aired following the evening news, and live transmissions, which, although they were relatively infrequent (no more than sixteen broadcasts in four months), seem to have left a profound impression on the Israeli public. At issue are two very different, even diametrically distinct broadcasting formats in terms of both production and reception: the former was the result of a regulated process of selection and prioritization with commentary to boot; the latter was more of a hands-off operation, without any proactive involvement on the broadcaster's side. In fact, Kol Yisrael presenters were instructed not to interfere with live transmissions in any way and to limit their presence to announcements at the beginning and end of the broadcast while keeping the microphones running throughout.[73] Such abdication, much like the phenomenon of dead air, would normally cause alarm in both producer and audience, not simply because of the possibility of technical failure, but, more dramatically, because it might signal the collapse of the authoritative presence of radio.[74] In the Eichmann trial, the result was an unfiltered transmission of the acoustic event as such and hence as inherently predisposed to surprises, accidents, and contingencies—the tumultuous noises of the Real.[75] While the daily recaps produced a mitigated, professional account of the course of the trial, the live broadcasts captured the uncontrolled, irruptive nature of the event, complete with all the sounds of its liveness.

That many Israelis remember the trial as broadcast in real time is a sign of the involvement it enlisted: to hear it live means to have access to the truth and authenticity of the event, in time if not in space.[76] Liveness compels vicarious participation, the possibility of bearing witness through the media. The false memory of liveness may therefore bear a hidden truth: the extent to which the event intervened in and impinged on the lives of those who listened to it on the radio. The Eichmann trial is one of those rare media events that fuse autobiographical and collective memory: almost everyone who heard it on the radio can recall the specific circumstances of listening—a classic case of "flashbulb memory."[77] Through the radio broadcasts, the trial entered into the lives and daily routines of the audience, interpellating each listener personally and the entire public collectively. This might indicate something quite significant with respect to the mediation of trauma: the interruption to programming schedule, and the consequent interruption to everyday life, produced a sense of exigency and momentousness that paralleled the articulation of private traumas in the courtroom. This is yet another sense in which media perform, rather than merely relate, cultural trauma.

The perceived experience of liveness complemented the sensation of discharge that emanated from the courtroom, the sense of something unprecedented happening, the interruptive force of the event. It is as though live transmissions re-enacted on a grand scale that which underlies the very experience of trauma—the persistence of something intangible yet invasive that haunts the present and is always experienced in the present. Two kinds of interruption were therefore at work in this trial, diegetic and extradiegetic: on the one hand, the sounds of corporeality clamoring within the broadcast testimonies, and on the other, the interruption of routine caused by the broadcast itself and experienced affectively by the audience. If in the former the body intruded into the disembodied voice, in the latter the body mortal intruded into the body politic. It was the combination of the two that contributed importantly to the mediation of cultural trauma during this historic trial.

CHAPTER 2
Videography and Testimony

Modern technological media and psychoanalysis are historically coextensive, so argues Friedrich Kittler. During the last decades of the nineteenth century, a profound transformation had taken place in the material conditions of communication—what Kittler terms *Aufschreibesystem* (literally "writing-down system," translated as "discourse network").[1] Prior to that transformation, writing, in its various manifestations, was the dominant medium of information storage and transmission. When writing was the prevailing writing-down system, all forms of data had to pass through the "bottleneck of the signifier."[2] With the technological transformation that followed, the symbolic mediation of writing was supplemented by the non-symbolic writing-down system of sight and sound: the audio channel of the phonograph and the visual channel of the cinematograph. As opposed to writing, these media are unselective inscription devices, capturing the intentional together with the unintentional, data and noise, indiscriminately as they come. It is against this background that psychoanalysis appears as a contemporaneous method of recording both intentional and unintentional expressions: the meanings conveyed by speech together with the halts, parapraxes, and stutters—which are rendered at least as meaningful as the intended meanings. Psychoanalysis has a technological counterpart in the form of late nineteenth-century media: the psychic and the technical constitute two parallel mechanisms for the inscription of traces, with the logic of the latter partially informing the former.[3] Sigmund Freud has an unlikely partner in Thomas Edison: the talking cure and the discovery of the unconscious are concomitant with phonography and the mechanization of nonsense.

Yet media and psychoanalysis, argues Kittler, do not only supplement the medium of writing; they also take on various tasks of cultural mediation previously under the monopoly of script.[4] One such task is the writing of the past, historiography understood most literally, which, following Kittler's reasoning, is also transformed by modern media to include the aural and the visual. That the past is experienced through its media traces was obvious enough to any citizen of the twentieth century. Less obvious, however, is the extent to which the conceptual correlation between media and psychoanalysis pointed out by Kittler continues to infuse recent thinking and writing on the past. Just as the science of the unconscious had its technological unconscious in late nineteenth-century media, recent psychoanalytically informed discourses, particularly in the humanities, have their own technological underpinnings in late twentieth-century media.

A case in point is the discourse of trauma and testimony as developed in the seminal work on Holocaust testimonies of Dori Laub, Lawrence Langer, and Shoshana Felman. Their studies bring together literature, history, and psychoanalysis to consider the challenges of language in testifying to the calamities of the Holocaust. The insights they provide have importantly influenced numerous accounts on other historical and personal tragedies; indeed, much of what is currently called trauma theory in literary, film, and media studies has its roots in these texts. Yet despite the wide application in various intellectual and artistic media, little attention has been given to the actual media behind this discourse. As I argue in the following, the technological unconscious of the trauma and testimony discourse is the videotape as an audiovisual technology of recording, processing, and transmission.

Ostensibly, there is no discovery in pointing out the technology at work. It is plainly clear that much of the source material for the authors above is videotaped testimonies, which is perhaps why this detail failed to attract special attention, with only a few exceptions. Among these are studies that explore the ways in which the audiovisual medium plays into the creation of a distinctive genre of testimony vis-à-vis other forms of historical knowledge and traumatic memory.[5] While providing important insights, this perspective tends to regard technology on the instrumental level, in terms of the challenges and opportunities the video apparatus introduces into the fraught question of representing the Holocaust. What is at issue here, however, is something different and more fundamental: not merely the media apparatus but the media a priori—the technological infrastructure from which such a genre can become meaningful in the first place. At issue, then, is what Hans Ulrich Gumbrecht calls the "materialities of communication": "those phenomena and conditions that contribute to the production of meaning, without being meanings themselves."[6] That the trauma and testimony discourse is underwritten by audiovisual technology of recording and replaying bears importantly on how both trauma and testimony themselves are consequently theorized. Read with videography in mind, these key texts bespeak the writing-down system—the videographic traumatography—without which the pains of testimony could not have come to signify as such, let alone be made available for scrutiny. It is only with an audiovisual medium capable of capturing and reproducing evidence of the fleeting unconscious that a discourse concerned with the unarticulated traumatic past becomes intelligible.

ARCHIVE, MEDIA, TRAUMA

The idea to videotape the testimonies of Holocaust survivors was initiated in 1979 by television producer and documentarian Laurel Vlock and psychiatrist and Holocaust survivor Dori Laub.[7] It began as a grassroots operation in New Haven, Connecticut, with the involvement of local figures from the Jewish community and Yale University, and soon took shape as the Holocaust Survivors Film Project (despite the name, filming was conducted from the start in videotape). In 1981 the project set itself under the auspices of Yale University as the Fortunoff Video Archive for Holocaust Testimonies, with the late Geoffrey Hartman as its academic director. To date, more than 4,500 video testimonies have been taped, all of which are available in the Sterling Memorial Library at Yale (a recording session of testimony in the early days of the Fortunoff archive is seen in Fig. 2.1.).[8]

As Laub later attested, the idea came after watching two films that attempted to relate to the Holocaust: the 1978 television miniseries *Holocaust*—whose "studio quality of Hollywood" he found appalling—and Marcel Ophüls's, *The Sorrow and the Pity*, whose employment of testimonies he found deeply impressive.[9] These two salutary checks on the cultural mediation of the Holocaust are the background for the development of a new form of testimony, one that combines oral history, the psychoanalytic session, and the television interview—what Geoffrey Hartman termed "videotestimony."[10] The founders' premise was "that the medium of video could be used successfully to document the personal memories of Holocaust witnesses."[11] From its inception, the Yale archive had a dual rationale: on the one hand, documenting the personal memories of survivors under the pressing conviction that "time

Figure 2.1. Interview for the Fortunoff archive. Image from *Those Who Were There* (HVT-8008). 1982. © Fortunoff Video Archive for Holocaust Testimonies, Yale University Library.

is running out and that every survivor has a unique story to tell"; and, on the other hand, employing videotape technology to capture the testimonies, as "it was felt that the 'living portraiture' of television would add a compassionate and sensitive dimension to the historical record."[12]

This rationale is far from obvious. Presumably, documenting testimonies could have been transcribed, recorded, or even filmed. Videotape technology had two important advantages for a project such as Yale's archive. It made it possible to carry out the entire process as an in-house production, including shooting, editing, and postproduction—all at a considerably lower cost than film. But more crucially, as a companion technology to television, the videotape, unlike film, can be easily preconfigured for televisual transmission. As such, the videotape constitutes at once a medium of archiving and a medium of potential broadcasting, as affirmed by Hartman:

> The principle of giving survivors their voice has been a sustaining one. Also that of giving a face to that voice: of choosing video over audio, because of the immediacy and evidentiality it added to the interview. The "embodiment" of the

survivors, their gestures and bearing, is part of the testimony. . . . Audiences now and in the future would surely be audiovisual. We decided to make video recordings of public broadcast quality, to build an Archive of Conscience on which future educators and filmmakers might rely. These living portraits are the nearest our descendants can come to a generation passing from the scene.[13]

Videotestimony thus performs two media functions: storage and transmission. It can capture the uniqueness and authenticity of the storyteller, the "embodiment" of the survivor bearing witness, while at the same time it holds the potential for future dissemination ("public broadcast quality"), for collective participation and intergenerational communication (what Hartman probably had in mind is television documentaries, such as the one produced in 1980 by Laural Vlock by the name *Forever Yesterday*[14]). The use of videotape in testimony intensified the potential brought by video recording more generally: the technology originally developed in the 1950s to facilitate synchronized broadcasting across different time zones ended up in the hands of private users as a means for singularized audiovisual experience, and further to document and preserve one's own biographical time.[15] In this sense, the videotestimony is a special kind of archival material: disposed to deposition inasmuch as distribution, it conflates the singularity of the testimony with the universality of its appeal. Such is the imperative of this archive, an imperative that is inseparable from the archive's technological infrastructure.[16]

As Jacques Derrida argued, the archive is about the past as much as it is about the future, and it is therefore both conservative and revolutionary. To archive something is not simply to consign what is already there waiting to be archived; rather, it is to shape the very construction of that which is archived and hence its future forms of distribution and signification. It is in this respect that the technology of archiving is intrinsic to the act of archiving: "the technical structure of the *archiving* archive also determines the structure of the *archivable* content even in its very coming to existence and in its relationship to the future. The archivization produces as much as it records the event."[17] Such is also the case with the archiving technology of the Yale archive; videography does not document testimonies as already formed and self-contained narratives but rather conditions the very structure of their signification, which allows them to signify precisely as testimonies.[18] In addition to and independently of the testimonial narrative itself, videography produces what might be called the audiovisual mark of trauma: the indexical and temporal markers of corporeality as captured by the video camera and recorded and reproduced by the videotape. If indeed the Yale archive could be said to be both conservative and revolutionary, it is by virtue of videography functioning as a medium for archiving testimonies and, at the same time, as a medium through which testimonies so archived redefine the scope of the archivable.

The Yale archive is the context of some of the most original theoretical developments around trauma in the humanities over the last decades. Indeed, the discourse of trauma and testimony owes much to the analytical possibilities opened by the archive—specifically, the lending of audiovisual testimonies to the professional analysis of literary critics, psychoanalysts, and critical historians. Focusing on three key representatives—Laub, Langer, and Felman—the analysis below sets out to explicate the intermedial exchanges among speech, writing, and videography in the work of each. In other words, under discussion is an ekphrastic process: the written interpretations of videotape recordings of survivors' oral testimonies. The analysis of the three accounts revolves around an apparent preoccupation of each author with a specific media function, corresponding respectively with what Kittler declared as the three elementary functions of media: recording, processing, and transmission.[19] What trauma comes to signify in these accounts will be shown to be connected with the way videography performs these three elementary media functions.

RECORDING

Dori Laub has made a crucial contribution to the understanding of massive trauma, both clinically and historically. His insights doubtless follow from his unique position as a child survivor, a psychoanalyst engaged in the treatment of survivors, and a cofounder of the Yale archive for Holocaust testimonies. According to Laub, bearing witness to trauma is facilitated by the recovery of an empathic listener who comes to partially participate in the reliving of the traumatic experience. The listener is not merely ancillary but is in fact fundamental to the process, serving a maieutic function by presenting him- or herself before the witness as an open and supportive addressee, as a Thou. As Felman, Laub's coauthor, puts it, "it takes two to witness the unconscious," or in Laub's words, the listener takes on "the responsibility for bearing witness that previously the narrator felt he bore alone, and therefore could not carry out."[20] The listener can be said to bear witness to trauma even before the witness does, heeding the narrative as it emerges from abeyance.

Given the emphasis on the listening party, it is curious that Laub's maieutics of testimony practically ignores the presence of the video camera on site. Yet, following his own logic, there is reason to believe that the camera's role is not unlike that of the listener; in fact, it may even be said to anticipate the listener's bearing witness to the witness and is hence indispensable to the process. If the listener is the facilitator of testimony, as Laub suggests, the camera facilitates the listener's facilitating; it serves as a technological surrogate for an audience in potentia—the audience for which many survivors had been waiting for a lifetime—providing them with the kind of holding environment that is unattainable in the solitude of an off-camera interview. If the listener acts as the Buberian Thou, the camera acts as the Levinasian *le tiers;* it imposes thirdness on the witnessing dyad. Bearing witness is from the outset bearing witness on camera, already with the dual prospect of safekeeping and dissemination. Hartman seems to come close to this realization when he suggests, invoking Maurice Halbwachs, that the video archive constitutes "a provisional 'affective community' for the survivor."[21] If for Halbwachs "affective community" meant the immediate social ties and common experiences from which collective memory emerges, in Hartman's rendering it is now the apparatus of the archive that doubles as the enabling context for the construction of a remembering community. It doesn't take just two to bear witness, but the promise of a whole congregation.

While focusing predominantly on the witnessing dyad, Laub's conception of testimony nevertheless discloses its technological setting through an apparent preoccupation with the issue of recording. This much is evident in the various inflections of *record* recurring in Laub's writing and, moreover, in the productive ambiguity of its meaning. Here is how Laub describes massive trauma: "the observing and recording mechanisms of the human mind are temporarily knocked out, malfunction." Hence the challenge for the listener is in searching for an experience whose registration is still pending, "a record that has yet to be made.[22] "Record" is sufficiently ambiguous to be read as the outcome of a psychoanalytic process by which an event is to be retroactively restored, but equally as the actual record, the video recording capturing the process of restoring the missing mental record—a record by which the testimony may also be retroactively replayed. Indeed, the two senses of "record" are inescapably linked; the technological observing and recording mechanisms work as restorative prosthetics for the once-blocked mental observing and recording mechanisms. Testimony is the search for a missing record, on record.

The recovery of memory through recording occasions rejoining the technical sense of "record" with its Latin etymology *recordari*, literally, "restore to heart" (*cor*) and, by extension, "call to mind." When tape-recorded memory combines with human memory the result is a technological anamnesis: a recollection feedback loop between mind and tape that brings back one's own memories as rediscovered memories, for ill or good, as poignantly depicted in Samuel Beckett's *Krapp's Last Tape*.[23] Technically speaking, with magnetic tape the operation of recording is concomitant with the operation of erasing: electromagnetic deletion takes place at the same time as recording.[24] With videotestimony, this technical detail takes on an allegorical meaning: the technological recording through deleting facilitates the undeleting of "a record that has yet to be made," the videographic recovery of a biographic memory. The witnessing scene has recording media at its base, as testimonies reordered at Yale "set in motion a testimonial process similar in nature to the psychoanalytic process, in that it is yet another medium which provides a listener to trauma, another medium of re-externalization—and thus historicization—of the event."[25] For this reason, Laub asks that the listener act as a "blank screen on which the event comes to be inscribed for the first time."[26] But there is in fact another screen—the television screen—on which this inscription comes to be inscribed in the first place. As screens and records occupy the process of witnessing, psychoanalysis and videotestimony become the correlating matrices of survivors' bearing witness to trauma.

And, yet, the added visual channel of videotestimony introduces problems foreign to the strictly audio channel of the talking cure. As Kittler notes, for Freud psychoanalysis was based on the separation of speech and vision. Analysis proceeds with the analysand speaking while lying down and the analyst sitting in the back, noting down all the minute halts, slips, and digressions in the flow of speech. Freud's aversion to the visual is particularly apparent in his writing on hysteria, where the talking cure is set to destroy the images inside the patient's head (typically the more "visual" women), decomposing the "inner film" into spoken words.[27] Videotestimony invokes the time-honored auditory bias of psychoanalysis by basing itself on what Hartman calls a "counter-cinematic integrity." While showing, it attempts to divert attention from what is shown to what is heard; it makes the image auxiliary to speech.[28]

Curbing the visual was indeed one of the first challenges of this enterprise. As Hartman affirms, after experimenting with different types of camera work during interviews, the decision was to give up the "expressive potential and remain fixed, except for enough motion to satisfy more naturally the viewer's eye."[29] Another decision was to record survivors in a neutral studio, rather than in the privacy of their homes, so as to minimize distractions. It was also decided that the camera should focus exclusively on the witness without showing the interviewer, deliberately producing the oft-disdained trope of "talking heads." "We were not filmmakers," Hartman insists, "even potentially, but facilitators and preservers of archival documents in audiovisual form. In short, our technique, or lack of it, was homeopathic: it used television to cure television, to turn the medium against itself, limiting even while exploiting its visualizing power."[30] In making the image an extension of the voice, videotestimony acts as an audiovisual amplification of the puncturing details of speech—gestures, postures, expressions, pauses, silences—all markers of what Hartman calls the survivor's "embodied voice."[31] The audiovisual serves to register the performing of trauma, capturing the witnessing body as its ultimate referent.

Consider Laub's often-cited depiction of a woman recounting her memories of the uprising in Auschwitz. Laub describes her as "slight, self-effacing, almost talking in whispers, mostly to herself." But then, "a sudden intensity, passion and color were infused into the narrative. She was fully there. 'All of a sudden,' she said, 'we saw four chimneys going up in flames, exploding'"; before long, the woman "fell silent and the tumults of the moment faded."[32] Laub then recounts a debate following the screening of this testimony at a conference where attending historians disqualified the testimony claiming that, historically, only one chimney was blown up, not four. Insisting on its importance, Laub argues that what the woman was testifying to was not empirical history but something more radical: "'an event that broke the all compelling frame of Auschwitz.'"[33] What the historians fail to acknowledge, according to Laub, is the performative aspect of testimony—the timbre and cadence of voice, gestures, expressions, and nonverbal cues—which arguably convey a more profound meaning than the merely historical. In challenging the historians' judgment, Laub effectively challenges their conception of what constitutes a legitimate historical record, a position that relies on the technological capability to record and reproduce spoken words together with their accompanying indexical markers. The debate between the psychoanalyst and the historians can be read as underwritten by their respective media of record.[34]

Laub's later work involves more explicitly video cameras in the therapeutic process itself. Together with his associates, Laub held a series of video interviews with Holocaust survivors hospitalized in mental institutions in Israel. Their postulation was that many of the survivors could have avoided the long hospitalization had they been given the opportunity to share their traumatic experiences. The aim of the study was therefore "to investigate the role of video testimony as a potential useful psychotherapeutic clinical intervention." The introduction of cameras into the therapeutic process proved remedial: "By videotaping testimonies of these patients' experiences before, during, and after World War II, we created highly condensed texts that could be interpreted on multiple levels going far beyond the mere narrative content of clinical medical history." The record produced thereby was born out of three "channels" captured on tape: the "cognitive channel," emphasizing "a detailed reconstruction of historical facts related to the traumatic events"; the "affective channel," reconstructing "feelings then and now"; and the "sensory channel," reconstructing "bodily sensations, sight, smells, and sounds."[35] Joint viewings of videotestimonies were then organized with staff and patients, ensued by group discussions that further contributed to the process.

Laub is of course not the first to use cameras in therapy; in fact, this practice harkens back to a pre-Freudian tradition in the form of Jean-Martin Charcot, Freud's teacher at the Salpêtrière clinic in Paris, who was among the first to admit cameras into the ward.[36] Indeed it is possible to situate videotestimony within a broader context of the late 1960s and early 1970s of employing videotape in psychiatric training and treatment. The technology opened new avenues for analysis, as one guide for videotape techniques in psychiatry affirms: "The use of video both compels the therapist to see more of what goes on nonverbally than he had previously realized and demands of him an increasing alertness to the nonverbal signs and communication which are ever present."[37] The same applies to videotestimony, which likewise rediscovers traditional talk therapy as an audiovisual channel ripe with hermeneutic possibilities. The videotestimony of hospitalized survivors removes the therapeutic scene from the seclusion of patient and doctor (typically with the latter writing notes only for himself to see). The two are now recorded during session, and the videotestimony is then shared with a small audience (the interviewer and patient among them). Even in such a restricted context, bearing witness on camera is a public event. Speech and writing give way to screen and camera—a taping cure in lieu of a talking cure.

In sum, recording for Laub performs a double redemptive function: restoring survivors' lost personal records and instituting historical records for future generations:

> Video testimonies of genocidal trauma are a necessary part of the larger historical record as well as of the individual's release from entrapment in trauma. The experience of survivors may be the *only* historical record of an event that has not been captured through the usual methods of historical record and public discourse. The event can literally be recreated only through a testimonial process. The process is a method of registering, perceiving, knowing, telling, remembering, and transmitting historical information about genocide that varies from traditional methods of academic historiography to a considerable extent.[38]

A medium of redemption at once private and collective, videotestimony is *Jetztzeit* caught on tape, complete with all its "chips of Messianic time."[39] A source and resource for a new historical record, videotestimony holds something that can never be fully narrativized. Recording and narrative are incongruous, as the one holds precisely what the other lacks: referentiality in the case of recording, chronology in the case of narrative. Whereas narrative constructs a sense of progress through time, recording captures the actual flow of time, along with the contingencies occasioned therewith. According to Kittler, media technologies do not simply extend sensory capacities but determine "recording thresholds," that is, the changing ratio between perception and inscription.[40] Not only is videotestimony a prime example for the shift in the recordable, it also records that very shift. For it is only with audiovisual media that the shortcoming of words can be documented as they surface from the fragments of traumatic memory. Recording bears witness to the gap between the spoken and the unspoken, between the Symbolic and the Real. And if the Real always returns to the same place, as Jacques Lacan used to say, that place is caught somewhere on tape.

PROCESSING

Lawrence Langer's *Holocaust Testimonies* is one of the most penetrating studies on videotestimonies written to date. Having watched hundreds of videotaped testimonies from the Fortunoff archive, Langer provides an exacting account of what he calls the "disrupted narratives" of Holocaust survivors.[41] Langer's preoccupation throughout the study is with two related yet distinct senses of processing. First, the word "process" figures importantly in his text, designating the actual performance of testimony, the process of recalling and recounting as it happens, a process whose temporal flow is shared by the survivor bearing witness and the audience watching the testimony. As its Latin etymology suggests, process implies advance or progress through time, the unfolding of sequential temporality—a key element in the temporal structure of videotestimony. The second sense of process relates to Langer's own analysis and interpretation, his *watching* of and *writing* on videotestimonies, his processing of the audiovisual in terms of the literary. This processing involves identifying, classifying, and explicating, with great acumen, the distinctive characteristics of videotestimonies according to narrative conventions of form and content, even if these eventually prove deficient.

For Langer, a traditional written account "is finished when we begin to read it, its opening, middle, and end already established between the covers of the book."[42] Videotaped oral testimony, by contrast, creates meaning through the very production of narrative; it "unfolds before our eyes and ears; we are present at the invention of what, when we speak of written texts, we call style."[43]

Until recently, he argues, we had to depend almost exclusively on the literary for addressing an audience with survivors' memories. Employing videotape technology to record survivors' testimonies calls for the development of new ways for the audience to engage with these accounts. Both written and oral forms involve an "imaginative space" between narrator and the audience. In the written, however, the author strives to narrow this space (by means of literary strategies such as chronology, analogy, imagery, dialogue); in the oral, the witness "confirms the vast imaginative space separating what he or she has endured from our capacity to absorb it."[44] Whereas written accounts draw on literary conventions and devices to engage the audience, videotaped testimonies draw on the mediated presence of the speaker, which "in addition to language includes gesture, a periodic silence whose effect cannot be duplicated on the printed page, and above all a freedom from the legacy of literary form and precedent to which anyone attempting a written narrative on any subject is indebted."[45] If the literary transforms the Real that it attempts to elucidate, the videotape performs the Real that it inadvertently captures.

A consistent theme in Langer's analysis is the double temporality of videotaped testimonies.[46] The paradigmatic case of this double temporality is the distinction between "deep memory" and "common memory," two terms Langer borrows from author-survivor Charlotte Delbo. Whereas common memory "restores the self to its normal pre- and post-camp routines" while offering "detached portraits, from the vantage point of today, of what it must have been like then," deep memory "tries to recall the Auschwitz self as it was then. . . . [It] suspects *and* depends on common memory, knowing what common memory cannot know but tries nonetheless to express."[47] Deep memory is the subterranean memory that lurks beneath common memory, the traumatic *then* infecting and intruding the habitual *now*, forever beyond proper articulation and comprehension.

Although emphasizing the importance of videotape, Langer nevertheless overlooks the more profound significance of the media technology at hand, an oversight that bears precisely on the double temporality above. While discussing deep memory, Langer proposes that what distinguishes video testimonies is their "'reversible continuity,'" which is "foreign to the straight chronology that governs most written memoirs."[48] Yet is it not the nature of the medium rather than of the narrative that Langer is referring to? Isn't the narrative always susceptible to the technological potential of halting and reversing the flow of time? After all, what better approximates the cotemporal *now* as it is interrupted by the traumatic *then* than a technologically reproduced narrative? Moreover, would it even be possible to detect and locate deep memory without the ability to pause, rewind, and replay? For how else could Langer analyze the moments where deep memory intrudes into the narrative, the pauses and silences that turn in his text into ellipses, without being able to reproduce these moments time and again? Consumed by the flow of the here and now, these intrusions are revived and rendered meaningful only as they are reproduced—only as reproducible—which means that deep memory is in fact an offshoot of videotestimony and, by extension, of the audiovisual archive. Referring to Langer's study, Holocasut historian Saul Friedlander asks whether on the collective level "an event such as the Shoah may, after all the survivors have disappeared, leave traces of a deep memory beyond individual recall, which will defy any attempt to give it meaning."[49] To the extent that deep memory is a byproduct of the audiovisual archive, this question seems only partially relevant. For deep memory is not properly an individual memory within the reach of personal recall; it is rather a mediated form of that memory, its recorded afterlife, which makes it not only safe from oblivion but also infinitely reproducible. To paraphrase Edison's (purported) quip on the phonograph, deep memory has become, as it were, immortal. Or to quote Kittler on this point: "the realm of the dead is as extensive as the storage and transmission capabilities of a given culture."[50] Far from disappearing with the survivors, the audiovisual archive is the ultimate depository of deep memory.

Interestingly, Friedlander's sole example of deep memory is the last frame of Art Spiegelman's autobiographical graphic novel *Maus*, where Artie's farther, in a slip of the tongue, calls Artie "Richieu," the name of his son who had died in the Holocaust before Artie was born. Significantly, that frame also reveals the technological backdrop of Spiegleman's memoir: "So . . . let's stop, please, your tape recorder . . . I'm tired from talking, Richieu, and it's enough stories for now."[51] Friedlander's coupling of deep memory with *Maus* rests on a hidden connection: both originate from tape recording. The deep memory of Richieu was captured on Artie's recordings before taking shape in his drawings. A slip of the tongue caught on tape becomes telltale of traumatic memory. As trauma transfers from one generation to the next, the unmediated becomes remediated. What defies literary memory is approachable only by means of nonliterary media.[52]

In one of the first accounts on the audiovisual archive, James Young likens videotestimony to "celluloid *megilla*": fragments of memory stitched together into a continuously unfurling scroll.[53] This metaphor calls for some unpacking because it further illustrates the confusion between narrative and medium (leaving aside Young's confusion between celluloid and magnetic tape). To understand the confusion, it might be helpful to distinguish between media that assume structure and media that assume time. In media that assume structure, the relation between retrieval and storage follows a fixed constructed order that is observed irrespectively of the original order of storage. Thus, in the Torah (presumably the source of Young's metaphor) Exodus might have been written before Genesis but it is still second in line. When reading a scroll, or any textual medium for that matter, it is possible to move back and forth, but the structure—that is, the narrative—is assumed even if not followed. Recording technologies, by contrast, are devices that capture the actual flow of time regardless of the contents. Here the relation between retrieval and storage follows a fixed temporal order. If structure-assuming media produce their own separate time, independently of the time of inscription, time-assuming media conform to the original pulse of recording. Synchronicity between playing and recording is therefore the condition for both faithful reproduction and mischievous tinkering (as in fast-speed playing, slow-speed playing, or reverse playing).

Although all storage media, as mechanisms for overcoming time, are reversible, the reversibility specific to text is structural while the one specific to recording is temporal.[54] It is for this reason that time-axis manipulation applies to media that assume time but not to those that assume structure; it would make little sense to say that reading fast or slow, backward or forward, amounts to manipulating the flow of time. Time-axis manipulation is particularly apt for revealing the hidden aspects of familiar reality as captured by recording devices. Thus, when sociologists such as Harvey Sacks employed tape recorders to record how people actually speak, human talk could be unraveled in all its wonderful everyday messiness—hence, sociolinguistics.[55] Similarly, when literary scholars such as Langer used the videotape to study the "disrupted narratives" of Holocaust survivors, testimony could be revealed as a discourse of silences as much as of words—hence, trauma theory. When recording technologies are applied to process the temporal flow of testimony, the Real takes precedence over the Symbolic. The "reversible continuity" Langer ascribes to videotestimonies is therefore a temporal reversibility—the technological condition for the emergence of deep memory.

One of the original uses of videotape technology was in closed-circuit surveillance systems designed for shopping centers, prisons, and other locations of panoptic power.[56] Although employing videotape in the context of testimony hardly has anything to do with surveillance, the logic of processing videotaped material in both cases is nonetheless comparable. Closed Circuit TV (CCTV) videorecording documents events successively so as to allow rewinding back to instances that went unnoticed in real time but are deemed important ex post facto (such as identifying a shoplifter). Langer's processing of videotestimonies is similar in that his reading is also concerned with key moments that are accessible only by means of rewinding and replaying—the puncturing moments in testimonies where the double temporality of the traumatic *then* and the narrational *now* is performed in actual time. By Langer's own admission, this is "a process difficult and perhaps impossible to detect on the printed page of a written text."[57] Deep memory, insofar as it is trauma captured on videotape, is a function of time-axis manipulation.[58]

When it comes down to allegiances, Langer's is clearly with the literary. His textual processing of the audiovisual treads on the verge of narrative inquiry, gesturing to the outside from the inside. William Shakespeare, John Milton, and Marcel Proust are occasionally invoked only to affirm the implausibility of any comparison between videotaped testimonies and traditional narrative forms. Langer's main literary inspiration comes instead from Maurice Blanchot's *The Writing of Disaster,* a fragmentary text poised to probe the extremities of language as it touches and skirts the disaster—an event so devastating that it leaves everything intact. To quote Blanchot, "We feel that there cannot be any experience of the disaster, even if we were to understand disaster to be the ultimate experience."[59] Drawing on Blanchot's insights, Langer nevertheless ventures a decisive conversion: "Although he calls his text *The Writing of the Disaster*, his language applies with equal precision to what we have been examining, the 'speaking of the disaster.'"[60] Thus, the writing of the impossibility of writing is transposed into the speaking of the impossibility of speaking; Blanchot's unwriting and the survivors' unspeaking are rendered equivalent. Yet what this conversion hides is a shift in the inscription system: from symbolic to indexical, from structural to temporal. Langer's ability to approach "the speaking of the disaster" entails the technological recording and processing of instances in which the survivor's body "speaks"—the audiovisual effects of the Real. A literary theory of trauma can make sense only insofar as it presupposes media that capture vibrations rather than representations.

TRANSMISSION

The seminal text of the growing discourse of trauma and testimony is undoubtedly Felman and Laub's *Testimony: Crises of Witnessing in Literature, Psychoanalysis and History*. The book brings together a literary scholar and a psychoanalyst—two narrative-based professions—to address the collapse of narrative in the wake of the Holocaust. With one of the authors as cofounder of the Yale archive, it should not come as a surprise that large portions of the analysis deal with survivors' videotaped testimonies. But no less significant are the circumstances that instigated the writing of this book for the other author. As Felman recounts, it was the story of one class in the fall of 1984: "The textual framework of the course included texts (and testimonies) by Camus, Dostoevsky, Freud, Mallarmé, Paul Celan, as well as autobiographical/historical life accounts borrowed from the Video Archive for Holocaust Testimonies at Yale."[61] Following the screening of a videotaped testimony "something happened, toward the conclusion of the class, which took me completely by surprise. The class itself broke out into a crisis."[62] The papers that students submitted subsequently turned out to be a "profound statement of the trauma they had gone through and of the significance of their assuming the position of the witness."[63] It was this event, Felman declares, "which determined me to write about it, and which contained, in fact, the germ—and the germination—of this book."[64]

That Felman ascribes such formative power to an event that, in her words, "broke the framework of the course" (that is, the textual framework) is indicative of the media backdrop of this theory of testimony. [65] Felman is preoccupied with transmission, an issue that spells simultaneously the predicament of testimony and its transcendence. Her model of transmission is inspired by Claude Lanzmann's monumental documentary *Shoah*; as he stated in a 1990 seminar at Yale: "I wanted really to address the intelligence of the viewer more than the emotions. . . . My purpose was the transmission."[66] By "transmission" Lanzmann might have meant a nonrepresentational mode of communication, the imparting of something beyond the imparting of knowledge. On this view, the truth of testimony lies not in the faithfulness of its representation but in the sense of bewilderment it transmits to the viewer. In her essay on the film, Felman suggests that the import of Lanzmann's achievement is in "performing the historical and contradictory double task of the breaking of the silence and of the simultaneous shattering of any given discourse, of the breaking—or the bursting open—of all frames" (the breaking of frames and frameworks is a recurring phrase of Felman's).[67] What the film dramatizes, then, is what might be called the transmission function of testimony, which emanates from the contradiction between the necessity and the impossibility of testimony.

Transmission informs much of Felman's work on testimony, with the story of that class serving as its so-called primal scene. It was the first time that Felman decided to move on "from poetry into reality and to study in a literary class something which is *a priori* not defined as literary, but is rather of the order of raw documents—historical and autobiographical."[68] The shift from the textual to the audiovisual spawned a crisis: none of the assigned readings had the shattering effect of the "raw" videotaped testimonies. Compelled to respond to the crisis, she prepared an address to the class, citing the feeling of one student: "We have been *talking* about the accident—and here all of a sudden *the accident happened* in the class, happened *to* the class."[69] Felman prefers to view the crisis as an accumulative effect, with the audiovisual building on the previous impact of the textual, finally resorting back to the literary as a way of working through the crisis. Yet is the crisis here not precisely that of the literary in failing to attend to a transmission that supersedes its impact and is outside its domain?

The term "transmission of trauma" entered the vocabulary of psychology in the early 1980s in the context of second-generation effects of the Holocaust.[70] Children of survivors exhibited pathological behavior (that is, post-traumatic), such as nightmares, acute anxiety, and overidentification with their parents' misfortune. The metaphor of transmission was initially chosen to denote some kind of traumatic transference from one generation to the next.[71] More recent speculations seem to have taken the metaphor to a new level of specificity:

> The transmission of sound waves in telecommunications is a commonly accepted phenomenon and may serve as a suitable analogy that also illustrates the process of trauma transmission. Thus, in the same way as heat, light, sound and electricity can be invisibly carried from a transmitter to a receiver, it is possible that unconscious experiences can also be transmitted from parents to their children through some complex process of extrasensory communication.[72]

If psychopathological transmission is still of the metaphorical order, a recent development is poised to turn metaphor into actuality. The latest edition of the Diagnostic and Statistical Manual of Mental Disorders (DSM-V) features the revised clinical criteria of PTSD, of which the forth criterion reads: "Experiencing repeated or extreme exposure to aversive details of the event(s) (e.g., first responders collecting human remains; police officers repeatedly exposed to details of child abuse). **Note**: Criterion 4A does not apply to exposure through electronic media, television, movies, or pictures, unless this exposure is work related."[73] As the discussion developed in Chapter 3 shows, this caveat narrowly recognizes, for the first time, the possibility of media to traumatize, a potential currently limited to work situations. Yet once admitted, the possibility of work-related trauma through media lays the ground for the possibility of that happening under different conditions as well.[74] In retrospect, the crisis experienced in Felman's class may well fit the criterion (and today could have possibly resulted in complaints against the professor). The point here is that what was proclaimed as the "germ and germination" of Felman's work on testimony—a case of audiovisual transmission of trauma—is now among the possible causes of trauma itself. Literary discourse anticipated clinical discourse in recognizing the traumatic transmissibility of the audiovisual.

In her more recent work on the Eichmann trial, Felman further extends the reach of the transmission of trauma, yet once again largely disavowing its media setting. Reading critically Hannah Arendt's account of the trial, Felman suggests that the significance of this extraordinary legal event was not only in the serving of historical justice but in "the granting of authority (articulateness and transmissibility) to trauma by a legal process of transformation of individual into collective trauma."[75] With more than one hundred witnesses, the trial provided release to survivors' silenced and untold traumatic memories, making them public for the first time. "The tool of law," argues Felman, "was used not only as a tool of *proof* of un-imaginable facts but, above all, as a compelling *medium of transmission*—as an effective tool of national and international *communication* of these thought-defying facts."[76] Similarly, when referring to one of the more memorable witnesses in the trial, who collapsed on the stand before completing his testimony, Felman declares: "it was precisely through K-Zetnik's *legal muteness* that the trial inadvertently *gave silence a transmitting power*, and—although not by intention—managed to transmit the legal meaning of collective trauma." Thus Felman concludes, "Once the trial gave transmissibility to silence, other silences became, within the trial, fraught with meaning."[77]

How could the testimonies heard during the trial gain such public impact and transform into a collectively shared trauma? Felman answers this question only in passing: "Broadcast live over the radio and passionately listened to, the trial was becoming the central event in the country's life."[78] This single reference to the media context in Israel of the early 1960s—where radio was the only broadcasting medium—reveals the technological conditions for the transmission of trauma during the Eichmann trial. As argued in the previous chapter, it was the acoustic medium of radio that allowed survivors to attain voice while taking to the airwaves. Although the verb "transmit" suffuses her text, Felman fails to spot the link between the two kinds of transmission occasioned with the trial—the traumatic and the radiophonic. Carried over from Lanzmann's *Shoah* to the discourse of testimony, the transmission function is finally brought to bear on the collective impact of the Eichmann trial—all the while unaware of its various media a priori.

Transmission, argues Régis Debray, is necessarily a violent act: "Every transmission is a combat, against noise, against inertia, against the other transmitters, and even—especially—against the addressees."[79] What is usually meant by communication is therefore the opposite of transmission:

"Communication is a transmission that has cooled, that is stable and calm."[80] Debray's observation seems to apply squarely to Felman's work, but coming from someone deeply concerned with material and technical mediation it also puts some strain on the relation between software and hardware in the trauma and testimony discourse. Testimony emerges as a historical and ethical concern profoundly implicated by the challenges of the transmission of trauma, including the possibility of transmission itself becoming traumatic (more on this in the next chapter). If testimony transmits something beyond the literary, it is owing to the intervention of media whose impact unsettles the literary. Felman's account thus appears as already out of joint with itself, having its germ and germination in an audiovisual moment. To use Derrida's words, the audiovisual is the *mal d'archive* of Felman's writing on testimony: "an irrepressible desire to return to the origin, a homesickness, a nostalgia for the return to the most archaic place of absolute commencement."[81] The literary gestures toward what it can never archive within textual means—the effect of its own collapse as captured by nonliterary media. It is when the affective transgresses the literary that the transmission function of testimony is set off.

MEDIA, TRAUMA, WAR

It will not have gone unnoticed that the present discussion has brought together, on the one hand, three Jewish scholars committed to narrative inquiry and whose collective work is devoted to the traumatic legacies of the Second World War and, on the other, a German media theorist born in Saxony in 1943 for whom all modern technological advancements are war driven.[82] One would be hard pressed to find two more diametrical discourses on the nature of history, subjectivity, and morality in the wake of war. If for the former war is the source of suffering both physical and mental, for the latter it is the origination of machines whose reign transcends both body and mind. Taken to the extreme, the choice they seem to leave us with is technics *or* civilization. That said, the one can be usefully read alongside the other as two postwar accounts on the collapse of narrative as a medium of history. Moreover, the post-trauma of the former and the posthumanism of the latter can be viewed as parallel effects of the medium overtaking the narrative. Rubbed against each other, they better expose their respective critical strengths; taken together, they both point to the conjunction of media and trauma in the postwar experience.

From a Kittlerian point of view, the three accounts on testimony and trauma discussed above are the result of inverted remediation—a written analysis of videotape recordings of spoken narratives. The outcome is a low signal-to-noise ratio discourse in which the background noise is as significant as the information conveyed. Just as psychoanalysis, with its insistence on recording all contingencies of speech, has a phonographic a priori, contemporary discourse of testimony and trauma, with its commitment to account for the unrepresentable and the unsayable, has an audiovisual—more precisely, videographic—a priori. In this sense, what Felman and Laub designate as the crises of testimony in literature, psychoanalysis, and history (three metanarratives rooted in the production of narrative) is coextensive with the expansion of modern audiovisual media; the failure of narrative in bearing witness is consistent with the technological mediation of that very failure.[83] If testimony performs its own crisis, audiovisual media bear witness to it. Or, as Kittler might have it, the discourse of trauma and testimony has literature summon its two successors in mediating reality— media and psychoanalysis—to examine conjointly literature's inadequacy in giving account of the horrors of war.

This might have some important implications for current debates on Holocaust testimony. Giorgio Agamben has famously opposed testimony to the archive, taking his lead from Michel Foucault's notion of archeology.[84] According to Foucault, the archive is the system that regulates what is sayable in accordance with the already-said: "The archive is the first law of what can be said, the system that governs the appearance of statements as unique events."[85] Subjectivity itself, argues Foucault, is a function of the archive; what is normally called the subject is a discursively conditioned and enacted subject-position. In Agamben's rendering, testimony in the wake of Auschwitz is the opposite of Foucault's archive. Rather than designating the regulation of speech insofar as it is a relation between the said and the unsaid, testimony refers to the relation between the possibility and impossibility of speech— that is, the possibility of the annulment or dispossession of speech. This move allows Agamben to reintroduce the subject—the witness—as the one that has the potential of not having language: "The subject is thus the possibility that language does not exist, does not take place."[86] Subjectivity reappears as the capacity to bear witness to an impossibility of speech through its very existence, that is, through the contingency of speech.[87]

Kittler, while influenced by Foucault's archeology, criticizes the latter's exclusive reliance on the medium of writing and utter disregard for modern technologies of storage and transmission. "It is for this reason," argues Kittler, "that all his analyses end immediately before that point in time at which other media penetrated the library's stacks. Discourse analysis cannot be applied to sound archives or towers of film rolls."[88] In this respect, the Yale archive introduces a significant reconfiguration of the archival formation whereby the audiovisual takes the role of the textual. What writing was to Foucault's archive, videography is to the Yale archive—both its technological condition and its logic of operation. This reconfiguration entails a profoundly different concept of the archivable: the audiovisual archive is designed to store precisely that which cannot be properly archived by writing—trauma. Rather than the system of everything sayable, the audiovisual archive is the system of everything recordable, which not only destabilizes Agamben's opposition between archive and testimony but ultimately makes the former the condition of the latter. The relation between the possibility and the impossibility of speech—the contingency of testimony, its capacity not to be—is not foreign to the audiovisual archive but rather thoroughly performed by it. Once the archive turns videographic, testimony and the precariousness of its articulation become simultaneous and compound. It is by means of videotestimony that the witness emerges as the subject bearing witness—on tape—to the impossibility that gives rise to testimony. Archive and testimony are inseparable.

What might Kittler make out of all this? Possibly, here is yet another example of how subjectivity is a product of technological-discursive regimes. What Kittler calls the "so-called man" is constituted by trauma, which in turn is constituted by a specific psycho-techno constellation. Subjectivity is rendered traumatic against the background of videotape playback. Yet even though Kittler's perspective allows us to understand how trauma is linked to media, trauma still can provide a critique of this perspective itself. In fact, the trauma framework might be the first step toward a dialectical critique of Kittler's media theory.

There is no escape from Kittler's technological singlemindedness; his efforts to subordinate history to technology are nothing less than, well, obsessive. His own technological a priori is that of computer engineering and information theory, invoking time and again Claude Shannon's mathematical model of communication.[89] Bearing in mind his preoccupation with World War Two technologies of the *Wehrmacht*, Peenemünde, and the *Luftwaffe*, this obsession ultimately amounts to blindness. As aptly put by Geoffrey Winthrop-Young: "there is no Hitler in Kittler's war, no war of aggression, no final solution, no complicity of military conquest and racial genocide, and subsequently no question of guilt and responsibility."[90] Kittler would probably regard such questions of guilt and responsibility as chimerical effects of the "so-called man," and hence as a further reinstatement of retrograde anthropocentrism under the guise of human moral agency.

But what if this blindness could be read as something that resembles a post-traumatic reaction? What if this technological monomania is but an elaborate form of acting out, relegating to the background precisely what cannot be dealt with and accounted for?[91] To the extent that media and trauma also intersect in Kittler's case, his would be the opposite of the three accounts above. Whereas their preoccupation with trauma suppresses the underlying media, his preoccupation with media suppresses the underlying trauma. It is as if there is a parallel mode of transmission of trauma at work in Kittler's meditations, the transmission of a secret that remains buried under a mass of technical information, transmitted but never properly communicated. Kittler's media legacy—especially his fascination with Third Reich media—is therefore inextricably linked with the erasure of the traumas wrought by the regime that sponsored the development of those media. Wartime technologies are divorced from wartime calamities. Mute are the channels that once carried lethal orders, blank are the records that once held murderous plans; the ends they served are nowhere to be found. Media are rendered amnesic, conduits of other media rather than of memory.

CHAPTER 3
Screen Trauma

Shortly after the 1989 Hillsborough Stadium disaster in Sheffield, England, sixteen people brought actions claiming to suffer a "nervous shock" as a result of learning from the media about the fatal human crush that occurred during a soccer match. The plaintiffs, most of whom were relatives of the victims, demanded compensations as secondary victims, arguing that their injury was within the "immediate aftermath"—a category recognized by British law as having been involved in the consequences of a tragic event. The court rejected the claim, but not before speculating on the hypothetical possibility of a traumatic live broadcast.[1] Numerous claims for psychiatric injury had been filed prior to this case, yet this is probably one of the first to consider whether media could cause trauma to viewers, and consequently be compensable by law. Were such a case to be heard today, however, it might find support from recent developments in psychiatric research. For there is now a growing acceptance among mental health experts that trauma could transfer, under certain conditions, through visual media. Referring to notions such as "distant trauma," "traumatic media exposure," and "vicarious traumatization," clinicians and researchers are now willing to acknowledge that witnessing disastrous events through the media could cause a reaction that complies with existing PTSD clinical criteria. How did this development come about? How does such mediated trauma manifest itself? What are its social, legal, and moral consequences? And what are the implications for our understanding of both media and trauma? These are the questions this chapter sets out to explore.

Psychiatry has long been in the business of understanding how external violence affects mental processes. While operating under various nomenclatures, modern conceptions of trauma have dovetailed with modern developments in technology and warfare. As already noted earlier in this book, trauma is a central theme in the grand narrative of the shock of modernity. In the latter half of the nineteenth century, conditions such as "railway spine" (British surgeon John Erichsen's term) and "male hysteria" (French neurologist Jean-Martin Charcot's term) were associated with inflictions of mechanized modernity, typically industrial and train accidents; syndromes such as "war neurosis," "shell shock," and "traumatic neurosis" (Sigmund Freud's term taking after Herman Oppenheim) followed directly from World War I; and more recently "gross stress reaction" and "PTSD" were the corresponding postwar psychopathologies of World War II and Vietnam, respectively.[2] From the very beginning, the science of psychic injury coincided with tort law jurisprudence and health insurance provisos; then, like today, causation is what determines compensation. Early conceptions of trauma restricted the affliction only to direct and immediate experience: there was no reason, and indeed no sense, in speculating about distant traumatic effects. In the last few decades psychiatry and psychology began to consider the possibility that traumatic behavior and symptoms could transfer across time from one generation to the next, a paradigmatic case being the second generation of Holocaust survivors.[3] The possibility of trauma through media, which is now beginning to gain purchase, further shifts the location of violence from direct to indirect, and from the immediate to the mediated.[4]

Media have long been accused of exposing the audience to violence. The 1930s Payne Fund Studies are notorious for having incriminated movies as propagating sex and violence among the young.[5] One of the first studies into the effects of mass media was on an alleged media-induced panic: the 1938 *The Invasion from Mars* radio broadcast.[6] Violence on television was a favorite topic for cultivation theory, which deemed it as contributing to the reinforcement of social order and conventions of morality at the expense of instigating feelings of danger and fear among viewers.[7] And studies in behavioral sciences on the impact of violence in the media on children are almost too many to count.[8] Despite the divergence, these and many other studies understand the deleterious effects of media as impinging on viewers' moral framework: how media violence affects people's attitudes, beliefs, and consequently social behavior. As I argue in the following, the psychiatric recognition of a technologically mediated trauma marks a qualitative change in the understanding of media effects: the impact is no longer regarded as symbolic but as literal, and the damage suffered is not only deemed emotional but clinical. The status of mediated violence shifts from obnoxious to noxious, making media influence a question for psychiatric epidemiology as much as for social psychology. As Ruth Leys explains in her genealogical study of trauma, the prevalent PTSD theory today is of a literal, often visual, imprint of the traumatic event, which is said to be registered in a special brain memory system.[9] That mediated images might be traumatic to the viewer complements this recent understanding of trauma, with the screen functioning as a potential locus of trauma.

The condition commonly known today as PTSD probably best encapsulates the story of trauma in recent decades. As Allan Young has argued, PTSD emerged as a distinctively contemporary pathology whose coherence and validity depend on "the practices, technologies, and narratives with which it is diagnosed, studied, treated, and represented."[10] In other words, PTSD is a pathology that is made real through historically specific material and discursive mechanisms—mechanisms that, because constituting the underlying conditions of the pathology, largely recede from its manifest reality. Ian Hacking speaks of traumatic memory in terms of what he calls "looping effects": the recursive classification processes whereby knowledge is produced between those who classify (doctors) and those classified (patients). Classifications create new knowledge about people, who then proceed to employ these classifications in their own reporting, which in turn leads to revising these classifications, and so forth. Looping effects can then explain how one would come to experience and remember one's own past under a category such as trauma.[11] Understanding the emergence of trauma by screen can certainly benefit from the dynamics described by Young and Hacking, and these dynamics do figure in the discussion below. Yet what this chapter seeks to emphasize is the media technological context of this development, which extends beyond, and indeed predates, current preoccupation with televisual exposure to potentially traumatic imagery (exposure being an operative term here, as we will see). The story of media through trauma thus reveals the media already in trauma—the way contemporary understanding of PTSD is implicated by visual media.

If in the previous chapter the capacity of video to impress itself on viewers was deemed a virtue, this chapter traces how this same capacity turns into a vice. As visual media become recognized as potentially traumatogenic, the screen becomes operative in redefining the threshold between inside and outside, creating the possibility for images of far-off tragedies to impinge upon the viewer's psychological well-being. In this sense, televisual mediation begets failure of psychological mediation. Yet the possibility of screen trauma, I argue, is linked with an understanding of trauma that, long before this recent development, was crucially informed by visual media. Rather than a new phenomenon, screen trauma is in a way already implicit within current clinical understanding of PTSD, and as such, is a logical extension of that understanding. The implications of screen trauma might be considerable: if the effect of what is seen on the viewer exceeds that of empathy or even identification, if the seeing of suffering becomes the suffering of seeing, then the viewer becomes a (vicarious) victim of on-screen violence. Once the vicarious and the direct are both within the traumatic spectrum, a whole new range of ethical and political questions opens up.

The chapter explores three key moments in the development of screen trauma. The first is an experimental research program that took shape in the early 1960s under the name "trauma film paradigm," which employed stressful films (often the same one) to simulate traumatic effects in subjects. The work of psychiatrists working with this paradigm came to shape some of the most basic tenets of contemporary understanding of stress and trauma. The second case traces the emergence of "distant trauma": the psychiatric study into the clinical effects of watching catastrophic events on television. A watershed event in that respect was the September 11 attacks in New York in 2001, after which "distant trauma" became an extensively researched—and increasingly accepted—clinical designation. The third case focuses on a current debate: according to U.S. Air Force reports, operators of remotely piloted aircrafts (also known as drones) exhibit PTSD symptoms at rates closer to those of ground troops than to pilots. Flying missions by remote, some drone operators claim to be traumatized by images of surveillance and killing seen thousands of miles away from the war zone, thereby making them victims of violence they exert on others from a safe distance (and adding a new dimension to the already vexing designation known as perpetrator trauma). While these three cases involve three different visual media (film, television, digital), from a psychiatric standpoint—which is the focus of this chapter—they are all equipollent instances of screen-based traumatic effects. Together they highlight defining moments in the progressive distantiation-through-visualization of trauma by technical means, with each case representing a different phase in the psychiatrization of media effects. Preceding the main discussion is a short interpretative reading of the recently amended PTSD diagnostic criteria, which for the first time include a direct reference to media. The media caveat introduced therein marks the culmination of a process traced by the three cases to follow.

DSM PRELUDE

The 2013 edition of the Diagnostic and Statistical Manual of Mental Disorders (DSM-V), published by the American Psychiatric Association, presents the revised criteria for PTSD. The first criterion stipulates the originating factors:

A. Exposure to actual or threatened death, serious injury, or sexual violence in one (or more) of the following ways:

1. Directly experiencing of the traumatic event(s).
2. Witnessing, in person, the event(s) as it occurred to others.
3. Learning that the traumatic event(s) occurred to a close family member or close friend. In cases of actual or threatened death of a family member or friend, the event(s) must have been violent or accidental.
4. Experiencing repeated or extreme exposure to aversive details of the traumatic event(s) (e.g., first responders collecting human remains; police officers repeatedly exposed to details of child abuse).
   Note: Criterion A4 does not apply to exposure through electronic media, television, movies, or picture, unless this exposure is work related. [12]

Consider the note that follows Criterion A4: while barring media exposure as a possible cause of trauma, the note nevertheless admits, by way of exception, that under certain conditions media may in fact have a traumatic effect. As the DSM supplies no further explanation, let us venture a short interpretative reading of this peculiar addendum.

First, it is instructive that of all things media are singled out to be excluded, as though the DSM is compelled to correct a supposedly existing misconception about the traumatic potential of media. Note also that the media specified (television, movies, picture) are all visual media, a detail with particular significance to the current understanding of trauma, as will be demonstrated shortly. The exclusion comes with an exception: media exposure in general is denied only to allow a special case—work-related media exposure. This is presumably because it would take a special kind of exposure, the kind that, unlike ordinary media exposure, is integral to the job and is most likely recurring and involuntary. Which line of work might that be? Conceivably one that involves working daily before a visual medium emitting potentially distressing images: jobs such as CCTV security guard, surveillance camera operator, drone operator, news reporter, film editor, perhaps even television critic.

Media exposure may now be narrowly declared as an occupational hazard with post-traumatic consequences.

The DSM is obviously much more than a diagnostic manual. As Ian Hacking observes, the primary readers of the DSM are not mental health professionals but bureaucrats of various governmental and cooperate branches, who rely on its categories to process mental health claims.[13] As a key tool in legislation, insurance, and policy, the DSM has been in the fray of a number of public campaigns that sought recognition for yet unacknowledged conditions. PTSD is an exemplary case in this regard. DSM-I (published 1952) included a broad entry of "gross stress reaction," which was later dropped from DSM-II (published 1968). PTSD was first introduced in 1980 with the publication of DSM-III, following a politically motivated effort to amend the psychiatric nomenclature of stress in the wake of the Vietnam War.[14] As Leys claims, it took Vietnam to learn the psychiatric lessons of World War II, and it took World War II to learn the psychiatric lessons of World War I.[15] Belated awareness of a traumatic past is not limited to victims but might also extend to experts. The recent reference to media in DSM-V can be seen as a belated response to events that redefined the scope of trauma over the last two decades.

A short comparative reading of PTSD entries in DSM editions reveals an expansion in the description of trauma impact. DSM III speaks of symptoms following a "psychologically distressing event that is generally outside the range of usual human experience."[16] DSM III-R largely reiterates the above but adds "serious threat or harm to one's children, spouse, or other close relatives and friends; sudden destruction of one's home or community; or seeing another person who has recently been, or is being, seriously injured or killed as a result of accident or physical violence."[17] DSM IV presents a more extensive revision: "The person has been exposed to a traumatic event" in which one "experienced, witnessed, or was confronted with an event or events that involved actual or threatened death or serious injury, or a threat to the physical integrity of self or others."[18] The impact of trauma seems to expand from one edition to the next: from personal to secondary, and from direct to indirect; from a relatively narrow definition of an event "outside the range of usual human experience," to an event experienced not only personally but also by significant others or "seeing another person" being seriously harmed, to being exposed to a traumatic event that one "experienced, witnessed or was confronted with." It is instructive that the term "exposure" appears only in recent editions, and as in the latest DSM-V definition above, assumes the general category from which the subsequent criteria ensue. Significantly, "exposure" is applied to both immediate and mediated traumatization, suggesting a common mechanism in both cases (more on this in Chapter 5). The inclusive exclusion of media exposure in DSM-V marks perhaps the farthest extent of traumatic impact yet to be officially recognized.

TRAUMA FILMS

In the early 1960s the understanding of stress and trauma became entangled with experimental psychology, and more specifically, with a research program that employed film as stress stimulus. This program, known as the "trauma film" or "stressful film" paradigm, provided a "prospective experimental tool" for investigating the mechanism of traumatic reactions in a laboratory setting.[19] In retrospect, what it also provided is a technical apparatus from which a transformed conception of trauma was to emerge. Experiments typically involved having subjects watch a film featuring stressful images while recording their physical reactions, using electrodes for measuring heart rate and a galvanometer for skin conductance (perspiration is an indication of parasympathetic arousal). This was supplemented with interviews and self-reports immediately after screening and over time. "Properly selected motion picture films," claims the pioneer of this paradigm, psychologist Richard Lazarus, "could have tremendous emotional impact upon subjects and, therefore, could serve as stressor stimuli."[20] Film, as Lazarus dubs it, is a "laboratory analogue" to real life conditions: it closely simulates processes at work in an actual event, sans the danger.[21]

Early experiments employed one film as a stress stimulus: the seventeen-minute silent documentary *Subincision Rites of the Arunta*, filmed in 1937 by the Hungarian anthropologist and psychoanalyst Géza Róheim.[22] A disciple of Freud, Róheim set out to study the aboriginal tribe Arunta, which figures prominently in *Totem and Taboo*. The film depicted scenes from puberty rites of crude surgical operations on male genitals. As the control, experiments used *Corn Farming in Iowa*, a documentary chosen specifically for its lack of distressful content. An initial experiment was designed to determine whether the *Subincision* film could actually produce viable stress indicators in viewers. It concluded that, despite some mitigating variables, the film "yielded consistent and marked evidence of psychological stress."[23] Stress effects were further ascertained from retroactive personal accounts; reportedly, a few were so distraught that they asked that the screening be terminated.

Subsequent experiments developed the schema to include the manipulation of the soundtrack as a way to modulate cognitive orientations toward the film. Three different soundtracks were produced: "intellectualization track" evoked a detached anthropological viewpoint; "denial track" downplayed the harmful aspects of the ritual and emphasized the possible positive aspects; and "trauma track" accentuated the major sources of pain, danger, and sadism in the film. The original silent version was retained as a fourth soundtrack. Results showed that the "trauma track" produced the highest degree of stress among viewers, with the "silent track" ranking second in effect. The two other tracks, "denial" and "intellectualization," produced a remarkable decrease in stress response (each ranking lowest with different groups). Thus if the visual track of the film acted as the source of stress—that is, the "laboratory analogue of stress processes"—the soundtrack acted as the corresponding evaluative process, "an analogue of the process of cognitive appraisal."[24] If images constituted the traumatic content, vocal narration constituted the evaluative response, which, according to Lazarus, regulates the degree of stress felt by viewers. Or as one psychiatry textbook summarizes the experiment: "What we tell ourselves about external situations (cognitive appraisal) influences our level of arousal."[25]

It is worth lingering on the term "analogue." As Lazarus explains, "analogue refers to the manipulations in the experiment which parallel, or are similar to, the processes that are postulated to take place in nature," and adds, "we assume that these conditions represent those in real life, and that the findings can be generalized to conditions like in nature."[26] Analogy implies an inference based on similarity. Logically speaking, the analogy Lazarus describes is proportional (Greek *analogon*: up to ratio): A is to B *as* C is to D; hence: stressful film is to subjects *as* a stressful event is to victims. Film is an effective analogue since its impact "is natural and appears to take advantage of the human tendency to identify with characters and their experiences in a dramatic portrayal."[27] Here psychiatry treads into film theory: the identification process enacted by cinematic depictions is not only assumed to be effective but is actively elicited for the purpose of objective recording and analysis. The effects of identification are not simply a matter of psychological association but are factual and literal—and hence, comparable to the point of generalization with respect to a real event.

Yet analogue could also be interpreted with reference to media. The underlying assumption, without which trauma film paradigm would be pointless, is that the visual medium of film can reproduce reality to the extent of producing discernible and tangible effects in viewers—and do so better than any other media (otherwise a different one would have been used). Film is the analog medium upon which the analogue experiment is performed. For the psychological processes to be analogous there must first be an analog(ue) medium to reality. Yet at the same time film is cast as a deeply split medium: the moving image gives it its gripping, "natural" impact, whereas the soundtrack serves a secondary, reflective function. The mental imagery arising from this analog(ue) apparatus is of a receptive visual sensory ("stress stimulus") and a cognitive voiceover (appraisal, "what we tell ourselves"). Trauma film constitutes a prime example of what Kittler calls (following Hugo Münsterberg) "psychotechnology" as that which "relays psychology and media technology under the pretext that each psychic apparatus is also a technological one, and vice versa."[28] And just as in Kittler's analysis of film, psychotechnology does not simply spell similarity between mind and media ("dreams are like movies") but deep correlation: the mental is bounded up and coextensive with the technical.

The trauma film paradigm achieved wide recognition with the work of psychiatrist Mardi J. Horowitz, who focused on the role of imagery in trauma and stress disorders. Horowitz builds on Freud's idea of the repetition compulsion but takes it to the computer age: "A traumatic perceptual experience remains in some special form of memory storage until it is mastered. Before mastery, vivid sensory images of the experience tend to intrude into consciousness and may evoke unpleasant emotions."[29] To study visual repetition, Horowitz repeated the method used by Lazarus, and even employed the same *Subincision* film as the stress stimulus (the control this time was *The Runner*, depicting a long-distance race). Films, according to Horowitz, can produce stress "minor to moderate in intensity" and "afford a well-studied and replicable laboratory device for providing visual stress events."[30] Unlike Lazarus, Horowitz was mostly interested in visual impact and its recurrence in the mind, and so had no use for soundtrack manipulation (in fact, both films were shown silent). His conclusion was that "a traumatic film is more likely to be followed by intrusive or unbidden visual images than a neutral film."[31]

Horowitz went on to develop an influential theory of image formation and cognition, classifying a range of images, from hallucinations to unconscious images. With respect to trauma, his theory was of a conflict between two processes: "one favors completion of unfinished business, i.e. translation, codification, and permanent storage, while the second favors continued inhibition to avoid emotional pain."[32] This mechanism explains the post-traumatic repetition of "unbidden image" as a byproduct of the second process undermining the first. Because it is hindered from being integrated into permanent memory, the traumatic experience remains stuck in "a kind of active memory storage that has an intrinsic tendency toward repeated representation of its contents until those contents are actively terminated."[33] Imagery became increasingly important in understating post-traumatic processes in the late 1970s and early 1980s.[34] Horowitz's work on stress response had earned him an invitation to join the working group whose recommendations ended up as the first PTSD nomenclature.[35] At the background of the introduction of PTSD in DSM-III lies a distinctive visual understanding of the condition and its mechanism.

It is only fitting that Horowitz was the first to introduce the term "flashback" into psychiatric discourse. The term made its debut in a 1968 paper on visual imagery in epileptics, whose visual seizures were described as "very vivid lifelike flashbacks of their past lives."[36] A full-blown use of the term came in Horowitz's 1969 paper on LSD use in San Francisco, where it designates "returns of imagery for extended periods after the immediate effect of the hallucinogenic has worn off."[37] The same year saw his above-mentioned trauma film study, titled "Psychic Trauma: The Return of Images after a Stress Film." The story of flashback in psychiatric literature is one of continuous dispute, and as Fred Frankel shows in his critical survey, the term initially had a fairly broad designation that overlapped with descriptions of other phenomena reported at the time. It was only on becoming associated with PTSD, especially following the Vietnam War, that the term came to signify a fixed stored memory—a "veridical recall" of past events. As Frankel further argues, the veridical nature of flashback was more assumed than proven since first appearing in PTSD criteria with the publication of DSM III-R in 1987.[38] That it might also be culture-bound is the conclusion of a more recent study suggesting that experiences resembling flashback were virtually nonexistent in medical reports of British servicemen treated for post-combat disorders in both the first and second world wars.[39] Curiously, the authoring clinicians ascribe the rise of flashback to television rather than film (which was already prevalent a century ago), the hypothesis being that whereas going to the cinema is a deliberate act, "television in the home can be a source of sudden and disturbing imagery in a familiar and apparently safe situation." This might explain why some patients now describe flashback "as being like the playback of a vivid video recording." [40] It seems that even if the media change flashback is always media-bound.

In her recent study on trauma, Leys highlights the centrality of imagery to the conceptualization of PTSD, particularly of what she calls the "*traumatic image*, defined as an externally caused mental content or 'icon.'"[41] She also notes the role of stressful films as used by both Lazarus and Horowitz (associating the latter with what she calls the antimimetic strand of trauma theory).[42] Yet her analysis downplays the media a priori from which the imagistic conception of trauma arises. That imagery has become central to the understanding of trauma must owe something to the film apparatus employed to approach trauma, both technically and conceptually. Resorting to film as an analogue presupposes the technical ability both to record stressful events and to replay those events so as to reproduces stressful effects—what might be called cinematic traumatography. The psychiatric use of films assumes, in other words, the technical iterability of the Real. Indeed, there is an obvious affinity between repetition and reproduction as two parallel mechanisms that converge on the centrality of the image with respect to trauma. For what makes film such an apt a device for the study of post-traumatic image repetition is the fact that it is itself a technology for reproducing images. Film emerges as a proleptic device, producing the flashforwards later to become recurring flashbacks.

The trauma film paradigm stands out as an important step in naturalizing the idea that visual exposure to violence could have clinically observable consequences. At its core is a double move of separation and integration. On the one hand, there is separation between perception and presence, between witnessing violence and being subjected to violence, which gives rise to the possibility of being affected without being directly threatened. On the other hand, there is integration between direct and mediated effects, between processes occurring in harm's way and those occurring at a remove, making the two processes varieties of a common post-traumatic mechanism. As the case of trauma films shows, it is the mediated that serves as a model for the direct. With the trauma film paradigm, the precedent is set for far-off images to cause a scientifically corroborated injury to the beholder's mind.

DISTANT TRAUMA

Is it possible to be traumatized by watching a catastrophic event on television? Can media exposure count as a legitimate cause of PTSD? While having little bearing in the past, these questions have recently become a focus of much debate and research. If there is a defining moment in this story it is the terrorist attacks of September 11, 2001, whose live television broadcasts have since been the subject of numerous studies. Although causality is still under debate, there seems to be an agreement that watching disturbing images on TV, such as those memorable pictures of airplanes crashing into the Twin Towers, might indeed cause post-traumatic symptoms in some viewers. Who might be most vulnerable and under which circumstances? What might be the explanatory personal, social, and cultural backgrounds? In a seminal study Allan Young discusses what he dubs as "PTSD of the virtual kind"—namely, the traumatic power of televised images during and after 9/11—in the context of the development of partial or subthreshold PTSD. According to this logic, while some features of the condition might be absent, the existence of others (say re-experiencing the event, automatic arousal, avoidance, and numbing) justifies the post-trauma nomenclature even if as substandard.[43] This important point should be complemented with a close examination of how the medium of television came to figure in the growing acceptance of traumatic exposure to mediated images.

Psychiatric epidemiologists have recently started rehearsing hypotheses on media effects much like those that have traditionally preoccupied the work of communication scholars. Yet unlike communication research, what psychiatry deems as effects is likely to carry far-reaching implications. Precursory studies began appearing in the early 1990s, and virtually all were concerned with traumatic effects of media on young children. One study on PTSD symptoms among Kuwaiti children during the 1990–1991 Gulf Crisis found that "the viewing of explicit graphic images of mutilation on television had measurable influence on severity of reaction."[44] Another focused on the impact of the televised explosion of the Challenger space shuttle in 1986 on American schoolchildren. The authors found lingering trauma-related fears, dreams, and plays, including cases that could qualify for PTSD diagnosis "if not for their failure to meet the first criterion for PTSD—having endured a traumatic event."[45] Attempting to find adequate terminology, the authors suggest:

> If we call what happened to the Challenger subjects "distant trauma," if we define their responses as "the reaction (memory, thinking, symptoms) to a disastrous event, experienced at the time of the event, but from a remote and realistically safe distance," we might also propose that distant trauma be considered part of a broad range of trauma-related conditions, or the "trauma spectrum."

They proceed to distinguish between different types of conditions on this "trauma spectrum," most of which are media-enabled. Their conclusion is that "for children raised from birth with television, the immediacy of the medium seems almost as real as pure, untouched reality."[46]

Still before 9/11, psychiatrist Betty Pfefferbaum and her colleagues held a series of studies of post-traumatic media effects on children following the 1995 Oklahoma City bombing. A clinical assessment conducted seven weeks after the bombing showed that for those with little personal connection to the disaster "the media appear to play a role in sustaining posttraumatic stress symptoms."[47] One of several follow-ups found evidence of impact as long as two years later: "The potential for media coverage to serve as a traumatic reminder and the potential for symptoms to endure cannot be overemphasized."[48] Another study suggests that television viewing itself may be a sign of an existing distress and so could become "a source of secondary exposure." Since this kind of exposure is largely in parents' hands, it may "constitute an important aspect of prevention."[49]

As noted, the September 11 attacks were a formative event in the study of distant trauma. Just two months later, a group of ten psychiatrists published a special report in the prestigious *New England Journal of Medicine,* featuring the results of a national survey on stress reactions immediately after the attacks:

> People who are not present at a traumatic event may experience stress reaction... After the September 11 terrorist attacks, Americans across the country, including children, had substantial symptoms of stress. Even clinicians who practice in regions that are far from the recent attacks should be prepared to assist people with trauma-related symptoms of stress.[50]

The survey showed that 44 percent of adults and 35 percent of children reported at least one of five substantial stress symptoms. Levels of stress were found to be associated with the extent of television viewing, especially with "repeated viewing of terrifying images." The conclusion is unambiguous: "the September 11 attacks, the shocking televised images, and the profound ramifications are unprecedented"—and so is the warning: "Ongoing media coverage may serve as a traumatic reminder, resulting in persistent symptoms."[51] Significantly, the special report goes beyond the previously studied impact on children and extends the impact to the entire population.

A wealth of studies ensued with a great many reaffirming the connection between television exposure and PTSD symptoms. Here is a small selection: "intensive exposure to the news coverage of such an intense disaster situation is associated with psychopathology";[52] people who watched television the most were 66 percent more likely to have "probable PTSD" than those who watched least;[53] stress in parents who watched the disaster on television was associated with stress in children;[54] television-related PTSD symptoms were found significant even when controlling for directly experiencing the attack, the kind of coverage seen, and sociodemographic characteristics;[55] each hour increase in television viewing resulted in a 5–6 percent increase in dreams containing references to the disaster, which "strengthen the hypothesis that there was a causal path from television viewing of these events, to increased stress and trauma."[56] In addition to television exposure, changes in viewing habits (such as avoidance or seeking out more coverage) were also associated with PTSD symptoms.[57]

And yet, whether television exposure fully merits trauma nomenclature remains a rather contentious issue. A pioneer on traumatic media effects,

Betty Pfefferbaum, presents a qualified view: "it is doubtful that media exposure alone, absent other forms of exposure such as physical or interpersonal relationship to direct victims, would qualify as witnessing."[58] Another commentator presents the opposite view, arguing that for numerous spectators, the collapse of the Twin Towers "was a trauma—without direct stress." What they witnessed, he claims, was "the unthinkable," which did "not stem from a threat to life but rather from *a threat to one's image of the world*." Trauma should therefore be conceptualized as the experience of "shocking novelty" and may include "exposure to extreme brutality, disfigured dead bodies, people jumping out of windows, or major loss."[59] For this commentator, distant trauma has bearing on rethinking trauma in general.

Nevertheless this debate should not obscure the underlying framework from which the question of media post-traumatic effects is approached. The operative term here is "exposure"—a term that subsumes an entire catalogue of orientations enfolded in the act of viewing and converts it into a largely passive stance. Such a stance persists regardless if post-traumatic effects are ascertained or not. Furthermore, on one point virtually all studies—including those that deem media's influence minimal—readily concur: that mental health professionals should be involved in future media coverage of disasters, both on the broadcaster's side and on the audience's. As one psychiatrist sums it up: "we have sufficient research in hand to develop guidelines and practices that limit the potential negative effects of excessive viewing of traumatic imagery. All parties—viewers, networks, and the scientific community—have critical roles to play in this prevention effort."[60]

This preventative intervention conforms to a development identified by Didier Fassin and Richard Rechtman of the rise of proactive involvement by mental health professionals in situations of crisis and disaster.[61] Such intervention, which would have been unthinkable three decades ago, relocates psychiatrists and psychologists from the clinic to the site of impact to supply on-scene preemptive therapy. From a mental health standpoint, the media present the risk of amplifying the site of impact, sending aftershocks far beyond the area of direct danger. In this sense, media coverage of disastrous events is a disaster site in its own sake, requiring an appropriate emergency protocol. A recent study conducted following the Boston marathon bombing in 2013 calls media outlets to "recognize that repeatedly showing gruesome, distressing images is not in the public interest." While "it is important to stay informed," the authors urge local healthcare provides to advise the public, especially those prone to stress, "to limit the time spent watching news coverage of events in the immediate aftermath of a highly publicized local or national trauma."[62] Taking a break from the news when disaster strikes is now the official advice of the American Psychological Association (as well as Dr. Phil's!).[63]

If media do indeed present a risk of trauma, those working in the media are most likely to be affected. As Carrie Rentschler argues, the language of trauma has penetrated journalistic labor, making journalists whose reporting touch death a species of "first responders," and hence prone to the same psychological afflictions that await those arriving promptly on the scene.[64] Psychiatric studies confirmed that war correspondents are as likely as combat soldier to develop PTSD.[65] Yet it now seems that journalists working in the studio are also at risk—the risk of excessive exposure to traumatizing images. A recent study found high rates of intrusive memories among newsroom employees who had been exposed to "violent video clips" during their work. The conclusion is that these "intrusive memories were similar to those occurring in PTSD patients."[66] The risk that newsroom workers face is more akin to that of the television audience than to on-scene reporters. The newsroom occupies a hybrid position on the "trauma spectrum": witnessing tragedy from afar but in proportions amounting to work hazard.

As per the DSM-V media caveat, it all comes down to whether exposure is work-related or not. Thus a newsroom reporter's claim might be valid but not one by a member of the audience. However, the growing acceptance of distant trauma among mental health professionals might portend otherwise, for neither risk of experiencing "shocking novelty" nor risk of overexposure are exclusive to the workplace. Indeed, warnings to limit television viewing during and after tragic events further confirm the plausibility of both risks at home. The point here is not whether the risk is real or not, but rather the rationale behind recognizing only one particular situation of media exposure. Children are a case in point: although virtually everybody in the psychiatric establishment agrees that young children are most likely to be affected, DSM-V unequivocally rejects media exposure as a post-trauma cause in children. As the note following clause A.2 in a section devoted to diagnoses for children stipulates: "Witnessing does not include events that are witnessed only in electronic media, television, movies, or pictures."[67] The risk narrowly accepted for adults is completely rejected for children. Ironically, children watching TV at home were the first research subjects of "distant trauma," but adults at work are the first to benefit from its clinical diagnosis.

The rationale behind the selective recognition might be found elsewhere. The inclusive exclusion of media in DSM-V comes at a time when the conditions and implications of distant trauma are still unclear and under debate. The restriction of work-related exposure has two consequences: first, in the event of a legal claim following traumatic media exposure, the employer becomes the designated party with whom to seek remedy for damages. Second, given the restriction of cause and liability, the possibility of audience PTSD is precluded from the outset, and therefore becomes, for all intents and purposes, an impossibility. The prospect of formally recognizing the risk of traumatic media exposure, irrespective of it being work- or home-based, may carry momentous economic, legislative, and social consequences. The media caveat in DSM-V effectively annuls that prospect. Granted, there may be good reasons to discriminate between different kinds and degrees of media exposure, but such discrimination is already premised on the notion that the screen is a potential medium of trauma. In today's media-saturated world, prioritizing between contexts of exposure might prove increasingly difficult, with various mobile screens performing both work and home activities. And so it remains to be seen if this restriction will hold in the future.

DRONE STRESS

According to recent studies conducted by the U.S. Air Force, remotely piloted aircraft operators flying missions over Iraq, Afghanistan, or Pakistan from ground stations in the American Southwest show stress symptoms typical more of ground troops than of pilots.[68] One operator describes the distinctive nature of his work: "You are going to war for twelve hours, shooting weapons at targets, directing kills on enemy combatants, and then you get in the car, drive home, and within twenty minutes you are sitting at the dinner table talking to your kids about their homework."[69] Remote-controlled warfare gives rise to a new constellation of psychology and technology, one that fuses extreme visibility with extreme distance. In terms of the cases discussed here, if the trauma film paradigm is about seeing distressing things happening to far-off strangers but not to me, and if distant trauma is about seeing distressing things happening to far-off strangers that could also happen to me, the situation of drone operators is about seeing distressing things happening to far-off strangers *because of me*.

Drone operators' occupation has recently been described as "the labor of surveillance and killing."[70] This combination is said to contribute to the combat-related stress some of them experience. Flying a drone can be an exceedingly monotonous task, sometimes involving surveilling a single target around the clock for days and weeks. In the process, operators become acquainted with local routine and terrain, as well as with ground troops deployed in the area, with whom they feel camaraderie despite the distance.[71] As one Air Force Colonel puts it, "These guys actually telecommute to the war zone . . . the band of brothers is built online."[72] But then there are those high-adrenalin moments when operators zoom in to launch and kill. Unlike fighter pilots, who fly thousands of feet away from the combat zone, drone operators have real-time high-resolution view of the strike—and its aftermath. Those who are farthest from combat can see more of it than those physically there, particularly when it comes to close-up details of civilian casualties.[73] Their vision is "'eighteen inches of the battlefield': the distance between the eye and the screen."[74] Balancing war on remote and life in suburbia, on the one hand, and maneuvering between mind-numbing observing and spasmodic killing, on the other—such are the makings of a new type of combat-related stress.

Air Force officials prefer to describe operators' condition in terms such as "burnout," "existential crisis," and "operational stress," distinguishing it from PTSD symptoms.[75] The cause, according to the official explanation, does not stem from visual exposure to combat.[76] However, when drone operators speak publicly, they tell a different story. Former sensor operator Brandon Bryant describes the following scene:

> And there's this guy over here, and he's missing his right leg above his knee. He's holding it, and he's rolling around, and the blood is squirting out of his leg, and it's hitting the ground, and it's hot. His blood is hot. But when it hits the ground, it starts to cool off; the pool cools fast. It took him a long time to die. I just watched him. I watched him become the same color as the ground he was lying on.

Upon discharge, Bryant was given a scorecard of his missions sporting a total number of kills: 1626. He was later diagnosed with PTSD resulting from "a soul-crushing experience. An experience that I thought I'd never have. I was never prepared to take a life."[77]

Heather Linebaugh, a former imagery analyst for the drone program, offers another account:

> I may not have been on the ground in Afghanistan, but I watched parts of the conflict in great detail on a screen for days on end. I know the feeling you experience when you see someone die. Horrifying barely covers it. And when you are exposed to it over and over again it becomes like a small video, embedded in your head, forever on repeat, causing psychological pain and suffering that many people will hopefully never experience. [78]

Still another account is brought by video artist Omer Fast in his film *5000 Feet Is the Best*, which features, among other depictions, an interview with a blurred-face drone operator:

You see a lot of death. You know, you see it all. As I said, I can tell you what kind of shoes you are wearing from that far away. It's pretty clear about everything else that's happening. I mean there came a point after five years of doing this that I just had to think about, "wow so much loss of life that was a direct result of me" . . . A lot of people look at me like, "how can you have PTSD if you weren't actively in a war zone?" Well, technically speaking every single day I was active in a war zone. I mean, I may not have been personally harmed but I was directly affecting people's lives over there every single day. There's stress that comes with that, with having to fire, having to see some of the death, to see what's going on, having anxiety, looking back at a certain situation or incident over and over and over, you know, bad dreams, loss of sleep. You know, it's not like a videogame. I can't switch it off. It's always there. [79]

What these accounts reveal is something other than burnout or operational fatigue: the story they tell is of witnessing in full detail the death of distant strangers whose killing was of the drone operators' own doing. Their post-traumatic symptoms all point to a moral conflict prompted by the increased visibility of the air strike and its aftermath. The technological ability to act from a distance, so argues Zygmunt Bauman, serves to eliminate "face-to-face contact between the actors and the objects of their actions, and with that neutralized its morally constraining impact." [80] Bauman refers to Stanley Milgram's experiments on obedience to authority, where the technological mediation of action (administering electrical shocks) accounted for the rate of obedience, which ranked highest when actors were kept separate from and blind to the effects of their actions.[81] Clearly this is not the case with drone operators, who embody a situation Milgram (and Bauman) did not anticipate: great distance combined with great visibility. Their actions are technologically mediated across great expanses but likewise are images of the carnage wrought.

Clinically speaking, drone operators' stress is arguably closest to what has recently been termed "perpetration-induced traumatic stress" (PITS): a form of PTSD caused not by being a victim to trauma but by being an active participant in producing trauma.[82] Although the psychiatric establishment has yet to recognize PITS classification, DSM-V parenthetically acknowledges the condition under "peritraumatic factors," which include "for military personnel, being a perpetrator, witnessing atrocities, or killing the enemy."[83] That one can be traumatized by the violence one inflicts on others is a possibility already entertained by Freud—traumatic guilt alongside traumatic fear.[84] Such is the trauma of killing, as Dave Grossman puts it: "Looking another human being in the eye, making an independent decision to kill him, and watching as he dies due to your action combine to form the single most basic, important, primal, and potentially traumatic occurrence of war."[85] For this reason, combatants killing at a distance, such as pilots, mariners, and artillerymen are consistently reported to be less encumbered by the psychological agonies of war.[86]

Following the Gulf War conflict, Jean Baudrillard famously commented: "The isolation of the enemy by all kinds of electronic interference creates a sort of barricade behind which he becomes invisible . . . it becomes impossible to discern whether or not he is dead." [87] The cutting-edge war technology at the time was the "smart bomb" with its on-board television camera transmitting images, later widely broadcast, of a continuous zoom-in descent, culminating with a blank screen: the destruction of both bomb and target. Drone technology presents a reversed relation between strike and image: visual surveillance not only precedes the strike but lingers long after to ascertain the kill. As opposed to the sterilized killing of the "smart bomb"—a prime example of Bauman's "distant technology"—high-resolution drone cameras supply the enemy in plain view before, during, and after the strike. In this version of panoptic power, images of the surveilled return to haunt the surveiller.

One remedy offered to this visually inflicted condition seeks to change the conditions of visibility by minimizing image definition:

> To reduce RPA operators' exposure to the stress-inducing traumatic imagery associated with conducting airstrikes against human targets, the USAF should integrate graphical overlays into the visual sensor displays in the operators' virtual cockpits. These overlays would, in real-time, mask the on-screen human victims of RPA airstrikes from the operators who carry them out with sprites or other simple graphics designed to dehumanize the victims' appearance and, therefore, prevent the operators from seeing and developing haunting visual memories of the effects of their weapons.[88]

Operators, on their part, resort to other coping techniques, which also rely on visual technology. A favorite pastime, as the operator in Fast's film reports, is video gaming: "A lot of guys over there, believe it or not, play videogames in their free time. I guess that's their way of unwinding. . . . I guess Predator is similar to playing a videogame, but playing the same videogame four years straight every single day on the same level."[89] If the mediated battleground is the origin of trauma, the pretend battleground is the outlet for its acting out. The screen is the primal scene of both the enactment and re-enactment of the mediated traumatic experience. The video game repeats, both in content and form, elements resembling a drone mission, albeit with the relief of "game over" with no casualties. In this, operators intuitively exercise principles of exposure therapy, the most advanced technique of which—Virtual Reality Exposure Therapy—is the subject of Chapter 5.

Drone operator's plight captures most distinctively the stakes involved in trauma through media. However controversial, their claim to PTSD fits squarely with recent DSM-V criteria, being a traumatic media exposure suffered in the line of duty. Theirs is the continuation of perpetration trauma by technological means. Yet perpetrator trauma, to the extent that such exists, is a condition that traffics on a problematic premise: it casts both aggressor and victim of aggression under the same category of psychic suffering. Here, moreover, the perpetrator is situated in an air-conditioned booth thousands of miles away from action while claiming to be affected by the combat situation. Being exposed to war-zone imageries but not to war-zone risks makes the perpetrator suffer from what some researchers now name "moral injury."[90] Yet in pleading for recognition of their plights, operators obscure the suffering of those targeted by them. Media-enabled violence leads to media-enabled guilt, which in turn leads to media-enabled post-trauma—the perpetrator ends up as a victim of his or her own mediated violence.

MORALITY FROM AFAR

Witnessing the pain of others from afar is a modern condition drastically intensified by modern media. At its core is a moral gap: those who witness distant suffering through the media do so from a safe distance, observing while remaining untouched by the misfortunes being observed. As Jean Jacques Rousseau argued long ago, the disparity between observer and sufferer is the condition for the rise of the moral sentiment of pity.[91] To pity the other, one must be free from the misfortune suffered by the other; one must not feel the other's suffering, for otherwise one would be compelled to pity oneself rather than the other. If there is a sense in which media can be said to implicate morality, it is by placing this disparity between observers and sufferers within a global context, thereby aggravating the disproportion between the ability to observe misfortune and the ability to intervene in the misfortune observed. This disparity remains key in recent debates about regarding the pain of others through the media. Whether it is Luc Boltanski's account of distant suffering in terms of the politics of pity, or Susan Sontag's plea that atrocious images continue to haunt the observers, or John Ellis's admonition to worldwide audiences: "you cannot say you did not know"—what these accounts presuppose is a clear distinction between those who suffer and those who observe suffering, between the unfortunate and the fortunate.[92] Only as long as this disparity persists can the situation be regarded as presenting a moral problem. The growing acceptance of trauma from afar marks a decisive shift: the observer becomes the sufferer. And with this shift, the moral problem in observing distant suffering is occluded.

As the psychiatric approach to media gains professional and popular traction, issues of public health become conflated with issues of the public sphere. Consider a recent controversy in the academia: a number of U.S. colleges are now compelled to issue "trigger warnings" alerting students that the material they are about to see in class might be upsetting, or even cause post-traumatic symptoms in victims of rape or war veterans.[93] That some expressions might be offensive is an old freedom of speech issue, and as many debates demonstrate, the very threat of legal sanction is often enough to bring about inhibition of expression. Under a mindset deeming the individual as needing protection from the media for psychological reasons, the traumatic effect might become the new chilling effect. Broadcasters' statements informing the audience before showing distressing images, or government agencies warning a susceptible populace against excessive media exposure to a disastrous event, can be seen as the first signs of acquiescence to the mental health standpoint. While the clinical status of distant trauma is still under debate, the popular discourse surrounding it seems to be already afoot. All this is not to say that audience protection against mediated violence is not warranted, but rather to call attention to the growing input of psychiatric considerations in public discussion on the issue. Whether observers can be wounded by what they see is a question that merits a critical history rather than clinical history.

Sustaining a moral position in the face of distant suffering seen in the media is increasingly difficult to maintain. Lilie Chouliaraki has traced a shift in humanitarian media practices from a paradigm of pity, in which solidarity is anchored on the image of the aching other, to a paradigm of irony, in which solidarity is anchored on the emotionality of the self and on self-reflection. This shift is the result of commercial, institutional, and technological changes, which together give rise to what Chouliaraki describes as "self-oriented morality, where doing good to others is about 'how I feel' and must, therefore, be rewarded by minor gratifications to the self."[94] The present discussion introduces a development that on one level aligns with Chouliaraki's analysis of the shift to self-oriented morality, but on another level undermines the very conditions for moral engagement through media. The ironic spectator is still concerned with the display of distant suffering, even if such moral engagement ultimately circumvents the pain of the other in favor of the sympathizing self. Conversely, the traumatic spectator, the observing subject arising from recent discussions on distant trauma in psychiatry and psychology, is one that altogether avoids the moral conundrum, for when seeing suffering becomes suffering in its own right, the spectator feels justified in claiming to be a victim, however vicarious, of mediated violence. This troubling prospect is yet to receive proper consideration in ongoing debates about media and morality.

Finally, what I call here screen trauma corresponds with Ruth Leys's critique of the literalist view of trauma—the prevalent view nowadays in clinical psychiatry according to her—which suggests a kind of iconic image-like imprint in the mind.[95] The problem Leys finds in the literalist view—that it sidetracks more complex processes, particularly those that imply the subject's collusion in the event or in what makes it traumatic—applies here yet on a social scale. Once psychiatry declares, however restrictively, media as potentially traumatic, it appropriates a complex social, cultural, and technical process and converts it into an individual mental condition multiplied to mass proportions. Focusing on the observing psyche obscures the conditions under which distressing images come to assume traumatic capability in the first place. The foregoing discussion serves to further denaturalize the literalist view by foregrounding the media context already at work within screen trauma—the implicit traumatic potential of visual media that accompanies psychiatric thinking since the trauma film paradigm. Visual media partake in the literalization of trauma, which leads to the decline of moral engagement through visual media. The shift in the status of mediated violence from obnoxious to noxious can now be seen as consistent with the shift in the observer's attitude from other-gazing to self-preserving, from pity through media to trauma by media.

CHAPTER 4

Virtual Testimony and the Digital Future of Traumatic Past

At the base of all Holocaust testimony projects lies a common commitment: to record and preserve the stories of those who survived the catastrophe as told in their own voices. When it comes to survivors' testimonies, the messenger is as important as the message. The first to subscribe to this reasoning was the American psychologist David Boder, who in 1946 set out to interview survivors in refugee camps across Western Europe. Equipped with what was then the state-of-the-art technology—an Armour Model 50 wire recorder—Boder went on to produce what was the first audio testimony of the Holocaust. The wire recorder, developed in the 1940s by Marvin Camras, Boder's colleague at the Illinois Institute of Technology, for the U.S. military, was a portable and remarkably durable device that utilized thin steel wires rolled into spools to produce an electromagnetic recording (see Fig. 4.1 below).[1] As Boder later commented, the device "offered a unique and exact means of recording the experiences of displaced persons. Through the wire recorder the displaced person could relate in his own language and in his own voice the story of his concentration camp life."[2] Studying wire-recorded narratives led him to devise a "traumatic index" by means of which "each narrative may be assessed as to the category and number of experiences bound to have a traumatizing effect upon the victim."[3] Boder's 1949 monograph, *I Did Not Interview the Dead*, invites readers to find indications of trauma implicit in selected transcripts of recorded narratives. The premise seems to be

Figure 4.1. David Boder with the Armour Model 50 wire recorder, Europe, 1946. Image Courtesy University Archives & Special Collections, Paul V. Galvin Library, Illinois Institute of Technology.

that, to the extent that such traumatic impact exists, it should be discoverable textually.

Yet the same technology that made Boder's project ingenious was also the reason for its relative obscurity. Wire recording was soon to give way to tape recording, consequently condemning Boder's wire spools to obsolescence and the testimonies they held to near oblivion. The short-lived medium precluded access to the recorded material. To be sure, access was never a concern for Boder, who saw no problem in adducing transcripts as equivalent to recordings. Today, however, we seem to have different expectations of the media of testimony, following the changing affordances of media technology. Preservation is no longer enough—access and availability are the norm (appropriately enough, Boder's wire recordings have recently been digitized and made available online[4]). Moreover, testimonies are now expected to reach out and address—to have an interpellating power on audiences. Testimony extends beyond documentation and preservations; it is now increasingly about connection and dialogue. And insofar as traumatic memory is concerned, its impact has become entangled with the performance of bearing witness itself, and especially with performing the inability to fully bear witness to the atrocity.

The origin of this transformation, as I suggest in Chapter 2, is to be found in the video archive for Holocaust testimonies initiated by Dori Laub and Laurel Vlock in the late 1970s. The collaboration between the psychiatrist and the documentarian is suggestive of the testimony genre they produced: a cross between psychoanalytic session and television interview. What began as the Holocaust Film Project in and around New Haven, Connecticut, and later became the Fortunoff Video Archive for Holocaust Testimonies at Yale University, was from the outset a videotape-based operation. Videography was the technological unconscious of this project in combining two media functions: recording and broadcasting. From the beginning, the "videotestimonies" (a term coined by Geoffrey Hartman, who served as academic head of the archive for more than thirty years) collected at Yale were meant to be more than an archival material; they were to transcend the "cold storage" of history.[5] Contrary to Boder's ethnographic motivation (in the literal sense, of documenting people's own voices and expressions), the testimonies produced at Yale were devised with the audience in mind, particularly a prospective television audience. This is the context from which developed Shoshana Felman and Dori Laub's influential speculations on the debilitating impact of trauma on testimony—the crisis of witnessing, as they put it—which plagues both its telling and reception.

If Boder's wire recorder represents the first generation of the media of Holocaust testimony, and if the videotape at Yale represents the second (to which we can add later projects, such as the Visual History Archive initiated by Steven Spielberg), the subject of this chapter represents the third generation. New Dimensions in Testimony (NDT) is a project currently under development at the Institute for Creative Technologies of the University of South California, in collaboration with the Shoah Foundation. Like the earlier projects in their time, it also makes use of the latest technology available as the media of testimony. Yet whereas the first generation of media of testimony was strictly about preservation, and while the second was a combination of preservation and reception, the third is concerned primarily with reception—more precisely, with interaction as a means for memorialization. The aim, according to the project's designers, is to "continue the dialogue between Holocaust survivors and learners far into the future."[6]

NDT presents itself as the next stage in the media of testimony by virtue of taking Holocaust commemoration into the digital age. While digitization of testimonies began in the early 2000s, previous projects tended to rely on the audiovisual model of testimony developed at Yale, reformatting it to benefit from digital platforms. What is novel about NDT is the entirely different logic of media of testimony it introduces by utilizing more fully the affordances of digital technology. Combining human-computer speech interaction capabilities with three-dimensional holographic imaging, the project promises to create an immersive experience of a live conversation with survivors long after they are gone. Interaction rather than narration is the premise of this new approach to Holocaust testimony. Much of the rhetoric surrounding the project comes from science fiction, celebrating the possibility of a simulated exchange between past and future—a veritable intertemporal exchange (the dialogue between Superman and his long dead father is mentioned as an inspiration[7]). Yet what makes this project worthy of serious critical consideration is not so much its high-tech futuristic gloss of testimony, but more importantly the way it aims testimony toward the future. As such, it makes for an exemplary case for investigating the transmission of painful experiences under conditions of digitization, including the digital status, if any, of traumatic memory therein.

But before delving into the specifics, it is important to consider the basic operational logic of NDT: the logic of the database. Lev Manovich has famously described the shift from narrative to database as the dominant cultural form of the computer age.[8] Whereas narrative operates according to a linear trajectory involving a series of causally interconnected actors and events, database operates according to functional principles of data organization irrespective of any previous relation among items. As Manovich argues, database has come to replace narrative as the basic paradigm for various creative processes. Although this assertion might be too far-reaching for some cultural objects, it seems quite accurate with respect to testimony—an eminently narrative form—as it undergoes conversion into digital database. Critical here is Manovich's insight about the reversed relation between syntagm and paradigm as occasioned by the digitization of data.

Narrative requires that all syntagmatic elements be preset and related (as in a written sentence) while leaving other paradigmatic elements (possible substitutions of nouns, verbs, adjectives, etc.) as associations in the narrator's mind. Under narrative form, syntagm is real and paradigm virtual. Thus, for example, both Boder's audio testimonies and the Yale audiovisual testimonies represent the centrality of syntagm in the narrative form, where the witness's actual articulations (and misarticulations) caught on tape constitute the entire scope of the testimony and its interpretative potential. Database logic reverses the relation between syntagm and paradigm: in order to construct a narrative from a given data set, all possible elements and substitutions must be structured and organized in it in advance. Hence database is a materialized form of paradigm while narrative becomes a resulting arrangement, one way among others of stringing together data. Under database form it is paradigm that is real while syntagm is virtual. This reversed relation between paradigm and syntagma will prove important in considering the status of traumatic memory in virtual testimony: as that which is made manifest not simply through narrative—that is, syntagmatically—but even more distinctively by unsettling narrative, by insinuating itself despite and upon narrativization, as a syntagmatic irritation.

Holocaust testimony has evolved as a distinct genre of oral history in the context of analog recording technologies—from the wire recorder to the videotape—whereby the performing of narrative has become inseparable from the testimonial narrative itself. These technologies allowed for an unselective inscription of both the sense and non-sense of testimony—the personal storyline together with the indexical cues along the storytelling—from which traces of traumatic memory could be retrieved. What is the fate of the irritation of narrative under the technical regime of data classification? Is it possible to transpose the narrative-based performing of traumatic memory into the digital database? And if possible, should it? Or maybe the question is altogether different, and rather than speculating about recreating discursive effects related to analog media, should focus instead on exploring new forms and formations of testimony as afforded by digital media. NDT provides an entry point for considering these questions as they arise from the shift from what Kittler calls the discourse network of 1900 to what might be called the discourse network of 2000.

I will argue that the digital configurations of testimony represented by the NDT project mark the uncoupling of traumatic memory from the testimonial narrative as its carrier. What was a defining feature of bearing witness in the context of the video archive—the acting out of traumatic memory upon testimony—becomes extraneous in the context of the digital database. The comparative approach I employ throughout the discussion serves to elucidate some of the consequences of this development. While opening new avenues for testimony, this project nevertheless presents a deeply problematic conception of the relation between past and present, and between absence and presence, as these come into play in the performing of testimony. Algorithmic-holographic testimony promotes a vision of unencumbered cross-generational interaction in which witnessing is devoid of pain—and of the essential difficulty in relating painful past experiences.

Designers of NDT are well aware of previous testimonial projects, and as much as they acknowledge that tradition, they are equally keen to break from it.[9] In their view, earlier employments of technology in testimony were strictly for the sake of documenting the process of bearing witness. From the vantage point of digital culture, this documentary concern seems lacking in terms of its interactive potential. Instead of the traditional documentary model, the NDT project follows a conversational model: a face-to-face dialogue between survivor and audience, the kind that would typically take place in a classroom or museum. Such encounters are said to have "created a connection and given those students an intimate experience with someone uniquely qualified to reflect on life, and about a very real part of history from an eyewitness perspective."[10] The conversational model of testimony is said to provide a firsthand personal experience, whereas the former documentary model is deemed as secondhand and derivative, permitting only to "hear the survivor's story in a linear way."[11] NDT can be seen, then, as combining the hitherto mutually exclusive functions of preservation and interaction by allowing for a cross-temporal storytelling. It does so by drawing on a database of multiple prerecorded clips that are used to simulate an interactive conversation with a survivor "through the fourth dimension of time."[12]

The first to partake in the project was Pinchas Gutter, a survivor of six concentration camps, born in Lodz and currently living in Toronto, who was seven years old when the war broke (recruitment and recording of additional survivors is currently underway). Gutter spent five days of filmed interviews in March 2014 answering several hundred questions presented to him by Stephen Smith, executive director of the USC Shoah Foundation. The questions were collected from experts in Holocaust and genocide studies, history, trauma specialists, and Holocaust museum education staff, as well as from specifically targeted audience of teachers and students, who had been asked to supply questions after watching a documentary about Mr. Gutter. A second round of interviews was conducted five months later following initial system trials.[13] Gutter's responses were then integrated into a human-computer interface to create what NDT designers call "time-offset interaction."[14] As opposed to telecommunicating, which requires synchronic participation (such as speaking over the telephone), time-offset interaction "removes this contemporaneity requirement while preserving the synchronous nature of conversation."[15] The working premise here is that testimony is a relatively circumscribed topic of conversation, and so interlocutors' questions and answers are largely predictable. Given a large enough selection of prerecorded responses, a computer program can successfully select and replay the most appropriate reply in each interactive session.

The NDT human-computer interface consists of two main components: automatic speech recognition module and natural language processing module. When the system receives a question, it first converts the utterance into a textual representation. Next, the system uses a statistical algorithm trained on a pull of questions and associated answers to build a model that predicts the most likely words to appear in an answer. It then ranks stored responses according to their closeness to the prediction and selects the most appropriate. Thus the system must have a representation of the answer's main variables before proceeding to locate the best match. If the result scores below a certain threshold (that is, when an appropriate answer cannot be produced given the input) the system resorts to an off-topic prerecorded response, such as "The question that you asked me, I'm afraid I won't be able to answer." Although failing to supply an answer, such replies (also called non-understanding) were found to be preferable to giving an inappropriate answer (misunderstanding).[16] To further sustain fluency of interaction, the system uses prerecorded neutral clips ("idle behavior") to interconnect conversational sequences, and in addition processes visual morphing of all start and end frames of each response clip so as to transition as seamlessly as possible from one to the next.[17]

The other half of this project's interactive promise lies in its visual rendering. During interviews, Gutter was filmed sitting at the center of Light Stage 6: an eight-meter geodesic dome lit by six thousand LEDs and mounted with some fifty high-resolution digital cameras capturing the survivor from multiple angles (see Fig. 4.2). Created by Paul Debevec at the Institute for Creative Technologies, the Light Stage technology has been used for special effects in films such as *Superman, Spiderman,* and *Avatar.*[18] It utilizes a technique called "light field rendering": multiple cameras capture the light rays reflected from the scene, each from a slightly different angle; the combined video feeds are then synthesized to create a three-dimensional projection. Unlike stereoscopic 3D projection, which requires viewers to use glasses, the system employs an anisotropic screen onto which vertical strips coming from multiple projectors produce a hologram of the survivor, one that can be viewed three-dimensionally from various points of view. The visual processing of the hologram can adapt to different lighting conditions and blend naturally into various settings (see Fig. 4.3). Clearly, no effort was spared to render the witness not only responsive but also virtually present at the scene of interaction.

The project received considerable media coverage since its announcement in 2012. Newspaper reports in the United States, Europe, and Israel hailed the futuristic testimony technology, and likewise television shows, including

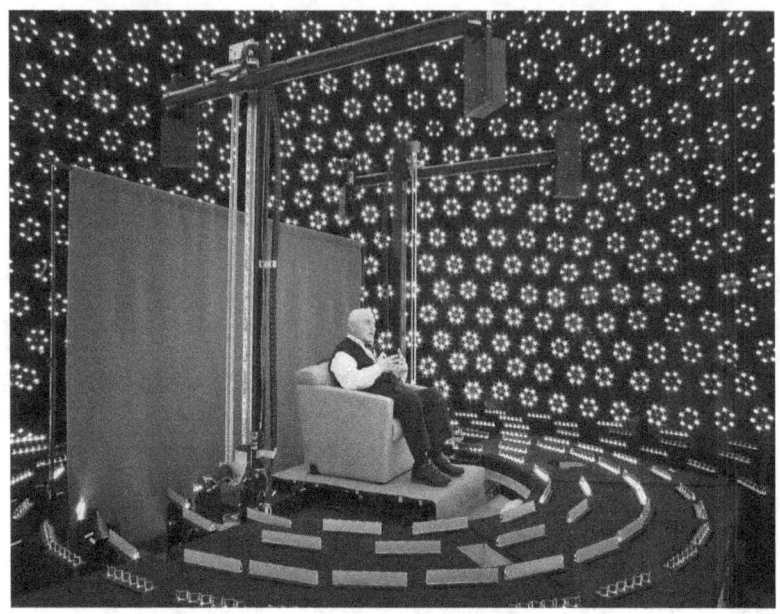

Figure 4.2. Pinchas Gutter being filmed on Light Stage.

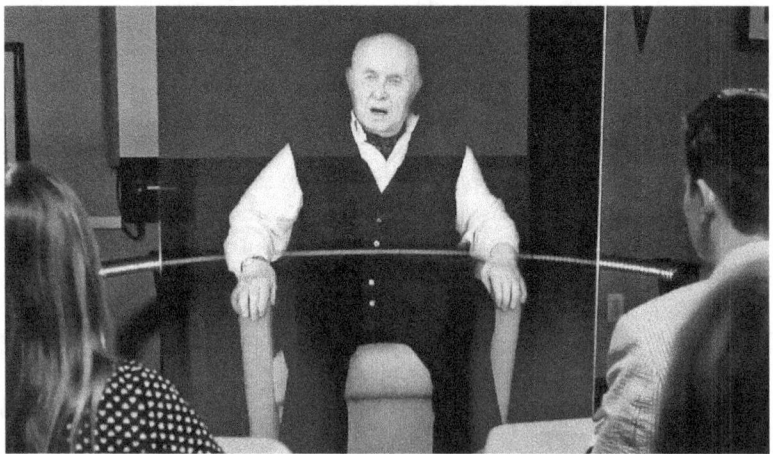

Figure 4.3. Pinchas Gutter's hologram interacting with a group of students. Images used with permission from the University of South California Institute for Creative Technologies.

a full demonstration of the system on NBC's *Today* show.[19] The Institute for Creative Technologies also released a short promotional clip featuring a group of teenage students sitting in a classroom around Gutter's hologram. "How old were you when the war ended?" asks one boy; "I was between the ages of 13 and 14 when the war ended in 1945," replies Gutter. "Do you remember any songs from your youth?" asks a girl; "This is a lullaby that my mother used to sing to me and I still remember it," and proceeds to sing in Polish.[20] In press interviews NDT team members Stephen Smith, Paul Debevec, and David Traum pledge to make Holocaust testimony "future proof," by which they mean not only secured for archival safekeeping but compatible with all foreseeable future media formats.[21] As opposed to the preservation rationale that characterized previous projects, which favored fidelity over accessibility (hence the problem of obsolescence), the reception rationale guiding this project revolves around the imperative of reaching out to future interlocutors. Making testimony "future proof" is thus a matter of ascertaining the conditions of prospective reception and interaction—ensuring transmission into the future in order to safeguard the memory of the past. Such is the "programmed vision" of NDT, to use Wendy Chun's term, whereby the future becomes "future simple," namely, a technologically predictable and manageable upgrade of the present.[22]

But not all are enthusiastic about the enterprise. One report quotes Holocaust historian Lawrence Langer as saying, "This is the craziest thing I have ever seen. . . . Why do we need these holograms?" Former chief archivist for the Fortunoff archive, Joanne Rudof, wonders, "What is the goal of this? Holograms make it less real," adding, "They're not getting a response from quote unquote 'person' . . . This is Siri, but artificially embodied."[23] Such comments are perhaps to be expected from those associated with the more traditional and well-established testimony project. Suspicion of the new is understandable among those committed to the dominant modes of preserving the past. (Personal note: when I showed the NDT clip to Dori Laub at a conference, his reaction was "this is not a testimony"). That said, it should be remembered that, much like NDT, the Yale project was also initiated with deep concern for the future of testimony and its reception by prospective audiences; and this concern, again like the digital project, was decidedly linked with a technological vision of testimony. As Geoffrey Hartman noted retrospectively, the premise at Yale was that "Radio Days were gone. Audiences now and in the future would surely be audiovisual. We decided to make video recordings of public broadcast quality, to build an Archive of Conscience on which future educators and filmmakers might rely."[24] Both projects are therefore geared toward future audiences as imagined through the dominant media platforms of their respective presents.

Yet the two projects diverge radically in the kind of performing of witnessing they promote, which amounts to a profoundly different conception of memory and of the relation between past and present. Specifically, instead of the fraught nature of memory arising from the analog-based Yale testimony, a memory that both prompts and troubles its recounting, the digital-based NDT testimony exhibits memory as a kind of transferrable data traversing and connecting past and future. Nowhere do these two versions of Holocaust memory diverge more dramatically as in the status of traumatic memory in testimony. If television and videotape were the media a priori for perceiving the impinging of trauma upon testimony, algorithm and holography are the media a priori of the removal of trauma from testimony. The type of testimonial narrative the NDT project introduces is one that is unburdened by the convolutions of traumatic memory, and is in this sense most literary "post-traumatic."

THE MEDIA TEMPORALITY OF TESTIMONY

Central to this discussion is the different media temporalities of the analog as opposed to the digital. By media temporality I mean the time that technical media produce through their operation. Media do not only refer or follow existing historical time; rather, they create their own time, what Wolfgang Ernst calls *Eigenzeit*.[25] Their operational processes generate autonomous temporal formations, which are not synchronous with those of human perception. Ernst refers to "time-critical media" as those technologies that abstract and disrupt human time by temporalizing independently of it.[26] They do so by registering physical rather than discursive effects, and by processing signals rather than semantic structures. This allows for an alternative epistemology of time by way of time-axis manipulation. It could be argued that all storage media, since the invention of writing, are means for manipulating time insofar as providing a record for future access—the ability to communicate across time. Yet it was only with the introduction of analog recording technologies, such as the phonograph, the photograph, and the cinematograph, that the flow of time itself could be subjected to storage and manipulation. This "real-time" inscription of the physical effects of light and sound allowed capturing the material traces of reality as temporal events—hence the ability to freeze, slow, and reverse the flow of recorded time—together with the ability to revisit captured moments, intentional as well as unintentional.

As the discussion in Chapter 2 shows, this quality of analog recording was key in the production of video testimonies. Video recording documented not only the narrative but also the event of telling: the details of survival together with the incidentals of speaking— halts, silences, slips, gestures, timbre, and tone. The latter are accessible only through non-symbolic technical inscription and, as such, coincide with what Kittler determined, following Lacan, as the (material) realm of the Real. Lacan's metaphor of the Real is pertinent here: "[it is] like a punctuation without a text . . . a noise in which one can hear anything and everything."[27] Hence Kittler's contention: "Only machines are capable of storing the real of and beyond all speech."[28] Video testimony is thus a medium for recording the testimonial narrative together with the punctures and punctuations of telling, the "non-sense" of testimony, which can then be retrospectively interpreted as indicative of vestiges of deep, or traumatic memory. It is for this reason that Boder's "traumatic index," which was based on converting audio wire recordings into textual transcripts, was strictly of the symbolic order. The linear access of recording was transformed into nonlinear, direct access of textuality. The way trauma came to signify in it was, to reverse Lacan's phrase above, like a text without punctuation. As wire recordings were converted into transcripts, the Real was transformed into the Symbolic. As we will see shortly, the re-symbolization of the traumatic effect through nonlinear access is now making a return with digitization.

The media temporality of the digital is entirely different from that of its predecessor. Whether textual, visual, or audial, all digital processing is underpinned by microtemporal calculations taking place at imperceptible intervals that are well below human perception. As Ernst suggests, such microtemporal operativity opens new capabilities of manipulating time, not only of capturing events, but also, due to its combinatory procedures, of creating new, artificial, or even artifactual events.[29] This is precisely the operation of the algorithm at the core of NDT in which microtemporal statistical calculations determine the most likely reply to any given question.[30] Gutter's "testimony" is based on statistical probability, its media temporality being microprocessual rather than chronological. Since the system already "knows" all the possible answers before receiving any question, the result is narrative ex machina: at each runtime a different stringing of responses depending on the queries presented. Paradigm transforms into syntagm through the "message bus": the element integrating speech recognition, language processing, and audiovisual rendering (see Fig. 4.4). If the Yale project was about documenting bearing witness as a process accompanied by the corporeal contingencies of speech, the NDT project is about eliminating contingencies so as to sustain functional human-computer interaction. If video testimony

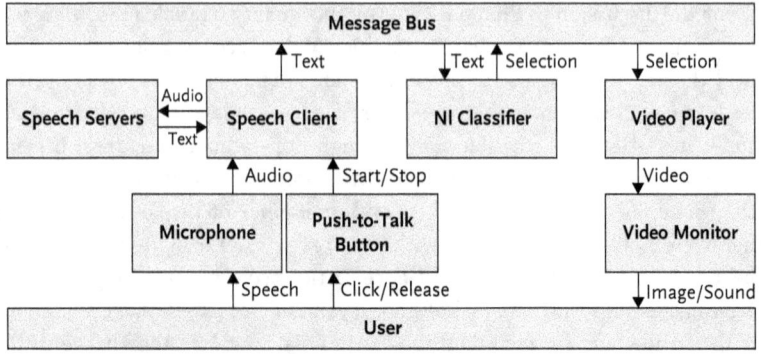

Figure 4.4. New Dimensions in Testimony system architecture. From: David Traum et al., "New Dimensions in Testimony: Digitally Preserving a Holocaust Survivor's Interactive Storytelling," in *Interactive Storytelling—8th International Conference on Interactive Digital Storytelling*, eds. Henrik Schoenau-Fog et al. (Heidelberg: Springer, 2015), 269–270. Reproduced with permission of Springer.

provides a repository of narrative-bound incidents and idiosyncrasies that are ripe with hermeneutical possibilities, the virtual testimony is based on discrete, semantically preclassified narrative units that are unsusceptible to real-time irregularities.

What is lost in the shift of media temporalities is the precariousness of the testimonial narrative, which no longer operates as a carrier of lapses and parapraxes as telltale of traumatic memory. This however does not mean that virtual testimony is devoid of lapses and parapraxes; these certainly exist, but when they occur they disclose a technical rather than psychic substrata. Designers of NDT have gone to great lengths to maintain the smoothness and seamlessness of the interaction. Clips of idle behavior, visual morphing, and off-topic answers are all devised to support interface fluency. Such fluency is the result of numerous micro-decisions executed algorithmically, which are of course determined in advance.[31] Yet it is precisely in moments when the simulation seeks to simulate the contingencies of human interaction that technology reveals itself most starkly. The more real is the virtual, the more jarring the glitches. What becomes apparent in such moments is not the overtones and undertones of bearing witness but the underlying computational procedures of the testimony algorithm, or to quote Ernst, "not physical but mathematical moments of the real."[32] What is revealed is not the alternative temporality of traumatic memory but the alternative temporality of computational operation.

An illustration to this is seen during a demonstration of the NDT project on NBC's *Today* show. Siting before Gutter's hologram, host Matt Lauer asks: "Is there any question you can't answer?" to which Gutter's hologram replies, "I have no comment about rap music." This line is an off-topic response to which the system resorts whenever failing to produce a statistically adequate response to the question presented. Lauer turns to David Traum: "It's amazing. It's almost haunting that he is looking directly into my eyes." The sheer technological achievement is indeed remarkable. But here and there it is possible to glimpse the hologram's programmed gestures, such as the repetitive nods when assuming a listening position, which are meant to simulate casual conversational behavior. Moments like these, as well as off-topic responses, are suggestive of what roboticist Masahiro Mori called in the early 1970s "the uncanny valley."[33] Mori speculated that as robots become more humanlike, the perceived familiarity they elicit increases steadily until reaching a sharp drop, where any subtle deviation from human likeness provokes eeriness and recoiling (see Fig. 4.5). In other words, comfort with human replicas, both moving and still, grows in proportion to their resemblance to human, or human parts, but then at a certain point the

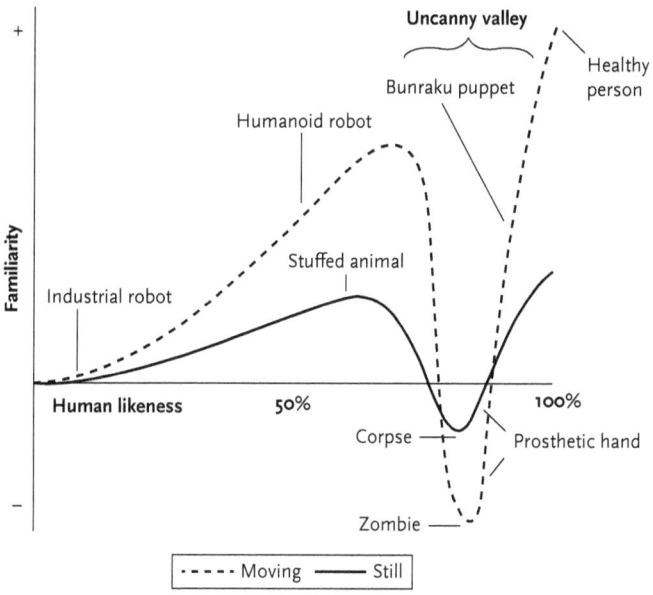

Figure 4.5. The uncanny valley (reproduced by permission from Masahiro Mori, "The Uncanny Valley," *IEEE Robotics and Automation*, trans. K. F. MacDorman and Norri Kageki 19(2), 98–100).

relation reverses radically, and any further increase in human likeness causes additional recoil from the replica. Being firmly within the territory of technological humanoids, the survivor's hologram is prone to the uncanny descent.

Mori's speculations draw on Freud's notion of the *Unheimlich* (the unhomely) as the frightening element "that was long familiar to the psyche and was estranged from it only through being repressed."[34] The uncanny spells the return of the repressed either when something already known but secret suddenly becomes revealed, or when a primitive (or childish) belief thought to have been long surmounted becomes confirmed once again. Both dynamics of the uncanny are connected to death, which explains why the appearance of doubles is a constant cause of trepidation: in their likeness they invoke the wish to overcome death, which inevitably turns them into harbingers of death.[35] Significantly, the two lowest points designating the "uncanny valley" (on the moving and still graphs) are not of artificial human likeness but of what was once, but is no longer, human life: corpse and zombie. It seems that with every human replication there is a reminder of the inanimate fate of all life. This aspect of the uncanny is suggested when failures to maintain believability reveal the underlying artificiality of the interaction. The holographic survivor evokes the uncanny most palpably by appearing as a species of the undead, which is indeed the designers' explicit intention—to surmount the survivor's demise.

Media technologies have long been portals for conjuring the dead, providing platforms by which ghosts emerge and the dead continue to live.[36] The rhetoric of NDT designers certainly ascribes technology with the power to hold what Amanda Lagerkvist calls "after-death communication."[37] To be sure, the very premise of Holocaust testimony is to outlive the survivors, to allow their stories to speak in their absence and in their stead. And yet whereas the videotestimonies produced at Yale reach to the afterlife dialectically by upholding the persistent inaccessibility of certain temporalities, both to the witness and to the audience, virtual testimony takes on the challenge most straightforwardly as a battle against the transience of the witness herself. The virtual witness is made to address future interlocutors by appearing to be present and speaking in the present. It is almost as though the hologram (complete inscription) purports itself to be a countermeasure against the disappearance of remnants of the Holocaust (complete incineration).

PRESENCING ABSENCE

Video testimony suggests a triadic relation among the witness, the interviewer, and the video camera as a stand-in for a prospective yet absent audience. Both interviewer and witness presuppose the promise of future dissemination as they proceed to bear witness. Thirdness is thus embedded within the secondness of video testimony. In watching recorded testimonies, the viewer assumes the position described by Thomas Trezise as "witnessing witnessing":[38] a third-party ex post facto view accompanying the emergence of the testimonial narrative. For all parties involved, delayed reception is the governing principle of bearing witness on videotape. The performing of testimony produced by the NDT, on the other hand, is one that collapses thirdness into secondness. Moving from two-dimensional viewing to four-dimensional immersive interaction (three-dimensionality plus contemporaneity, or "time-offset interaction," as NDT designers dub it), the viewer becomes a pseudo interviewer, assuming a second-person perspective and a simulated face-to-face mode of address. Immediacy replaces delay and presence takes over absence.

According to NDT designers what distinguishes their project is "the ability to connect on a personal level with a survivor, and the history, even when that survivor is not present."[39] To them, the technological effort to simulate "face-to-face" and "first-hand" experience stands against what they regard as the secondary experience of traditional recorded testimonies. While every kind of technical memorialization is in one way or another about making the absent present, the NDT version proceeds to take the extra step of counteracting the absence of that which is made present. Hans Ulrich Gumbrecht proposes the notion of "production of presence" to describe instances that bring forth the embodied and material aspects in phenomena rather than the semantic and hermeneutic. While such "presence effects" are always inextricably linked with "meaning effects," their specific configuration is determined by the materialities of communication at hand.[40] Both video testimony and virtual testimony are apt cases for the production of presence, however with each representing a different type of the effect. Consider NDT chief visual officer Paul Debevec's description of the effect of virtual testimony:

> Feeling them be part of your own environment, lit by the same light that you are so they really feel present, there's this potential to be that much more connected to what they're saying and to break away this frame that puts them in one place and puts you in another, and put you in the same place, which is where all great storytelling can happen.[41]

Clearly presence is understood here in terms of the reception context, referring both to the hologram's extensive immersion within the projection environment as well as to the production of a cotemporaneous exchange, simulating live conversation. The feeling of co-presence is what drives this project with the explicit aim of breaking the frame—that is, the iconic metaphor for the image seen on the screen—which supposedly separates witness and audience.

Curiously enough, the metaphor of frame is also used in the trauma and testimony discourse, most notably by Laub when referring to a videotaped testimony of a woman testifying to the explosion of four chimneys in a failed Auschwitz revolt. When criticized by historians saying that only one chimney had been blown up, Laub retorts that the explosion of one or four chimneys is as incredible: "The woman testified to an event that broke the all compelling frame of Auschwitz"; what she testified to, he adds, was the unbelievability of what she had seen: "this bursting open of the very frame of Auschwitz."[42] Felman employs the same metaphor to describe what she regards as the unique testimony performed by Lanzmann's *Shoah*: the "double task of the breaking of the silence and of the simultaneous shattering of any given discourse, of the breaking—or the bursting open—of all frames"; indeed the film itself, she argues, "bursts open even its own filmic frame."[43] Felman takes up the phrase again in a later work when discussing the collapse of the writer Ka-tzetnik on the stand while giving his testimony at the Eichmann trial. As discussed in Chapter 1, Felman deems this event as profoundly significant since it encapsulates the failure to give voice to trauma through legal procedure, and simultaneously the performing of that failure within that procedure. What Ka-tzetnik's testimony ultimately signifies is "a rupture in the legal frame" of the trial, for it is "through this inadvertent breakdown of the legal framework [that] history uncannily and powerfully speaks."[44]

This digression into the figuration of the trauma and testimony discourse captures in a nutshell the fundamental difference between the two approaches to testimony. For Debevec, as a representative of the NDT view, breaking the frame denotes breaking what allegedly separates witness and audience—namely, the screen—so as to create a sense of shared presence. In this Debevec seems to celebrate what Mark Andrejevic has recently termed "framelessness": the contemporary cultural logic of big data that promotes immersion instead of representation, being thrown into media environments rather than being able to select and assume a point a view within these environments. In the virtual realm, framelessness has become the ideal: freeing the image from the constriction of the frame serves "to fulfill the promise of total information capture and to overcome the biases of partiality and selectivity."[45] Of course what the move toward framelessness as represented by NDT ignores is that the frame not only separates but also connects; indeed, connects because it also separates. For Laub and Felman, to be sure, breaking the frame designated testimonial moments that transcend the sayable, exigent articulations that come to signify precisely by failing to fully mean. Only audiovisual recording and framing can account for these articulations. In testimony the frame is indispensable in its own breaking. If for Debevec the motivation is connecting past and present, and replacing absence with presence by eliminating the archetypal rectangular shape of visual media, for Laub and Felman there is the opposite motivation of upholding the disconnect between past and present, and yielding to the haunting of presence by absence as captured and performed through and despite the frame.

Holocaust scholar Lawrence Langer provides a most cogent description of this latter logic:

> We as audience experience an existence defined not merely by its own survival but also by the destruction of others. It is a revelation fueled by the vitality of its insight and the gloom of its finality . . . [videotape] testimonies are not based on common experience or an imaginable past, real or literary. Though eager to participate with sympathetic understanding, we are driven by the nature of the material to the periphery of comprehension. Odd as it may sound, we need to search for the inner principles of incoherence that make these testimonies accessible to us.[46]

The presence effect, to use Gumbrecht's term, of video testimony is achieved by way of emphasizing, rather than diminishing, the separateness between witness and audience. In contrast to the fabricated co-presence of virtual testimony, video testimony evokes the non-synchronicity between the event of testimony and the event of viewing the testimony (not to mention the event testified to). It produces a presence effect inasmuch as it produces an absence effect. If virtual testimony involves the simulation of testimony (simulation, strictly speaking, is making the absent present), video testimony might be said to involve a countervailing effect of dissimulation (that is, making the present absent)—a way of referring to what cannot be fully re-presented and carried into presence. Whereas virtual testimony maximizes the impulse to "participate with sympathetic understanding," video testimony minimizes that impulse, pushing the audience to the "periphery of comprehension." It seems that Debevec, together with the other NDT designers, sees the potential of producing meaning from testimony, of making it meaningful, as contingent on the technical possibility of producing presence, or more precisely of producing a presence effect. Conversely, Langer (as well as Laub and Felman) presents the opposite logic whereby the presence effect of video testimony is plagued by absence and separation, and its meaning effect, the way it becomes meaningful, is punctured by the occasional failure to mean, sending the audience to scramble for "the inner principles of incoherence" with which to connect to testimonies. Such is the limbo of videotestimony: neither entirely in the past nor completely in the present but somehow in both. NDT seems to operate under a contrary assumption, namely, that absence and separation are technologically resolvable predicaments. The goal is producing just enough suspension of disbelief in the survivor's presence to keep the interaction going.

FROM WITNESS TO WITNESSEE

NDT can be placed within a broader context of contemporary Holocaust testimony projects that emphasize the side of the recipients. As we move closer to the day when all living survivors will disappear, issues of secondary witnessing, of bearing witness to witnesses, become more acute. To be sure, this concern has long accompanied documentation and preservations efforts, certainly since the establishment of audiovisual testimony archives. And yet, as Trezise argues, the time has come for a careful critical evaluation of the fraught practice of "witnessing witnessing" as one that is irredeemably bounded up with the lure of identification and the perils of overidentification.[47] In the context of new media, the problem of the reception takes on new dimensions, not least in the case of the New Dimensions of Testimony. There seems to be a trend, encompassing a range of media platforms drawing on the affordances of digital technologies, of involving recipients in the very production and reproduction of testimony. Such platforms typically consist of user-centered design, which shifts the emphasis from the witness as the deliverer of testimony to what might be called the "witnessee"—the digitally enabled participatory recipient.

Clearly this is not an entirely new phenomenon. Several scholars have drawn attention to the ways contemporary mediated memory practices, especially in the wake of catastrophes and calamities, produce new experiential dimensions for remembering publics. Thus, for instance, Alison Landsberg speaks about "prosthetic memory" as the memory produced by technologies of popular culture that invite people to form their own personal sensory experience of events they themselves did not live through (Steven Spielberg's *Schindler's List* being a key example).[48] Marita Sturken discusses embodied practices of memorialization of public events as these are experienced individually through technologies, images, and objects.[49] Marianne Hirsch introduces the notion of postmemory as the received post-traumatic memory of the second generation to the Holocaust, which is artistically and medially created.[50] And José van Dyke focuses on the ways digital technologies give rise to new formations of "personal cultural memory."[51] The shift to the witnessee suggested here extends from the developments cited above, but it also marks a distinctive transformation in that it involves a thorough reconfiguration of the relation between addresser and addressee of testimony as redefined by the affordances of digital technology.

Central to this shift is N. Katharine Hayles's conceptualization of embodiment and its relation to technology. Hayles distinguishes between the body and embodiment, suggesting that whereas "the body is always relative to some set of criteria," embodiment is "contextual, enmeshed within the specifics of place, time, physiology and culture, which together compose enactment." [52] In other words, if the body refers to a generalized concept and construct, outside any specific context, embodiment refers to specific instantiations of experience and action within a particular material context. Although interconnected, body and embodiment never completely coincide but make up a polarity wherein the former spells an idealized form and the latter a messy bundle of varied activities. Hayles introduces the notion of "incorporating practices" as those practices that "cannot be separated from their embodied medium."[53] Being both culturally and physiologically constituted, they include repeated learned performances, a kind of encoded bodily memory, such as a goodbye wave. Incorporating practices are particularly important in understanding the lived experience of technology and the way technological changes are linked with situated, embodied activities. In terms of the present discussion, to the extent that the development pointed out above of the turn toward the witnessee is now gaining dominance, this would mean a corresponding shift in the incorporating practices of the media of testimony, in their embodied, lived experience. And this would consequently mean a shift in the status of traumatic memory and its relation to the embodied testimonial narrative.

Consider two examples. The first, also created in collaboration with USC Shoah Foundation, employs a mobile application, *Broadcastr*, to deliver audiovisual testimonies related to the location of the user. Thus when visiting Auschwitz-Birkenau, relevant camp survivors' testimonies can be played automatically based on the visitor's GPS position. The app's developer, Scott Lindenbaum, likens it to Proust's madeleine, acting as an involuntary memory device by which memories "leap up on us." The injunction "never forget," he adds, compels us to use media that "help us remember to remember," in this case by linking in situ experience with a cloud-based archive.[54] The second example is a 2013 campaign by an Israeli advertising agency for raising Holocaust awareness among adolescents. It involved distributing removable number tattoos coupled with postcards displaying a QR code that when scanned by a mobile device application links to an audiovisual testimony by a survivor marked with the same number tattoo. Executives at the advertising agency explained that with many survivors passing away and Holocaust memory becoming dimmer, the only way to reach the younger generation is by creating "a strong icon" that comes from "the world that they know."[55] Innovative or in bad taste, the campaign relied on the centrality of mobile devices in today's social life. In both examples technology figures in the challenge of making the absent present by inviting users to assert their own embodied presence as a way to invoke, and perhaps even compensate for, the increasing disappearance of survivors. The employment of digital platforms in creating new ways to engage with testimonies is consistent with a set of incorporating practices that shift the focus of testimony from the witness to the witnessee. It is also consistent with the transformation identified by Lilie Chouliaraki in the relation to the suffering of distant others on media, a shift from a perspective of pity, where the plight of the other takes center stage, to a perspective of irony, where the focus is put on the spectating self's emotions and gratifications.[56]

This shift has important moral implications, as two recent studies of the Visual History Archive demonstrate. Producing computer-generated data from digitized testimonies poses a moral problem insofar as this might imply converting human suffering into quantifiable data. And yet, Todd Presner suggests that algorithmic processing may actually present new and deeply ethical engagement with testimonies, owing to the capability of integrating large-scale data over a small selection. He proposes "distant listening" as a computational practice that "moves away from the close, hermeneutical reading of texts in favor of an algorithmic approach that presents overarching structures and patterns."[57] The transformation of testimony from narrative to database reaches its limit with "indeterminable data" such as tone, expression, and emotion, which require interpretive intervention to be enumerated. It is precisely the nonmeaning of trauma—the contingencies of telling and failing to tell—that calls for close rather than distant listening. Here Presner pins his hope on users' engagement, speculating on the possibility of participatory collective indexing and dynamic browsing based on "communities of experience, narrative structure, or even silences, gaps, and so-called nonindexical content."[58] Transcending the calculative logic of the database is sought outside the database, with users supplying the hermeneutical excess needed to counteract definitive categorization. The alterity of trauma once gleaned on tape is now crowdsourced online.

Another account of users' moral response to online testimonies comes from Paul Frosh, who examines the graphic interface of the Visual History Archive. Being an embodied arrangement of eye, hand, and screen, the graphic interface elicits an action-oriented attitude toward testimonies streamed online. In contrast to predigital conventions of prolonged empathetic involvement with filmed testimonial narrative, engaging with testimonies through the graphic interface, argues Frosh, promotes a generalized state of responsiveness and restlessness in the face of on-screen manipulatable objects. While this sensorimotor alertness might cause distractedness and even agitation, it might also give rise to new modalities of moral response, "the ethics of kinaesthetics," allowing for alternative explorations of data and metadata through connective responsivity, akin to Presner's ideas of participatory user engagement.[59] Frosh depicts a shift in the media of testimony whereby what points or stabs (as in Roland Barthes's photographic definition of the punctum) is not the intensified, indexical moments of testimony as captured on tape, the conventional markers of traumatic memory, but the literal index—the user's finger—operating various mouse activities: pointing, clicking, and dragging objects on the computer screen.[60] This reversed indexicality exemplifies a shift in the incorporating practices of testimony: from embodied enunciation to embodied interaction, from the punctum to the pointer, and from the survivor's face to the user interface.

The NDT project takes this recent trend even further by completely customizing testimony to fit the recipient's context, from conversation topics all through lighting conditions. In this new arrangement of technology and embodiment what is being asserted is the intervention of those observing rather than the articulation of those depicted. It is as though the embodiment of the witnessee comes to replace that of the witness—and with it the removal of the mediation of traumatic memory. The two developments are therefore interconnected: the phasing out of continuous registration of narrative by discrete processing, on the one hand, and the precedence of reception and user-generated criteria on the other. Although it is technically possible to recreate the condition for extended linear, analog-like, viewing of testimonies, this is not the dominant and certainly not the principal mode of operation of the digital archive. The logic it promotes is of direct rather than linear access, of interactive rather than interruptive experience. In her account of testimony Shoshana Felman recalls the crisis felt by her class after watching a Yale videotaped testimony, resulting in "a sort of *panic* that consisted in both emotional and intellectual disorientation."[61] It is hard to imagine something like that happening to a class interacting with Gutter's hologram. The traumatic pangs of testimony are not native to the digital testimony apparatus.

REMEDIATING TRAUMATIC MEMORY

What if the audiovisual markers of traumatic memory, "the silences, the gaps, the so-called non-indexical content," to repeat Presner phrasing, could somehow be coded and indexed into an algorithm—would that serve to recreate the traumatic dimension of testimony within the digital database? What would be the digital status of such audiovisual markers of trauma once rendered as data? This is really a question of remediation, the representation of one medium within another, and as is always the case with remediation, it involves both the naturalization and denaturalization of the remediated content.[62] Speculating about the digital fate of traumatic memory in terms of "indeterminable data," as Presner does, therefore already assumes the analog depiction as the paradigmatic reference point for digital rendering. It assumes, in other words, the notion that traumatic memory manifests itself in testimony latently and enigmatically, a notion that could have only arisen from an analog audiovisual media setting. Yet such remediation of the traumatic content—the conversion of analog-based traumatic markers into metadata, a transition from videographic to algorithmic traumatography—inevitably results in an altogether different configuration of testimony.

To begin with, indexing the non-indexical would entail representing the so-called unrepresentable and determining the supposedly indeterminable; in order to be coded, such latent content would have to be made definable and identifiable. But this would further mean not only a process of classification but also of discretization, of making the coded content classifiable only as discrete. The digital remediation of audiovisual markers of trauma, to the extent that such is possible, would result in the tagging of such markers alongside other, more "determinable" content: silences, halts, and parapraxes as classifiable—each individually and all together—as trauma designators, just like keywords such as "hunger," "ghetto," and "liberation." Once classified, these markers are no longer imbricated within the unfolding of testimonial narrative. They become uncoupled from narrative as their carrier, and as such, recast from the syntagmatic axis to the paradigmatic, and from symptom to sense. Similar to Boder's "traumatic index," this would mean a complete relocation of trauma from the Real to the Symbolic.

As mentioned before, Holocaust historian Saul Friedlander has raised the concern of whether the event of the Shoah could, in the absence of survivors, leave traces of "deep memory," the kind of memory that "will defy any attempt to give it meaning."[63] In Chapter 2 I suggest that this concern may not be entirely warranted since these memory traces, nebulous as they might be, are not only safely stored within the videotape archive but are in a sense the product of it. When it comes to the digital archive, however, Friedlander's worry might become justified again, though for a different reason. At stake is not the loss of deep memory but its reification; not the disappearance of memory traces together with their bearers but the coding of such signifiers under fixed signifieds; in other words, not oblivion but objectification. Indexing testimonial instances that "fail to mean" cannot but collect them under a concrete designation, and thereby turn them into an operationally and semantically quotable formula. What was incidental in the performing of narrative on tape becomes overdetermined in the coding of narrative by algorithm.

The point can be further explained using Emmanuel Levinas's distinction between the Said and the Saying as developed in his philosophy of language. The Said is the content of language, the meanings given and received in interaction; it is the representational modality of language, the ability to name and thematize for the sake of exchange. The Saying, in contrast, is the relational modality of language, the event of addressing and being addressed, which signifies beyond the Said, beyond thematization and content, as "the approach to another."[64] While the Said is given to another, it can never fully represent and grasp the other. Hence speaking involves an experience with otherness, with someone who is approached but never completely known. Serving the relation with another as Other, the Saying remains unthematizable, beyond the Said, but nevertheless comes to signify through the Said, even if by way of its interruption.[65] Taken to testimony, Levinas's concepts apply directly to a point repeatedly made by Laub, Fleman, and Hartman, among others, that testimony is not exhausted in what is said but extends to the event of saying, to the performative act of testimony. And it is in moments when testimony "fails to mean," when the Said comes short of thematization, that the Saying arises most distinctively, if fleetingly, beyond the Said. To index such moments is to thematize them, and thus to reduce the Saying to the Said. The advantage of video testimony is in the mediation it performs of the precarious process by which these two modalities come into play in bearing witness.[66] Once formulized that precariousness is inevitably lost.

Having said all that, this discussion should not be taken as an extended lament for the loss of the analog traces of traumatic memory in the digital age. One lesson to learn from Walter Benjamin's classic assessment of the work of art in the age of mechanical reproduction, is that the aura of originality is discoverable only retrospectively. As Andreas Huyssen has noted, in contemporary memory culture, it is digitalization that endows the analog with an auratic effect.[67] The same could be said about the audiovisual markers of traumatic memory, whose significance is becoming apparent just as the technical media of their emergence is becoming obsolete. Indeed, the problem of "latent content" may itself be symptomatic to the shift in the media of testimony from narrative to database. Just like Benjamin's notion of the aura, it is the retroactive residue produced as one form of media regime takes over another. It is therefore critical to point out the mistake in endowing the analog modality of traumatic memory the status of an original, and then proceeding to devise ways to carry it over to a different media logic. This suggests not only a simplistic understanding of remediation, as though content could simply be extracted from the context of its materialization and transferred en bloc to another context, but moreover, the risk of enshrining the analog within the digital, as a relic of a lost original.

One of the greatest challenges for the future of Holocaust testimony is exploring new ways to accommodate the past within digital platforms. The vision that NDT portrays may or may not become the norm in the future, but for now it is important to analyze this vision and point out what is problematic about it. As said, the primary concern of NDT designers is the imminent disappearance of Holocaust survivors, which they proceed to tackle head-on. What they seem to celebrate most is the technical capability to compensate for the absence of witnesses by simulating their presence. This I find to be deeply misguided. That survivors will soon be gone is indeed a challenge, but not so much as a problem to overcome but more as a condition to be reckoned with. Their disappearance in and of itself does not necessarily bode ill for the future of Holocaust memory. The question is how to involve this fact creatively and meaningfully within memory platforms.

Dominick LaCapra distinguishes between absence and loss as two processes related to trauma.[68] Whereas absence refers to a foundational lack at the level of the origin, which is not a function of history (hence not the absence of what was once present), loss refers to some lost object and is therefore always historical—what is lost once was. LaCapra warns against conflating the two terms, and in fact ties their conflation to post-traumatic impact that similarly collapses past and present, and self and other. With respect to testimony, the imminent disappearance of survivors should be dealt with as a loss. As LaCapra further argues, acknowledging loss may open the way to social mourning, the path that leads from the sometimes delimiting process of acting out to the more enabling process of working through.[69] Acknowledging loss does not amount to forgetting but instead encourages developing alternative ways of remembering that embrace the unbridgeable gap between past and present. It allows for renewed interpretation and meaning making over time from a critical distance. Indeed loss is implied in every act of recording testimonies. As Jacques Derrida (and Barthes before him) claimed, recording is a form of spectography: every footage produces and reproduces the loss of its subjects in advance, thus making them apparitions already in their own lifetime.[70] Especially given today's technological capabilities, Holocaust remembrance calls for a modicum of release: survivors should be allowed to pass on so as to be survived by their testimonies.

Absence comes to signify in testimony through the incommunicable and inarticulate aspects of bearing witness, which in themselves serve to corroborate the impossibility of full reception and the irrecusible gap between survivors' experiences and those of their audiences. The recording of testimony further negotiates the ontologies of presence and absence—and their effects. Videotestimony is exemplary in bearing out the interplay of absence and presence that infuse bearing witness, and the limitation of calling into presence. One is reminded of the folly that Barthes ascribed to photography as manifesting "absence-as-presence": that is, not calling the absent into presence (it is not about, strictly speaking, re-presentation) but, bewilderingly, making absence as such present.[71] Absence is a creative possibility in testimony, involving not simply the relating of experiences but also the relating of the impossibility of relating certain experiences.

No technology can compensate for the disappearance of survivors, nor should it. The question is how to involve both absence and loss creatively in whatever shape digital testimony might take. It remains to be seen whether the preoccupation with traumatic memory will wither under the discourse network of 2000. Yet, to repeat, it is not traumatic memory itself, as a special kind of content, that necessarily demands preservation, and even less its potential to impact a future audience (the dangers of trauma at a distance are detailed in Chapter 3). There is little sense in attempting to remediate the analogically produced traces of traumatic memory within the digital, as this naively assumes—or worse, imposes—the discursive effects of one media context onto another. If there is anything that might be taken from the analog context to the digital it is the function that traumatic memory has served under videography—namely, the insertion of absence into presence as a reminder of the incommensurability of past and present. With this, a radical form of remediation of traumatic memory may after all come about—of function rather than of content—and consequently, an alternative way of inheriting and at the same time transcending the former media of testimony.

CHAPTER 5

Virtual Therapy and the Digital Future of Traumatic Past

Post-traumatic stress disorder (PTSD) presents a puzzling pathology of memory. An event, usually experienced with great fear and distress, is remembered not through typical recollections of past occurrences, upsetting as they may be, but instead as repeated and intrusive re-experiencing of the event as if happening once again. This is more or less the description of a disorder officially recognized by the American Psychiatric Association in 1980, but whose history can be traced back to the middle of the nineteenth century. As critical accounts by Ian Hacking, Ruth Leys, and Allan Young have shown, the very notion of traumatic memory is a distinctively modern development, which introduced new dimensions to the understanding of human memory more generally.[1] In the spirit of modern progress, pathology of memory calls for therapy of memory, and the question of how to treat post-trauma inevitably involves the question of how to penetrate traumatic memory. That this memory is such that resists normal memorization renders any therapy a form of intermediating between past and present. In fact, it might be possible to run through the history of trauma therapies as a story of the challenge of accessing and retrieving traumatic memory. This chapter ventures no such enterprise. But its subject matter might be considered as a most recent episode in that story, in which access and retrieval of traumatic memory are performed by means of digital media technology.

Virtual Reality Exposure Therapy (VRET) is a clinical therapy project that employs digital virtual reality platform for treating war-related PTSD. Developed chiefly by psychologist Albert "Skip" Rizzo at the Institute for Creative Technology of the University of South California, the project draws on principles of exposure therapy, a cognitive-behavioral method whereby the patient is exposed to stimuli associated with the fearful event in order to achieve habituation. Its most recent configuration is Virtual Iraq-Afghanistan: an Xbox videogame-based platform currently in use at more than sixty locations, including hospitals, military bases, and university centers.[2] A typical therapy session involves the patient wearing a head-mounted three-dimensional display with surround sound playing various virtual combat scenarios, which can be customized individually. The immersive experience is designed to "transport" the patient back to the original traumatic event, with the therapist monitoring the session and introducing relevant evocative cues into the scenario as treatment progresses. Proponents of VR therapy celebrate it as an evidence-based method that offers an effective exposure medium for confronting difficult and hazardous situations in a safe and controllable environment. While its clinical effectiveness is still under debate, VR therapy merits a critical consideration beyond and outside the strictly psychological purview. This is the aim of this chapter: to propose a media analysis of the technological mediation of traumatic memory performed by VR therapy.

The prospect of curing PTSD with a cutting-edge technology that combines videogame and hard science has attracted attention from various quarters. The project has received wide press and media coverage, complete with vivid imagery of the treatment procedure—a detail with particular significance when taking a media perspective on this project, as the following discussion shows. An important critical voice was filmmaker and artist Harun Farocki, who created a video installation on Virtual Iraq as part of his 2009/10 work *Serious Games*. In an accompanying text, Farocki notes the videogame aesthetics of the project and makes the point that the computer-generated images do not seem to refer to any external reality: "They are something that is generated, not something that is reproduced."[3] The generative imagery of virtual scenarios (as opposed to the reproductive imagery of photography and cinematography) will prove important in the analysis below. In terms of scholarly attention, Virtual Iraq has been the subject of a small number of studies, among the most notable are: Pasi Väliaho's discussion on the neoliberal biopolitics underlying this project;[4] Kathrin Friedrich's analysis of the design of trauma relevant virtual environment;[5] Elisabeth Losh on the militarization of traumatic images through government-sponsored videogames;[6] and

Marisa Brandt's ethnographic study on the making of virtual therapy.[7] This study continues from where others left off but focuses on a key aspect largely missing from previous accounts: the VR-generated mind-media interchanges by which traumatic memory is technologically accessed, retrieved, and processed. I will argue that the recursive channeling of mind through media and of media through mind gives rise to a changed understanding of traumatic memory, one that is consistent with the logic of digitization.

In this chapter I consider VR therapy as a prime example of what Friedrich Kittler calls psychotechnology. Borrowing the term from the German-American psychologist Hugo Münsterberg, Kittler intends the term to describe the way psychological processes and media-technological operations are coupled together and inform each other in continuous feedback loops.[8] "Psychotechnology," Kittler states, "relays psychology and media technology under the pretext that each psychic apparatus is also a technological one, and vice versa."[9] In his analysis of the discourse network of 1900, Kittler shows how particular media technologies emerged from research in physiology and psychology, and once finalized, these media technologies became in turn models for physiology and psychology. As per Kittler (with inspiration from Foucault), this recursive process brought a paradigmatic shift in the understanding of the human itself, which transformed from a romantic vision of a transcendental being epitomized by spirit or soul, into a scientific vision of an empirical being characterized by observable and analyzable functions. Accordingly, human capabilities ceased to be associated strictly with cultural setting and upbringing (*Bildung*), becoming related instead with functional psychophysical processes.[10] Media technologies of the late nineteenth and early twentieth centuries—specifically phonography and cinematography—figured prominently in these psychotechnical transferences. Writing—the epitome of human invention—was taken up by writing machines (suggestively bearing the "graphy" suffix) capable of registering non-symbolic data streams—the "white noise" of reality that alphabetization can never capture. Although referring originally to analog media context, I suggest that psychotechnology also applies to the digital context, where such psychological-technological feedback loops not only persist under a different technological regime but are arguably even more thoroughgoing.

But before we proceed to the digital context of VR therapy, further elaboration on psychotechnology is needed. What better example for the mind-media interchanges Kittler spoke of than the man who coined the term, Hugo Münsterberg. As head of the Psychological Laboratory of Harvard University (a position for which he was recruited by William James in 1892) Münsterberg conducted numerous experiments in what he called "applied psychology."

These experiments involved various instruments designed specifically for measuring perception, memory and other mental activities, representing an "epistemological architectonics" of shared processes between psychology and technology (Fig. 5.1 shows one such experiment).[11] The goal was to develop practical psychological knowledge to be implemented in fields such as medicine, law, business, industrial efficiency, and advertising.[12] Münsterberg keenly distinguished between psychohistorical and psychotechnical knowledge: whereas the former—with psychoanalysis as its key representative—has its reference in the past, the latter refers to the future and to realizing practical ends rather than explaining historical events. As he writes, "Psychotechnics is really technical science related to causal psychology as engineering is related to physics"; and it could prove particularly useful "to foresee what mental development may be expected from a patient or a criminal or a pupil."[13]

A most concrete articulation of Münsterberg's psychotechnology is found in his 1916 *The Photoplay: A Psychological Study* in which he regards cinema as

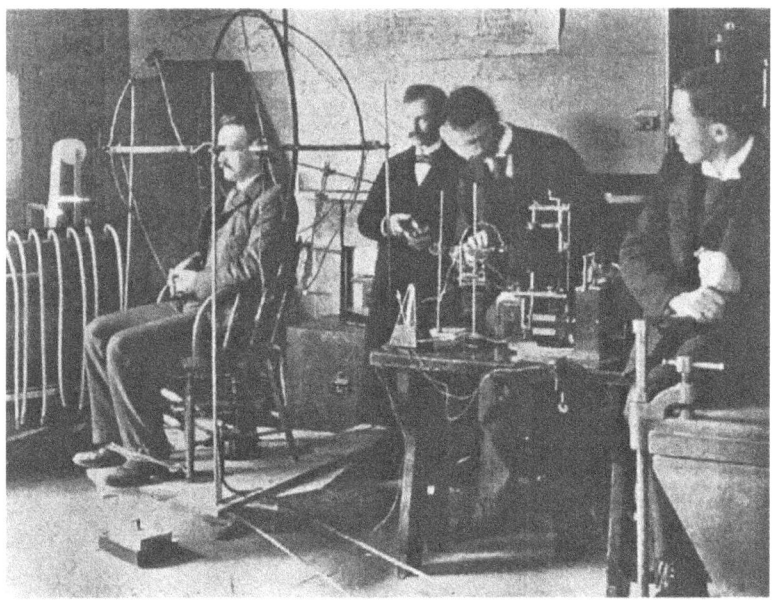

INTERIOR OF A LABORATORY ROOM.
(INFLUENCE OF DIZZINESS ON LOCALIZATION OF SOUND.)

Figure 5.1. An experiment in the Psychological Laboratory. From Hugo Münsterberg, *The Psychological Laboratory at Harvard* (Cambridge, MA: Harvard University Press, 1893).

an apparatus that best approximates the inner workings of the mind. When discussing memory processes, he suggests that whereas the theater can only refer to the past discursively while letting the audience imagine the events narrated, film displays the image of the past as such before the audience: "We see the jungle, we see the hero at the height of his danger; and suddenly there flashes upon the screen a picture of the past." He calls this filmic device "cut-back," which is essentially "an objectification of our memory function."[14] Film follows the laws of the mind rather than those of the physical world insofar as it actualizes visually the temporal multiplicity of mental reality. What it presents before the eyes is the memory mechanism inside the head. It is as though inner processes were exteriorized, and events normally removed in space and time were now "fusing in our field of vision, just as they are brought together in our own consciousness."[15] Münsterberg's psychological analysis of film can just as well be read as a filmic analysis of psychology. The equation, as Kittler puts it, can be read from both directions, for what psychotechnology fundamentally reveals is "that experimental psychological theories of film are also mechanical media theories of the soul."[16] As the viewer's psyche finds its parallel on the screen, it also comes to know itself through its twin technology—it becomes knowable precisely as seen. Henceforth it would be hard not to imagine remembering as cutting-back (or what is now commonly called flashback). As Kittler notes, it is not coincidental that around the same time people's descriptions of near-death experiences began to take the form of a rapid time-lapse film projecting one's life in the mind's eye.[17] The psychotechnological process came full circle with memory becoming a motion picture.

    VR therapy makes for an apt case of psychotechnology, and this is for three reasons. First, analyzing the discourse surrounding VR therapy makes evident multiple transferals between psychology and technology, such that confirm the inter-referentiality and codependency of mind and media as observed by Kittler in his discussion of nineteenth-century discourse network. This is not to say that the current psychological-technological constellation replicates that of the historical precedent. Rather, it is to point out similar recurring dynamics of the channeling of mind through media and of media through mind as these occur in a digital context while taking their own distinctive form. Second, VR therapy shares with psychotechnology an applicative rather than interpretative approach to psychology. Consistent with Münsterberg's definition, VR therapy is a technologically-enabled applied psychology designed to achieve concrete goals, and as such, similarly distances itself from the schema of psychoanalysis and from the practice of the "talking cure." Finally, VR therapy, true to the form of psychotechnology, is brazenly future-oriented, and in its forward-looking vision predicts a future where PTSD is technologically curable. In fact, the digital future of traumatic memory this vision affords is not only of successfully treating PTSD with VR technology but also of preventing the development of the condition in advance, using the same technology for preemptive treatment.

Like its adjacent project at the ICT, New Dimensions in Testimony, which is the subject of the previous chapter, the project at the center of this chapter also presents a view of the digital future of traumatic past, only here in terms of therapy. Tracing the junctions between psychiatry and virtual reality, the following discussion advances an argument about the status of traumatic memory as a function of the mind-media correlation and interconnection materialized by VR therapy. Specifically, I suggest that, through these digitally-enabled psychotechnological transferences of mind and media, traumatic memory undergoes discretization, becoming segmented and modular in its structure. If for Jacques Lacan the traumatic Real is that which impacts outside symbolic and imaginary significations, here the traumatic Real is re-symbolized—yet not in order to produce meaning but rather data streams. To use Kittler's formulation, the Real, understood as "the stochastic disorder of bodies," is rechanneled into "the world of the information machine."[18] That which resists coded meaning is subjected to encoding and programing—contingencies become probabilities, the Real becomes computerized. VR therapy thus sets itself up against traditional talk therapy by purporting to provide an immediate access to the "fear structure," the mental arrangement by which traumatic memory is said to be stored and activated in the brain. Access to traumatic memory is achieved by short-circuiting neurobiology and technology: reaching deep into the psych through multisensory immersiveness while altogether circumventing recourse to narrativization and social communication. Such interfacing therefore has implications beyond strictly therapeutic considerations insofar as it entails the de-articulation and de-socialization of trauma.

A SHORT HISTORY OF VR THERAPY

Computer artist Myron Krueger was probably the first to speculate about the therapeutic potential of VR. In his 1991 book *Artificial Reality II*, Kruger lists various possible applications, including teleconferencing, telerobotics, military training, science education, and finally psychotherapy. Among Krueger's designs was VIDEOPLACE, an interactive computer environment developed in the 1970s that integrated movements and gestures into video-projected graphic simulations. Its novelty was in introducing a computer-generated environment into the relation between action and perception, allowing "researchers to intervene between a subject's behavior and the consequences he perceives." As for the therapeutic potential, "artificial reality" provided "a flexible tool for presenting stimuli and analyzing behavior; it is a generalized Skinner box." Following on Skinner's conditioning rationale, Krueger suggested the technology could be used to reinforce desired patterns of behavior whereby "elements of change could be phased in slowly." As therapy proceeds, "the patient could venture from the responsive womb, returning to it as often as he needed." Krueger speculations remarkably anticipate the basic tenets that informs current employment of VR in psychotherapy; specifically, the marriage between technicity and conditioning, which in the case of PTSD treatment translates into the ability to bypass the mediation of language and act affectively on visceral sensations "burnt-in" as traumatic memories. Or as Krueger puts it, artificial reality is "a medium that can resist interpretation . . . [it] can take steps to individualize response and thwart analysis."[19]

Kreuger's vision was one of many in the early 1990s predicting that computer-generated artificial worlds would revolutionize society. With the privilege of hindsight more than two decades later, the initial hype seems premature. The vision of people wearing VR headsets for multiple everyday purposes proved to be farfetched. Yet if there is a place where the technology never fell out of grace and continued to attract attention and exploration, it is in psychotherapy of the behavioral and cognitive strands. As many have noted, VR technology developed from the dual sponsorship of military research and the entertainment industry.[20] Experimenting with manipulations of sensory experience and their psychic and somatic effects bring the production of fun and war closer than might be expected. VR therapy not only draws from both military and entertainment enterprises, but moreover, conflates the two into the fold of psychotherapy—a particular type of psychotherapy, to be sure, one that, much like fighting and gaming, relies on visual, auditory, and kinesthetic training. If virtual reality, to follow Mark Hansen's claim, reasserts the body within digital media, VR therapy harnesses this embodiment to recondition its responsive circuits.[21]

Michael Heim provides a tripartite definition of VR: immersion, interactivity, and information intensity.[22] Immersion made its debut with the 1950s Sensorama Simulator, which played 3D film with stereophonic sound, vibration, smell, and wind blowing. Its creator, Morton Heilig, situated the machine as the latest development in the legacy of Lumière, Griffith, and Eisenstein, declaring it as the future of cinema. As he put it years later, with Sensorama "You *feel* the experience, you don't just *see* it."[23] The interactivity and information intensity components of VR became apparent with devices developed by Ivan Sutherland for NASA and the Advanced Research Project Agency (ARPA) in the 1960s. The head-mounted three-dimensional display, nicknamed "The Sword of Damocles" due to its prominent overhead construction, began as a servo-controlled camera for helicopter pilots that moved in synch with the pilot's helmet. In an early experiment, which demonstrated the technology's immersive potential, a rooftop camera was connected to a head-mounted display worn by a viewer insider the building. When a ball was thrown at the camera, the inside viewer ducked, and when the camera tilted down to show the ledge, he reportedly panicked.[24] Sutherland and his colleagues proceeded to develop a head-tracking device employing computer-generated graphics instead of video feed to create a virtual wireframe "room" into which the viewer could enter.[25]

The term "virtual reality" was coined in 1989 by computer scientist and artist Jaron Lanier, founder of VPL Research (Visual Programing Languages), the first company to develop VR equipment such as goggles and gloves for popular use. The ensuing years saw intensive preoccupation with the emerging technology and its prospects. VR was declared a medium of telepresence, constituting the highpoint of vividness and interactivity as compared to traditional media technologies.[26] It came to represent the epitome of what Jean Baudrillard called the hyperreal: "the generation by models of a real without origin or reality."[27] As such, VR was seen by many as opening up avenues to new experiential worlds, to alternative realities restricted only by the powers of imagination. Fittingly, Howard Rheingold's 1992 bestseller *Virtual Reality* sports a blurb by Jerry Garcia that reads, "They made LSD illegal. I wonder what they're going to do about this stuff." While popular culture was celebrating VR as a computer-age hallucinogen, researchers in psychology and psychiatry began experimenting with the technology for exactly the opposite reasons. It was not the possibility of opening the doors of perception that made VR so useful for psychotherapy; it was the ability to create hyperreal experiences of actual realities, especially those that are pathologically avoided or inhibited. Far from escaping reality, the virtual served to return to reality, recovered.

In their 1996 book *Virtual Reality Therapy: A Innovative Paradigm*, Max North and his colleagues at the Clark Atlanta University declare themselves as the first to launch a research program utilizing VR in psychotherapy.[28] North discovered VR's therapeutic potential while working on a flight simulator for the U.S. Army and Boeing.[29] One of the team members began to feel anxious when the flying mode was in operation, an experience that was consequently explained by her preexisting acrophobia. The team experimented with the flight simulator for several weeks, recruiting university students to participate in what they called "virtual environment desensitization." North later traded desensitization for a cognitive approach, which supplied new perspective and vocabulary to explain Virtual Reality Therapy:

> Disturbing memory is stored by a picture, cognition, affect, and physical sensations. VRT reveals that these factors are stored by association and linked together. VRT appears to activate the visual memory, in case only visual stimuli are presented, and in turn activates other related memories and experiences such as cognition, affect, and physical sensation. Under VRT, many of the subjects report physical and emotional symptoms associated with these stored memories. They report having sweaty palms and shaking knees, feeling scared, and feeling uncomfortable. In general, VRT appears to provide a link between the reality of the client and the objective world.[30]

These words, which precede the more recent employment of VR in PTSD treatment, describe a fundamental association between psyche and techne as two interconnected mechanisms that operate according to corresponding media logic of storage and retrieval. Virtual visual stimuli activate neurophysiological visual memory and in turn symptoms associated with traumatic "stored memories." Importantly, VR therapy is seen as mediating between inner reality and the "objective world," short-circuiting the visualities of client and therapist.[31]

The link between VR with PTSD came through the involvement of Barbara Olasov Rothbaum, an Emory University psychologist recruited to the project by North's colleague Larry Hodges, a leading VR researcher at the Georgia Institute of Technology. Rothbaum's expertise was exposure therapy, a cognitive-behavioral technique developed by her mentor Edna Foa. The technique will be discussed in detail later, but suffice now to say that it involves exposing the patient repeatedly either to actual objects of anxiety (when possible) or imaginally to objects envisioned mentally. The goal in both methods is achieving habituation to anxiety triggers. Initially collaborating on research projects for treating acrophobia and aviophoboa (fear of flying), Rothbaum and Hodges sought to extend the use of VR to other psychopathologies.[32] Rothbaum had previously worked with Foa on sexual assault trauma, but this condition was deemed too difficult to test and generalize using VR technology. The decision fell on the next-largest PTSD population with which Rothbaum had worked with: Vietnam War veterans.[33]

Virtual Vietnam was introduced in 1997 with a case report of a fifty-year-old veteran who had undergone a fourteen-week treatment program. The team led by Rothbaum and Hodges designed the virtual environment following interviews with veterans and consulting visual material from the period, including news footage. They decided to focus on two scenarios that seemed to fit most veterans' experiences: a jungle clearing with jungle sounds, gunfire, explosions, helicopters, and battle cries; and the interior of a flying Huey helicopter with the sound of rotors, radio chatter, gunfire, explosions, and battle cries.[34] Rothbaum submitted virtual therapy as "a new medium for exposure therapy for veterans with PTSD," having the potential to replace standard imaginal exposure (which proved unsuccessful for this population) and actual, in vivo, exposure (which was impractical). She noted that virtual therapy supplies "a sense of presence," which is "also essential to conducing exposure therapy."[35] Treatment sessions had the patient wearing a head-mounted display with high quality headphones while alternating between seating on a "Thunder Seat" with a built-in subwoofer to simulate helicopter vibrations, and "walking" through the environment on a raised platform. Having determined the patient's most traumatic memories prior to treatment, the therapist gradually prompted elements associated with these memories as sessions progressed. After each session the patient was asked to describe in detail, in the present tense, the traumatic memories triggered by the virtual scenarios, and to do so repeatedly until anxiety decreased.

A new war motivated the reemployment of virtual reality for PTSD treatment, this time with substantial support from military and government agencies. With the continuation of Operation Iraqi Freedom, a research team at the ICT led by psychologist Albert Rizzo initiated in the early 2000s a virtual reality therapy project featuring a Middle-Eastern environment as a setting for PTSD exposure therapy. While referring to Virtual Vietnam as his model, Rizzo and his team sought a different approach, and rather than creating a virtual system from scratch (as was the case with Virtual Vietnam), they opted to utilize an existing application created by the ICT for tactical combat simulation called *Full Spectrum Command*. This application, developed under close consultation with U.S. military personnel, was the platform for the commercial award-winning Xbox videogame, *Full Spectrum Warrior*.[36] Thus gaming, training, and therapy converge psychotechnologically.

Virtual Iraq features a number of scenarios: city scene, checkpoint scene, building interior, rural village, desert base, and desert roadway. Navigation through scenarios is made possible from a number of perspectives, including walking on a patrol, alone or with a solider companion, and driving in a Humvee vehicle (see Figs. 5.2 and 5.3 below).[37] In its basic configuration, the system comprises of components similar to those used in Virtual Vietnam, only more up to date. A new feature of Virtual Iraq is a scent generator for releasing pertinent smells, such as burning rubber, diesel, Iraqi spices, and body

Figure 5.2 BRAVEMIND VR head-mounted display.

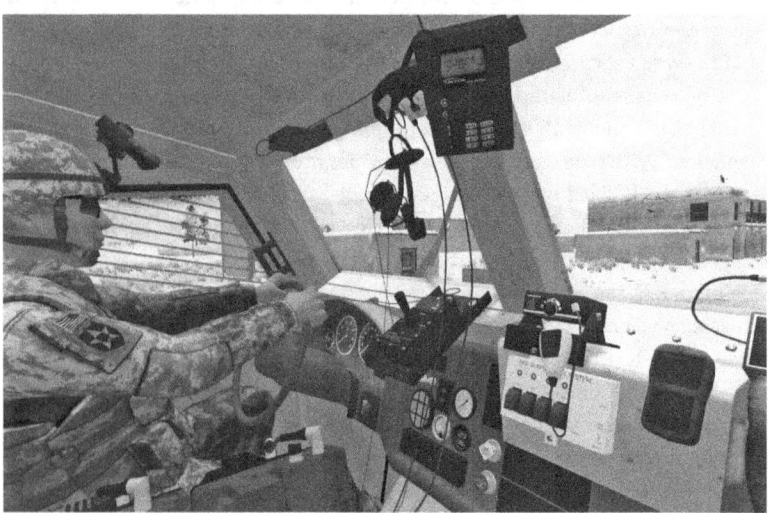

Figure 5.3 Virtual Iraq inside Humvee scenario. Images used with permission from the University of South California Institute for Creative Technologies.

odor. During a session, the clinician introduces elements into the scenario—visual, audial, corporal, olfactory, separately or in combination—intended to evoke the patient's traumatic memory. The system records the patient's physiological data such as heart rate, respiration, and skin conductance, and displays them on the clinician's interface. Through the interface (suggestively called "Wizard of Oz," evoking the contraption used to send Dorothy back to Kansas) the patient is "teleported," to use Rizzo's term, to a scenario closest to the original traumatic event.[38]

Virtual Iraq—recently rebranded as BRAVEMIND (Battlefield Research Accelerating Virtual Environments for Military Individual Neuro Disorders)—not only responds to a different war setting, it is also geared toward a different kind of potential patient. Today's recruits are members of the digital generation, and as such are drafted with awareness as to their gaming literacy, having developed skills that are translatable into training and combat situations (such as simultaneous attention, fast reflexes, and hand-eye coordination).[39] Recruits nowadays engage with videogame simulations during training; they are likely to continue playing while on active duty; and if diagnosed as suffering from PTSD symptoms (10 to 20 percent of Iraq and Afghanistan veterans according to recent reports[40]) might end up undergoing videogame-based VR therapy. In this way gaming culture interweaves with contemporary warfare, blurring the lines between combat and entertainment, and between military and civilian realities.[41] Both gaming and therapy draw on what Mark Andrejevic calls framelessness: the production of full immersion in media environments while suspending the subject's critical faculties—the ability to discern, to select, and, most critically, to relate experience.[42] The technological capability to create a sense of presence, of being immersed—so crucial to the entertainment industry—is here adopted for therapeutic purposes, together with the loss of narrativity.

To Rizzo, this is actually a selling point for VR exposure therapy, for having been raised around gaming technology, young military personnel "may actually be more attracted to and comfortable with a VR treatment approach as an alternative to traditional 'talk therapy.'"[43] VR therapy can then pass as recreation rather than therapy, and so reduce the stigma of mental health treatment and attract more patients in need: the gaming cure instead of the talking cure. Yet posing VR therapy as an alternative to "talk therapy" also suggests that mere talking does not cut deep enough when it comes to a condition such as PTSD. As will be shown shortly, the radicality of treatment supposedly achieved by immersive technology corresponds closely with a particular neurobiological understanding of traumatic memory. The congruity of digital therapy and the digital generation may therefore be taken as a sign of the changing nature of traumatic memory, which is far from being a stable object. Access to the brain is always historical, and the means of access—that is, media technologies—often end up discovering their mental correlates in the process.

Virtual Iraq has attracted considerable media attention with television reports on a variety of networks, including CNN, CBS, ABC, Discovery, BBC, and PBS, as well as numerous YouTube clips.[44] Virtually all portray a success story of a veteran struggling with PTSD symptoms and finding a cure through VR therapy. A recurring segment in these reports is of a VR therapy session in progress shown as a series of intercutting images: the veteran wearing full VR gear, the virtual scenario being played inside the veteran's head-mounted display, and the therapist monitoring the session while watching the same scenario on a computer screen. Popular culture is replete with representations of PTSD and traumatic memory, most typically through the device of flashback, which, as per Münsterberg's psychotechnology, traverse cinematography and psychopathology. The media coverage of VR therapy seems to introduce a new dimension into the condition's visual representation: it is as though the patient, the clinician, and the audience conjoin on the same visual depiction of traumatic memory. A new phase in the psychotechnology of trauma makes its debut whereby the same image, seen on multiple screens, connects the clinic and the public. Not only does this depiction portray VR as a revolutionary, science fiction-like therapy for PTSD, it further substantiates the intervention of media technology as practically offering direct access into the recesses of traumatic memory. Digital visual mediation plays a key role in making PTSD analyzable medically, treatable clinically, and explicable socially.

EXPOSURE MEDIA

The foregoing short review already reveals some transferals between mind and media, but in order to fully appreciate the psychotechnological processes associated with VR therapy—and particularly their significance with regard to traumatic memory—it is important to take a closer look into the theory and practice of the exposure therapy upon which VR therapy is based. Prolonged Exposure (PE) therapy was developed chiefly by psychologist Edna Foa in the early 1980s to treat obsessive-compulsive disorders and specific phobias such as fears of heights, flying, and animals. Her reports of effectively treating PTSD with the technique have made her a leading authority in the psychology of stress and anxiety disorders (she served as chair of the committees that worked on PTSD and Obsessive-Compulsive Disorder chapters in DSM-IV).[45] Exposure therapy, as the name suggests, involves exposure to anxiety-producing objects or situations in order to achieve habituation and retrain brain mechanisms activated by fear. This is done either by in vivo exposure, that is, directly experiencing the feared object or situation (e.g., climbing a high-rise with a patient suffering from acrophobia); or by imaginal exposure, whereby the patient is instructed to imagine the feared object or situation and retain that image in mind as long as possible (e.g., instructing a social phobic to imagine speaking in front of a large audience). In both in vivo and imaginal methods, the patient is asked to narrate in detail her thoughts and feelings throughout the exposure session. Such treatment is repeated (hence prolonged exposure) over a series of sessions (typically ten to fifteen) until relief in anxiety symptoms is attained.

A short excursion into the current neurobiological understanding of traumatic memory will also prove helpful. Psychiatrist Bessel van der Kolk provides a concise explanation:

> When memory traces of the original sounds, images, and sensations are reactivated, the frontal lobe shuts down, including . . . the region necessary to put feelings into words, the region that creates our sense of location in time, and the thalamus, which integrates the raw data of incoming sensations. At this point the emotional brain, which is not under conscious control and cannot communicate in words, takes over. . . . Under ordinary conditions these two memory systems—rational and emotional—collaborate to produce an integrated response. But high arousal not only changes the balance between them but also disconnects other brain areas necessary for the proper storage and integration of incoming information, such as the hippocampus and the thalamus. As a result, the imprints of traumatic experiences are organized not as coherent logical narratives but in fragmented sensory and emotional traces: images, sounds, and physical sensations.[46]

According to this explanation, traumatic memory is located in the "emotional brain," the brain areas that comprise the reptile brain and the limbic system—the more primitive brain parts that control, among other things, basic sensations, emotions, and drives. When experiencing a horrific event, the physical arousal caused by the secretion of stress hormones might reach a level that incapacitates the higher conscious brain levels. Thus, unlike typical memories, which include both cognitive and emotional components, traumatic memory lacks the cognitive and is "etched" in what van der Kolk calls the "somatic memory" (hence his title "The Body Keeps the Score" as well as frequent use of "imprint," "trace," and "engraved" to describe the way trauma is "stored" in memory—a veritable traumatographic description of that memory).[47]

Drawing on Pierre Janet (Freud's contemporary and occasional critic), van der Kolk describes traumatic memory as non-declarative memory. Declarative memories, he argues, are the result of cognitive integration of information, and are accordingly organized logically as narratives with a beginning, middle, and end. These memoirs are essentially communicable and therefore social, capable of being related and shared with others. Traumatic memories are fundamentally different: lacking cognitive processing they are stored as isolated images, sounds, and sensations (the proverbial flashback) and are consequently fragmentary and devoid of logical and temporal structure. Because non-declarative, traumatic memory is often inexpressible, and hence non-social: "there is nothing social about traumatic memory . . . Reenactments are frozen in time, unchanging, and they are always lonely, humiliating, and alienating experiences."[48] This brings van der Kolk to conclude that despite more than a century of belief in talk therapy, trauma is the starkest proof of this method's shortcoming, since no matter "how much insight and understanding we develop, the rational brain is basically impotent to talk the emotional brain out of its own reality." Treating PTSD depends on gaining access to the emotional brain and performing "limbic system therapy": "repairing faulty alarm systems and restoring the emotional brain to its ordinary job of being a quiet background presence that takes care of the housekeeping of the body."[49]

This division between two memory systems follows a distinction between two logics of registration, or two traumatographies. The one proceeds through the operation of a conscious level of sense making, ordering, and symbolizing; having narrative memories as its output, it involves the mediation—and hence the filtering—of the symbolic order. Conversely, the other system registers sensation rather than sense, fragments rather than narrative, and hence operates indexically rather than symbolically. These two registration logics, representing two mutually exclusive memory systems, normally work in conjunction. But faced with a traumatic event, the logical system breaks down, leaving the somatic as primary registration. There is a striking structural similarity between this dual neurobiological memory system and the dual technological memory system of symbolic and non-symbolic registration: the dichotomy that Kittler draws between the selective inscription of meaning by signs and the nonselective inscription of audiovisual effects by media. Indeed, it seems that with the use of media technology in exposure therapy these two memory systems, the neurobiological and the technological, come to intertwine and mutually implicate each another.

The foundational text of the prolonged exposure technique was written in 1986 by Foa and Michael Kozak and has since become a key reference in VR therapy research. While discussing the psychopathology of fear in general, it nevertheless corresponds closely with van der Kolk's theory, and may well be considered as a form of "limbic system therapy." Foa and Kozak frame their discussion as a theoretical investigation into the employment of exposure in psychotherapy. Exposure, they suggest, has always been part of treating phobias, starting with psychodynamic and Gestalt orientations, and more emphatically with behaviorist stimulus-response approaches. While influential, the latter have only provided a limited explanation of the acquisition and reduction of fear, and so their intervention seeks to present a more comprehensive theory. Fear, they hold, "is represented in memory structures that serve as blueprints for fear behavior, and therapy is a process by which these structures are modified."[50] Foa and Kozak posit "fear structure" as a hypothetical construct that encompasses both stimulus-response elements and the meanings associated with these elements; in other words, "fear structure" is a propositional structure containing information about reaction to and interpretation of the feared stimulus. Exposure therapy requires, first, the activation of the fear structure, and next, the incorporation of information incompatible with the existing "program to escape or avoid."[51] This allows for "emotional processing" of fear to take place whereby elements in the fear structure, both conscious and unconscious, undergo modification.

Exposure therapy is explicated in terms of access, retrieval, and reprograming of fear memory formation. There are obvious—and declared—links between this cognitive theory of fear and cybernetic computational models, links that in and of themselves make for a credible case of psychotechnology.[52] Yet the mind-media relations in this case are even more concrete and straightforward. Foa and Kozak make the function of media in exposure therapy patently clear: it is by means of what they call "evocative media" that fear memory is accessed and activated. Media is integral to exposure therapy insofar as constituting the platform for introducing fear stimuli. Their understanding of media is nevertheless wide, covering almost any form of delivering evocative information. Media here include in vivo exposure, that is, confrontation with the actual fear; imaginal exposure, where the patient is asked to imagine the feared situation; and finally, but no less effectively, employing audio and visual technologies as evocative media. As they state, "Verbal descriptions, visual displays, or lifelike enactments can contain the required information to access an existing fear structure. Indeed, novels, films, plays, and so on can evoke a range of emotions when the information they contain provides a good match with some affective memory structures in the audience." Foa and Kozak express no overt preference for one medium, stating that the efficacy of different media varies across disorders. What determines the choice of a particular exposure medium is its adequacy for "depicting the information required to match" the specific fear structure.[53]

This media constellation calls for further unpacking. To begin with, this theory presupposes the possibility of direct access to the fear structure, which is in fact what "exposure" suggests: an immediate contact with the fear elements to be activated. Insofar as the fear structure is concerned, exposure media are such that act as if there is no mediation between mind and feared event, as if the feared situation is *hic et nunc*, present and not simply re-presented. Exceeding figuration and symbolization, exposure media are what have the power to produce the Real, even if by means of technical reproduction. It follows that exposure therapy is constitutive upon its media: it assumes and depends on media as the high road to the fear structure. The low road would presumably be talk therapy, or to use van der Kolk's terms, a declarative approach to reach non-declarative memory strata. Now despite the equivalence that Foa and Kozak express with regard to exposure media, it is clear that the principal medium underpinning their theory is in vivo exposure, while the alternative exposure media are its derivatives. This is because imaginal and media technology become optional only when they can produce effects comparable to those of in vivo, that is, function as adequate substitutions to actual, real exposure. This is the perspective from which to understand the role of media technology as potential exposure media; namely, as media that insofar as the fear structure is concerned can produce an effect that is felt as if unmediated.

Prior to virtual reality, a favorite medium in exposure therapy was the tape recorder. In their book on treating rape victims, Foa and Rothbaum incorporate tape recording in therapy routine: the therapist records the patient detailing her thoughts and feelings during exposure sessions (in this case, imaginal), instructing her to listen to the recordings repeatedly between sessions.[54] In her self-help book, *Stop Obsessing*, Foa upgrades the use of tape recording to something almost comparable to a full-fledged exposure session. The self-help version involves writing down a detailed description of the feared event, recording the description on an audiotape, and listening to it repeatedly every day for forty-five minutes or longer.[55] The use of tape recordings provides a clear example of the function of media in exposure therapy. It is not the articulation of fear itself that confers the therapeutic value, but rather, and chiefly, the accumulated impact of repeating the articulation. To the extent that exposure is achieved, it is not by means of either writing or speaking, and any meaning produced thereby serves no revelatory function in dispelling symptoms. Rather, exposure works on the level of conditioning where meaning is subjected to somatic reaction, to attaining habituation to fear-triggering meaning. The repetitive retraining of the fear structure through emotional processing conforms to the mechanical reproduction of speech by the tape recorder. Mind and media interact therapeutically on the automatic level without having to engage the full interpretative capacities of the conscious level.

Exposure therapy all but anticipates the use of virtual reality technology, a technology that might be said to convert in vivo into *in virtu*. All the more when it comes to treating combat-related PTSD: with in vivo exposure being too dangerous or impractical, and with imaginal exposure being difficult to maintain given the purported complexity of the condition, often involving guilt and shame, it is easy to see why Barbara Rothbaum and her colleagues announced virtual reality in their Vietnam case study as "a new medium of exposure therapy."[56] What this means, then, is that in being a medium of exposure VR can impact the fear structure as though without mediation. Indeed, the very understanding of traumatic memory as set in non-declarative strata already comports itself toward a technological rather than a conversational therapeutic medium. Hence the psychotechnological recursion of mind and of media: the correlation between neurobiological and technological memory systems, which informs the use of media to access and activate pathological memory, which affirms the understanding of such memory as prone to immediate technological mediation, which calls for the employment of immersive exposure media, and so on and so forth.

DIGITAL PTSD

How does traumatic memory appear from the standpoint of VR therapy? Proponents of this therapy tend not to speculate about the nature of the condition, following instead the current DSM definition and diagnostic criteria. What they are keen to emphasize, however, is that the therapy is evidence-based, by which they mean meeting the standards of experimental protocols for determining and validating the effectiveness of treatment. Whether VR therapy is an effective treatment program is of less importance here (research reports by Rizzo and his team show success; others, such as van der Kolk, are less enthusiastic).[57] What is important for the purpose of this discussion—which concerns the media of therapy—is that according to those practicing the therapy, VR constitutes a verifiably effective medium of exposure, which means that it can successfully produce scenarios that closely match the traumatic fear structure. Yet such effectiveness of the medium necessarily, if implicitly, reveals something about the condition it targets. It is by virtue of functioning as an effective exposure medium in therapy that VR provides a portal into the presumed mental state of PTSD.

And the shape of traumatic memory so revealed is one that is consistent with digital media context.

Practitioners of VR therapy make special effort—and take special pride—in explaining the procedure of using the technology in treatment. The procedure is detailed not only in clinical studies but also, in lay terms, in television reports and online promotional clips, which once again demonstrate the coincidence of mass media and therapeutic media in this case. The key interventionist feature is the ability to introduce specific details into the scenario as the session progresses. As Rizzo and his team explain in a Virtual Iraq case report, such details include "location, time of day, weather, significant events (ambush, explosion, medevac), and other stimuli such as particular sounds (AK-47 gunfire) and smells (diesel fuel, cordite), which were components of the memory." This mnemonic collection "served to inform the therapist around appropriate cues to be introduced during VRE sessions." Later on, more intense cues were phased in, such as a helicopter flyover and background radio communications. In this way, "the therapy experience was customized to meet the individual needs of the participant via systematic real-time delivery and control of trigger stimuli in the environment."[58] True to exposure therapy tenets, the patient was instructed to describe his emotions and recollection while immersed in the scenario. The clinicians report that the patient showed strong affective reaction to the scenario, which is taken as evidence of its matching with the fear structure.

It is here, I suggest, in what the customizability of the system denotes, that a changed understanding of traumatic memory comes to the fore. For if this treatment is successful in triggering and consequently processing traumatic fear structure by means of introducing distinct elements into the generic scenario, then the memories so evoked must be assumed to be organized correspondently as distinct mnemonic items. If paradigmatic manipulation of cues in the generic scenario is capable of accessing the fear structure, then that structure is bound to be paradigmatically constructed, that is, comprising separate and substitutable elements. What the psychotechnological recycling of mind and media through VR therapy produces, then, is the discretization of traumatic memory. Rather than the all-at-once of unselective repetition of the past epitomized by the iconicity of the flashback, here traumatic memory undergoes structural disassembling and reassembling. Critically, such discretization of traumatic memory could only have emerged from a digital media context. It seems that both the therapeutic medium and the condition undergoing therapy operate according to the principles of database as the dominant symbolic form of the digital age, as explicated by Lev Manovich.[59] For what VR therapy demonstrates is the privileging of paradigm over syntagm and the phasing out of individual experience in favor of generic yet modular scenarios.

This development can be further explicated using Bernard Stiegler's conceptualization of human memory as shaped by a process of grammatization. By grammatization he means the conversion of experiential continuities into discrete units (thus writing is the grammatization of the flux of speech). This process is "the history of the exteriorization of memory in all its forms,"[60] which amounts to the history of human memory in general. Following Derrida's reading of Plato's *Phaedrus*, Stiegler deems living memory, or *anamnesis* (recollection), as subtended by technical, so-called dead memory, or *hypomnesis* (memory aids, principally writing). Plato's writing on Socrates's mistrust in writing is of course an ironic confirmation of the argument. It follows that external-technical memory is not opposed to internal-living memory; rather, any access to human memory is necessarily mediated through artificial means, which are what constitutes internal-living memory as knowable. There is therefore no static division between exterior technicity and interior retention but a constant displacement. What this ultimately means is that human memory is intrinsically technical, always already externally reliant.

As per Stiegler, there are three, historically discernable types of grammatization: literal, analog and digital. The literal is textual inscription, the various forms of symbolic writing; as above, the Platonic alphabetization of the Socratic dialogization. Analog grammatization largely corresponds to what Walter Benjamin described as the principles of mechanical reproduction, the analog mass media circulation of the audible and the visible by prevailing cultural industries. Digital grammatization refers to the information society of the digital age, beginning in the last mid-century and continuing to the present, in which all forms of knowledge are subject to informational processing. Whereas analog grammatization imposed collective reception based on mass-scale industrial logic (hence the Frankfurt School criticism), digital grammatization personalizes users as both senders and receivers, giving rise to new participatory platforms and new formations of service economies. But Stiegler is keen to connect this development with a general process of cognitivization as a fundamental logic by which to understand memory, behavior, and feeling. He anticipates that digital technology will bring up to a point where "*all* form of knowledge will be grammatized in the guise of cognitive mnemotechnologies. From linguistic knowledge—technologies and industries of language processing—to knowledge-how-to-live or behavior in general, knowledge becomes discreticized through technologies and industries of language processing, user profiling, and the grammatization of affect."[61]

While Stiegler does not refer to traumatic memory per se, it is tempting to apply his schema to this special type of human memory—to link the idea of grammatization to what I call here traumatography. Indeed, traumatic memory takes the question of technology as shaping the conditions of knowability to the extreme: it might be described as a condition of *hypomnesis* in the sense of impaired memory that requires *hypomnemata*, or memory aids, in order to render it knowable. Hence, its literal grammatization would be a conversion into linguistic signs, spoken or written, with psychoanalysis being the signification scheme: its inscription perhaps corresponding with Freud's description of the mystic writing-pad (the Wunderblock as carrier of unconscious memory imprints), and its retrieval and processing presumably corresponding with free association through the "talking cure" (which harks back to Socrates's maieutic method for facilitating anamnesis).[62] To paraphrase on Kittler's phrase, here the traumatic Real is filtered through the bottleneck of the signifier. An analog grammatization of traumatic memory, or what might be called analog traumatography, would be the mechanical reproduction of impact, the function ascribed by Benjamin to film and photography in mediating "the disintegration of the aura in the experience of shock" brought about by mechanized modernity from the factory to the frontline.[63] Flashback is the epitome of such analog grammatization insofar as constituting a technical mnemonic of traumatic memory common to both cinematography and psychopathology. And as to the digital grammatization of traumatic memory (or digital traumatography), this finds a clear demonstration in VR therapy insofar as the retraining of the fear structure by means of its discretization and modularization. More generally, this latter phase correlates with Stiegler's point about the rise of cognitivism (exposure therapy is based on cognitive-behavioral precepts) and the development of what he calls "cognitive technologies," which refer to contemporary digital knowledge production that traverses and assembles mentalities and collectivities.[64]

The digital grammatization of traumatic memory is further corroborated by a most recent application of VR therapy. A project called STRIVE (Stress Resilience in Virtual Environment) employs a VR therapy platform to offer pre-combat psychological preparation said to provide protection against future trauma. The premise is that combat post-trauma might be preempted by pre-deployment exposure to "a pivotal trauma event" such as "witnessing the death of a child or squad member."[65] Such training is said to also strengthen resilience, and allow for quick recovery after a stressful event. In an online video Rizzo says that he hopes the project will put him "out of a job at the back end by doing a better job at the front end."[66] The prospect of producing trauma-free soldiers opens a host of moral questions, some of which are addressed in the final section of this chapter. For now, let us focus on the undergirding logic of this preventative operation, which exemplifies most patently the future-oriented dimension of pscyhotechnology (as opposed to Münsterberg's labeling of psychoanalysis as past-oriented). That potential trauma could be averted by immersive VR exposure to "a pivotal trauma event" presupposes what was identified above as the discretization of traumatic memory. Whatever "pivotal trauma event" might be, it is one that could be coded into the system through psychotechnological feedbacking of distinct cues already known through PTSD VR therapy to be associated with traumatic impact. Once recycled as pivotally traumatic, these cues are made available for variable insertion into training scenarios, targeting in advance the trauma-prone elements of the fear structure. Pre-trauma VR treatment draws on the modular understanding of traumatic memory as gleaned from post-trauma treatment: the ability to dismantle that memory into distinct components and then reconstruct from these components hypothetical scenarios with immunizing potential.

Such pre-trauma conditioning is digital grammatization of traumatic memory *par excellence*. A short comparison with analog grammatization may help to explain the point. Recall the famous *A Clockwork Orange* scene where the protagonist Alex undergoes an aversion treatment to make him recoil from his predilection for violence. He is strapped and forced to watch a film of a man ruthlessly beaten by a gang of youngsters. Although the goal of the fictional treatment is repulsion rather than habituation, if taken as a form of therapeutic exposure medium *avant la letter*, this scene represents analog grammatization. Presumably the film had to be made specifically to fit Alex's tendencies, and so the redness of the blood, which initially excites him before causing him nausea, is embedded in the film's composition so as to trigger him, and only him, like a punctum emerging from the image. Were this conditioning to be performed through a VR therapy platform, the process would have been completely different. Rather than the personalized filmic *mise-en-scéne* viewed from specular distance, a virtual scenario would combine a generic scenario with an immersive experience. The personalization of the generic scenario would be achieved by introducing various triggers into the scene at different times with varying intestines. The analog grammatization is fixed once and for all; the digital is flexible and manipulatable from within. To the extent that these two exposure media, the fictional analog and the existing digital, are held to be effective, they each bear out, through their operation, a different understanding of affecting the mind, and consequently of the affected mind itself.[67]

This brings us to the question of the suggestive nature of VR therapy imagery. As Marisa Brandt explains in her ethnographic study of VR therapy, the decision to employ a design that can only provide a sketch and not replica of the trauma scene—or in the designers' jargon, "generic realism" as opposed to "mimetic realism"—was the result of development constraints rather than a premeditated preference.[68] In other words, it was the technical impossibility of creating personal scenarios for each and every case (as for Alex in *A Clockwork Orange*) that led to resorting to approximation. Yet once put into practice this generic realism was found to be effective and, in some respects, even preferable. VR therapy practitioners began reporting a phenomenon they call "immersive fill," where patients seem to fill in details in the scenario from their own imagination and memories. One research report takes this rationale a step further, suggesting that VR system design should follow Masahiro Mori's notion of the "uncanny valley," according to which the effectiveness of a simulation grows in proportion with its realism until reaching a sharp drop. Hence too much reality in VR therapy might be counterproductive. Instead, the goal should be reaching "the sweet spot on the suspension of disbelief curve," and this is by favoring "the suggestive over the specific" and by designing scenes "that can be interpreted in a number of different ways." Adaptation to a specific patient can then be done by carefully introducing disambiguating information, such as a sound file that can "pin down the meaning of the scene."[69] Thus the ambiguity imposed by the technology is said to have therapeutic advantages in both concretizing and abstracting the virtual environment.

That suggestive content (even if coupled with a strong sense of presence) can provide an adequate and even favorable exposure medium seems to stand in contrast with principles of exposure therapy. If in vivo exposure involves directly experiencing the feared event, and if imaginal therapy involves purposefully imagining the feared event, VR therapy involves inferring the feared event. If exposure therapy entails an encounter with the traumatic Real, VR therapy produces this encounter symbolically. Indeed, what the notion of "immersive fill" suggests is that the lack of mimetic operation on the side of the system is taken up on the side of the patient. VR therapy seems to reinstate deductive, interpretative processes—precisely the processes exposure therapy set out to circumvent in the first place. Whatever might be the psychological explanation for this apparent contradiction, its very existence already bears out the psychotechnological feedbacking between media and mind at work here. In remediating exposure as compatible with computer-generated suggestive content, VR therapy redefines the logic of exposure therapy, and with it, the principles of activating traumatic memory.

Presumably, the ambiguity of virtual scenarios could lead to an interpretative process and perhaps even to reflexivity on the part of the patient. If scenarios invite different interpretations some of those might be inconsistent with the therapeutic agenda. VR therapy inserts a mimetic streak into the prevalent understanding of trauma that Ruth Leys identifies as largely antimimetic (that is, resulting from an external event unmitigatedly stamping a helpless subject).[70] It is clear, however, that such ambiguity is restricted to the therapeutic agenda, and the possibility of interpreting scenarios in different ways is bounded by the objective of retraining the fear structure. Nonspecificity and open-endedness of scenarios are not designed to solicit free association; they are rather operational resources for maximizing the usability of one platform for multiple patients. The mimetic streak, the insertion of suggestive content into the inner-workings of trauma, is subjected to the overall antimimetic rationale of exposure therapy, which in this case is oriented to achieving symptom resolution. This military-therapy platform imposes structural limitation on how far interpretation could actually go.

Katherine Hayles has speculated on the structural affinities between code and trauma, seeing both as depth operations taking place on the physical level, as occurring outside conscience awareness, and as operating below the linguistic surface while having the power to affect that surface.[71] VR therapy reveals these structural affinities as a functional synthesis: trauma is rendered as code, and code renders the traumatic. VR therapy is premised on the notion that the mechanism of PTSD is already known, and furthermore, that the basic elements of the disorder can be technologically simulated and stimulated. As Brandt argues, "the 'traumatic' is built into the system, available to be put on a screen."[72] Yet what allows the traumatic to be so produced—indeed what makes this possibility conceivable—is a digitally grammatized notion of traumatic memory. VR therapy does not merely treat PTSD but reprocesses traumatic memory as a modular arrangement predisposed to selection and manipulation. If the traumatic is built into the system, it is by virtue of having been recycled in terms of the system, which precisely describes a psychotechnological process. Trauma becomes encoded: digital processing—the conversion of intensities into discrete data—is imported into the post-traumatic condition itself.

TALK BEYOND THERAPY

Trauma is not only a clinical question; it is also a moral one. Whatever its theoretical conceptualizations may be, what trauma fundamentally denotes is an experience of being exposed to and taken by the outside. That the subject is one that can be traumatized, can be undone by external violence, is evidence to the profound vulnerability of the subject. Emmanuel Levinas took this point to the extreme when placing exposedness as the condition of an ethical relation with another.[73] It is the possibility of being claimed by violence and suffering that brings trauma into the realm of morality. Trauma may therefore open the way for acknowledging the fragility of life and mind. While violence and suffering are never equally distributed—which makes their existence profoundly political—the fact that everyone, at one point or another, can be subjected to violence and suffering holds universally. Sharing one's pain is impossible, but that everybody can feel pain is grounds for common humanity (in fact, inclusive of all living beings). Viewed in this way, trauma summons social and moral reckoning beyond and outside clinical and therapeutic considerations, important as they are. In concluding this discussion, I suggest that VR therapy represents a development that is inimical to such social and moral engagement with trauma. For at its core it is a project that pits technology against discourse as a medium for accessing traumatic memory.

There is a broader context to consider here. VR therapy is one member in a family of techniques, usually grouped under cognitive-behavioral therapy, which advocate short-term intervention instead of extended talk therapy. The purported effectiveness and conciseness have made these methods expedient for various corporate and governmental agencies, first and foremost, as seen in the case of VR therapy, for defense and military agencies. It is easy to see the advantages of exposure therapy for PTSD, being an evidence-based method, over extended and costly individual psychotherapy, whose effectiveness is notoriously difficult to assess. A recent contender along these lines is Eye Movement Desensitization and Reprocessing (EMDR), a method that employs eye movement stimulation to process post-traumatic memories.[74] Clinical debates aside, what is common to these techniques is the displacement of speech in favor of direct, proactive intervention. While talking is still going on in exposure therapy sessions, it is subjected to the overall habituation scheme, functioning as auxiliary to the exposure medium, as in when instructing patients to recount their feelings through a session, and listen to audio recordings between sessions. VR therapy constitutes an extreme case of anti-talk pro-technology therapy, as Rizzo states in a recent interview: "the current generation of soldiers grew up digital. And they may be more apt to seek treatment within a treatment environment that has digital technology. And so we hope we'll be able to draw in folks to treatment that would never go one-on-one, 'tell me about your mother' type therapy."[75]

While supposedly superfluous clinically, the exclusion of talk has significant moral consequences. For it is through talk that one is able to address one's experience to another and thereby take a stand with respect to violence and suffering, one's own as well as another's. Engaging with trauma discursively takes it out from clinical considerations and into social and moral concerns. As Pasi Väliaho claims in his study of VR therapy, this technology generates an image of war that is oriented to internal brain processes, to "the media technological regulation of basic affect programmes and the endogenous imagery they produce," rather than to external socially shared reality.[76] In terms of the present study, this internal processing of war and its effects is part of the recycling of mind and media that gives rise to a new formation of traumatic memory, one that is amenable to technological intervention. The vision that VR therapy portrays is that of the possibility of accessing each traumatic memory individually while rejecting the possibility of engaging with it discursively. To be sure, at stake here is not the fate of the "talking cure" per se, or the question of whether trauma can find appropriate articulation by means of speech. Rather, it is the potential of approaching trauma outside the realm where computer and brain circuits interconnect, engaging it in the realm of social communication. Specifically, it is the prospect of recovering what Judith Butler calls "the structure of address": "the situation of being addressed, the demand that comes from elsewhere, sometimes from a nameless elsewhere, by which our obligations are articulated and pressed upon us."[77] By addressing and being addressed the subject becomes a moral agent capable of being called upon to take responsibility. For all the pains it causes, trauma may summon moral reckoning.

No doubt alleviating trauma is a noble and worthy cause. But it is one thing to seek a cure for the pains left by traumatic events, and it is another thing to apply the cure in ways intended to prevent moral compunctions stirred by such events. The future trajectory of BRAVEMIND and STRIVE is one of quick and efficient recovery from combat trauma coupled with the prospect of its eventual inoculation. The same system used for treating post-traumatic veterans is the platform for training recruits before deployment. Put bluntly, post-trauma treatment makes the effects of killing more bearable on the back end, and pre-trauma training makes killing more bearable on the front end. This hands-on approach to trauma is directly connected to its decontextualization and de-narrativization by means of technological mediation. Walter Benjamin famously lamented the loss of narrative by those who returned from the battlefields of the First World War "not richer, but poorer in communicable experience."[78] A century later, trauma is once again bound up with postwar non-communicability. Only this time it is not owing to the dumbfounding, overwhelming effect of mechanical warfare, or in Benjamin's words, "a field of force of destructive torrents and explosion": in this case it is owing to the explication of trauma as technologically treatable—the virtual reality, rather than the reality, of war.

Conclusion

Wounding Transmissions

"Transmission" is a term used, curiously enough, in both technology and psychology. In the former, it denotes the transfer of messages from one point to another, a view that was principally theorized by Claude Shannon and Warren Weaver.[1] Technologically speaking, transmission names the conveyance of information from sender to receiver through a designated channel by means of symbols or signals. This technical formulation of transmission constitutes the operational basis of numerous media technologies. In psychology, transmission is often used to describe the way behavior and symptoms of traumatized parents are transferred to their children, causing transgenerational trauma. Such transmission can be direct or indirect, overt or covert; indeed, transmission of trauma might be the result of either over-disclosure of knowledge and facts, or of under-disclosure, even of persistent silence, which "can often communicate traumatic messages as powerfully as words."[2] In both technological and psychological uses, transmission denotes a unilateral handing over across space and/or time. But clearly psychological transmission implies more than the mere delivery of messages: it involves a delivery that exceeds that of meaning or information proper, a transmission taking place as though beyond words, on the affective rather than on the cognitive level. This book has posited media as linking the two senses of transmission above by virtue of the technological capability of effecting impact in excess of message, and contact in excess of content. And nowhere are the stakes in linking technological and psychological transmissions higher than in the mediation of trauma.

In this book I have advanced an argument about the deep association of media and trauma. The media discussed here—radio, videotape, television, digital, and virtual—comprise different instantiations of the mediation of trauma: the ways media technologies sustain and convey the experience of unsettling experience. Media reach to the Real, and in so doing make available a register whose registration is of corporeality itself. Bodies find expression through media in the Real, revealing materiality as a common substratum. Thus, while trauma is a condition epitomizing human vulnerability, it is one that is remarkably made tangible by media technology. What the mediation of trauma as developed in this book ultimately amounts to is the imparting of human vulnerability in the wake of violence. Media shape the social life of trauma: living through it, reliving it, relating it, remembering it, overcoming it—all in ways that exceed individual consciousness. From this arises a theme running throughout the book: the incompatibility and sometimes conflict between semiotic and somatic channels, between the delivery of meaning effects and presence effects (to rehearse once again Hans Ulrich Gumbrecht's distinction), between transmission of content and transmission of contact—all as enacted and re-enacted through media technology.

Of special importance here are the threshold operations between inside and outside, or what I named traumatography: the mediatic logic informing the registration and recollection of trauma. This logic goes deeper than designating trauma as a crisis of representation, as it encompasses the ways that crisis itself is registered, retrieved, and disseminated. Media are instrumental in bearing witness to the human failure to bear witness, as each of the preceding chapters demonstrates. Radio provided an acoustic channel for the disembodiment and re-embodiment of voice during the Eichmann trial, recasting the status of trauma between private and public. Video constituted the audiovisual unconscious of the trauma and testimony discourse initiated at the Yale Fortunoff archive, shaping both the experience and the conception of traumatic memory in the wake of the Holocaust. Media screens have played a key role in the recent history of trauma, with the trauma film paradigm setting the ground for the visual bias of PTSD. This bias has become ever more pronounced with psychiatric research into televisual trauma following the 9/11 attacks, culminating with the recent acceptance of trauma through media in the DSM-V, and the ongoing debate about drone operators claiming to suffer from post-traumatic symptoms supposedly as a result of killing by remote. Digital technology marks a traumatographical shift with the traumatic Real undergoing re-symbolization into code so as to fit the logic of a database.

Virtual testimony provides a contrastive case to that of videography insofar as demonstrating the elimination of traumatic memory from testimony as brought by the subjugation of witnessing to algorithm, and the complementary shifting of emphasis from the witness to the witnessee, the recipient of testimony. Virtual reality therapy for PTSD attempts a direct access to the traumatic brain fear structure through a combination of gaming and exposure therapy, and in so doing renders traumatic memory discrete and modular while circumventing and discrediting talk as a medium of therapy. Despite the variety, in all cases media partake in activating the threshold operations by which trauma is approached and experienced.

The perspective expounded in this book allows considering the vicissitudes of narrative with respect to trauma in a circumferential manner, as though from the outside. Two modes of narrativity figure prominently in the foregoing chapters: testimony and psychotherapy, either separately or conjointly. Broadcasting and videotaping testimonies present two cases where media bear out the performative power of narrative in reaching out to what escapes narrativization, disclosing the way traumatic memory acts upon narrative. This is by means of linear capture and relay of the temporality of narrative, of the event of telling together with all its verbal and nonverbal incidentals. The shift from analog to digital mediation of trauma marks the eclipse of narrative in favor of nonlinear access to psychic pain. Virtual testimony dismantles the agency of the witness as narrator, granting priority to algorithmic stringing of questions and answers. Virtual therapy altogether disposes of narrative in seeking to directly target and retrain affected brain areas. That media technology now emerges both as a possible cause of and potential cure for trauma further substantiates the decline of narrative as a therapeutic resource. What becomes evident through all this is the loss of empathetic social discourse around trauma. Trauma might be redemptive of human vulnerability as a basis for morality—with testimony and therapy serving as two key discursive modes for acknowledging vulnerability. My point here is not so much to rehabilitate the priority of narrative as to invoke the addressability underlying both testimony and therapy, an addressability that is fundamental to moral concern. The status of narrative in relation to trauma may then be indicative of the potential for moral engagement with pain, one's own as well as others'.

Two parallel trajectories run across this book, both mixing the ironic and the tragic. In the first, the growing preoccupation with trauma in various therapeutic, literary, and popular outlets have brought to the democratization of the traumatic experience, making it collectively recognizable and relatable. Media play a key role in this process by making the traumatic palpable through affective channels, allowing for the possibility of being affected from afar and ex post facto. This is the context for understanding the stakes involved in what clinicians call secondary traumatization. The crisis reportedly experienced by Shoshana Felman's class after viewing videotestimonies from the Fortunoff archive seems to have anticipated the clinical recognition in the transmitting power of media images during and after the 9/11 attacks. The figure of the drone operator as both perpetrator and victim of mediated violence marks the far end of such democratization of trauma. The other trajectory charts the history of the attempts to deal with the traumas of the twentieth century in various therapeutic, literary, and popular outlets as leading to government- and military-sponsored efforts to absorb and neutralize the mental cost of waging war.[3] Media are equally instrumental here, but in promoting a situation where trauma is treated as a collateral damage to be routinized and minimized. This is therapy at its most utilitarian and standardized level. The figure of the soldier undergoing preventative pre-traumatic VR exposure treatment marks the far end of this trajectory. Between the two ends, the democratization of trauma on the one hand and its neutralization on the other, a range of unprecedented ethical and political questions unfolds.

In a different yet related vein, the mediation of trauma presents an extreme case for the logic of mediality. According to Sybille Krämer, the functional logic of media depends on their withdrawal from what they mediate: "A medium's success thus depends on its disappearance, and mediation is designed to make what is mediated appear unmediated . . . The implementation of media depends on their withdrawal."[4] The basic function of media, then, is to make something appear while making themselves disappear in the process. Media dissolve through their operation: they can render immediate what they mediate only inasmuch as in so doing they recede to the background. Once the medium becomes perceptible (noises in reception, blots on the screen, illegible writing) transmission is compromised. It follows that there is no contradiction between mediation and immediacy, to the contrary: a medium makes something perceptible to the point it appears immediate, which is also the point where the medium becomes imperceptible, eclipsed by its own activity. All this gives a new sense to the status of the medium as being in the middle, in-between, both connecting and separating, and connecting because separating, heterogeneous domains. Media must dissipate between in order to operate betwixt.

Yet Krämer's conception of immediacy is not sufficiently discerning. To her, a written text makes meaning immediate just like a screen makes image immediate, just like an audio player makes music immediate. At one point, she even argues that immersion does not begin with virtual reality but in fact "already takes effect in the reading of a book, which grips and transfixes the reader."[5] Clearly, there is much to say here about media specificity and how different media produce different kinds of immediacy. But the problem seems to come down to the distinction between hermeneutic and non-hermeneutic immediacy; or to pursue a mythological personification, the difference between the mediation performed by Hermes and the one performed by Iris. As Alexander Galloway suggests, Hermes, the messenger of Greek gods and patron of boundaries (as well as of messengers, travelers, merchants, and thieves) typifies the relaying of messages across space, sending by means of going the distance. The mediation performed by Hermes, to which he gives his name, is hermeneutics: the art and practice of interpretation, of handing over meaning, which expands the figure of the go-between from physical to discursive. In contrast to Hermes, the mediation performed by Iris—also a messenger of the gods, goddess of sea and sky, and the personification of the rainbow—is that of iridescence. Her mediation is of the annihilation of distance through ecstatic immediacy: "To tell is to touch, no matter how far away, and thus for Iris any mediation is mediation in the here and now."[6] Iris is decidedly non-hermeneutic: she is a model of immanence rather than of meaning, of the distant as made near rather than as made intelligible, of contact rather than content.

While the distinctions above do not typically manifest themselves separately and may often be intertwined, there are instances where the two types of immediacy not only diverge but are patently at odds with each other. This is indeed the gist of my argument in this book, which suggests that the mediation of trauma comes about when the non-hermeneutic exceeds the hermeneutic, and when presence effects overwhelm meaning effects. In fact, it is possible to imagine the two immediacies as constituting two opposite poles of mediation: on the one extreme, the dream of perfect communication, an angelic union brought about by transparent message exchange; on the other extreme, the nightmare of fatal shock, a bringing together that culminates in a crushing impact. In both cases the medium mediates so excessively that it virtually vanishes, resulting in radical immediacy: the melting of souls in the former, the collision of inside and outside in the latter. It is in this sense that the formula proposed in the introductory discussion, the mediation of failed mediation, bespeaks the capacity of media to encompass the traumatic effect as the surplus of the non-hermeneutic over the blockage of the hermeneutic. And what better confirmation is there to that capacity of media than psychological discourse itself, which often resorts to media technological terms and metaphors to describe both the etiology and symptomatology of trauma.

Perhaps one of the most poignant dramatizations of a medium effecting contact in lieu of content is Franz Kafka's short story "In the Penal Colony." It features a harrowing depiction of an apparatus whose function is to inscribe the sentence of a condemned prisoner directly on his skin. The prisoner does not know the sentence before being tied to a bed with an elaborate system of needles looming over. But during the excruciating hours of inscription he begins to decipher it "with his wounds," finally bleeding to death as understanding sets in.[7] The killing writing machine represents a most severe separation between the delivery of contact and the delivery of content. As Steven Connor suggests, this "epidermal fable" can be read not only as "the figuration of a traumatic assault on a surface, but also as the dread of a failure of the surface, the giving way of embodiment."[8] Crucially, the wounding inscription anticipates the deadly message (of justice, no less), while full reception is fatally late to arrive. The transmission of contact postpones indefinitely the transmission of content, ultimately eliminating both message and recipient. Kafka's lethal writing machine provides an extreme illustration as to what is implied in the notion of traumatography—the writing down system of trauma. For there is something in the way that trauma gets inscribed, in the way it leaves its mark and impresses itself, that evokes visceral inscription (the Latin *inscribere* draws from the Indo-European root *skribh*, which means to cut or incise), which has its correlate in technical indexical marking. That Kafka's machine may have been inspired by an actual one—the Hollerith Tabulating Machine, the 1890 information processing device in which a system of electric pins passed through punched cards to record data for a national census—further suggests the prevalence of the "contact apparatus" across body corporeal and body politic.[9]

Kittler suggests that Kafka's short story is revealing of the bond of technology and physiology when it comes to material inscription. In a node to Nietzsche, who speculated on the human as forgetfulness in the flesh, Kittler states: "Only a scratch or a cut into the flesh of forgetfulness itself can be unforgettable."[10] These very same words can be used to describe traumatography. It is not by chance, then, that wound, prick, and cut are the main attributes of Barthes's punctum, which as a form of photographic signification has repeatedly been associated with the structure of trauma. Inscrutability and latency are integral to the punctum, which unlike the studium, stabs but does not inform: "What I can name cannot really prick me. The incapacity to name is a good symptom of disturbance."[11] (This also explains why attempts to code "latent content" as telltale of traumatic memory is doomed to failure, as I argue in Chapter 4). Barthes substantiates photography as comprising both hermeneutic and nonhermeneutic valences, semiotics and somatics, content and contact. The punctum as index touches like a finger. Yet this indexical touch, to be sure, is a product of mediation; it can only come to pass as mediated immediacy, a wounding transmission. Only non-symbolic inscription of the temporality of the event is capable of effecting such a transmission; only media capable of intervening in the flow of time can produce presence effects—effects, not presence as such, which is another way of saying mediated immediacy. The mediation of contact bears out the material bond between physiology and technology, which bears out a common basis of vulnerability. Only the material is vulnerable, and mortality being the human subset of this general vulnerability of the material. This is what the transmission of contact transmits.

What ultimately connects the different cases analyzed here, from the radio broadcasting of testimonies in the Eichmann trial to VR therapy, with video testimonies, distant trauma, and algorithmic-holographic testimony in-between, is human vulnerability as made tangible by and through media. Trauma reveals vulnerability as a basis for morality—a minor morality of media; minor, because it does not involve concrete edicts or elaborate guidelines but rather the precondition and opening for moral concern. This minor morality is distinctively a morality of media, not in the sense of standards and regulations, but, more profoundly, in the sense of media as fundamental to producing an inclination toward vulnerability. The introduction of vulnerability into the framework of media materiality might help redeem Kittler's media theory from its anti-human streak—a redeeming, to be sure, much against his own thinking.[12] But to the extent that such redeeming is warranted, it would entail neither the technologizing of pain nor the humanizing of technology, but rather approaching trauma through the recursive loops of technology, physiology, and psychology that give rise to it. The mediation of trauma thus allows relocating the preoccupation with trauma beyond clinical discourse, taking it into the realm of moral concern. While being vulnerable makes for a propensity to be traumatized, what actually makes the traumatic is always historical, and as such calls for moral scrutiny. Trauma may be too telling of our situation to be left only to clinical consideration.

NOTES

INTRODUCTION

1. Christopher Hope cited in Fiachra Gibbons and Stephen Moss, "Fragments of Fraud," *The Guardian*, October 15, 1999. https://www.theguardian.com/theguardian/1999/oct/15/features11.g24; Jonathan Kozol, "Children of the Camps," *The Nation*, October 28, 1996. http://www.writing.upenn.edu/~afilreis/Holocaust/children-camps-bk-review.html.
2. Binjamin Wilkomirski, *Fragments: Memories of a Wartime Childhood*, trans. Carol Brown Janeway (New York: Schocken Books, 1996), 155. The historical study of the case is by Stefan Maechler, *The Wilkomirski Affair: A Study in Biographical Truth*, trans. John E. Woods (New York: Schocken Books, 2001). For more on the Wilkomisrski case, see Michael Bernard-Donals, "Beyond the Question of Authenticity: Witness and Testimony in the Fragments Controversy," *PMLA* 116(5), 2001, 1302–1315; Andrew S. Gross and Michael J. Hoffman, "Memory, Authority, and Identity: Holocaust Studies in Light of the Wilkomirski Debate," *Biography* 27(1), 2004, 25–47; Jay Geller, "The Wilkomirski Case: *Fragments* or Figments?" *American Imago* 59(3), 2002, 343–365; Stefan Maechler, "Wilkomirski the Victim: Individual Remembering as Social Interaction and Public Event," *History and Memory* 13(2), 2001, 59–95.
3. Wilkomirski, *Fragments*, 4–5.
4. Elena Lappin, "The Man with the Two Heads," *Granta* 66, Summer, 1999, 61.
5. Janet Walker, *Trauma Cinema: Documenting Incest and the Holocaust* (Berkeley and Los Angeles: University of California Press, 2005), xix.
6. Ann Kaplan, *Trauma Culture: The Politics of Terror and Loss in Media and Literature* (New Brunswick, NJ: Rutgers University Press, 2005), 69. Another example is Elaine Showalter who speaks of "hystories," the cultural narratives of hysteria—including of traumatic memory—which "multiply rapidly and uncontrollably in the era of mass media, telecommunications, and e-mail." Here, too, media are seen as conveyers of content already deemed to be traumatic, while the question of what makes them so apt for the task never arises. See, *Hystories: Hysterical Epidemics and Modern Media* (New York: Columbia University Press, 1997), 5; on the media circulation of traumatic memory, see 144–158.

7. Hans Ulrich Gumbrecht, "A Farewell to Interpretation," in *Materialities of Communication*, eds. Hans Ulrich Gumbrecht and K. Ludwig Pfeiffer (Stanford, CA: Stanford University Press, 1994), 389–404.
8. John Durham Peters, *The Marvelous Clouds: Toward a Philosophy of Elemental Media* (Chicago: Chicago University Press, 2015), 15.
9. Cathy Caruth, *Unclaimed Experience: Trauma, Narrative, and History* (Baltimore and London: The Johns Hopkins University Press, 1996), 59.
10. Sigmund Freud, *Beyond the Pleasure Principle*, trans. James Strachey (Mineola, NY: Dover, 2015) 21, 23.
11. Sigmund Freud, *General Psychological Theory: Papers on Metapsychology*, trans. James Strachey (New York: Touchstone, 2008), 214.
12. Ibid., 216.
13. On the transmission and storage functions in Freud's conception of the psychic apparatus, see Jacques Derrida, *The Postcard: From Socrates to Freud and Beyond*, trans. Alan Bass (Chicago: Chicago University Press, 1987), 344–353; Friedrich A. Kittler, *Literature, Media, Information Systems*, trans. Stefanie Harris (Amsterdam: Overseas Publishers Association, 1997), 133–135; Thomas Elsaesser, "Freud as a Media Theorist: Mystic Writing-Pads and the Matter of Memory," *Screen* 50(1), 2009, 101–113.
14. The "protective shield" (*Reizschutz*) makes a final appearance in Freud's last work, Sigmund Freud, *An Outline of Psychoanalysis*, trans. James Strachey (New York: W. W. Norton, 1969). In summarizing his life's project, Freud reconsiders the definition of the ego: "From what was originally a cortical layer, equipped with the organs for receiving stimuli and with arrangements for acting as a protective shield against stimuli, a special organization has arisen which henceforward acts as an intermediary between the id and the external world. To this region of our mind we have given the name of ego" (Freud, *Outline of Psychoanalysis*, 14). The ego performs the task of "self-preservation" by coping with outside excitations as well as with internal instincts; its striving after pleasure and avoiding displeasure is achieved by virtue of its "intermediary" position between inside and outside. Read in conjunction with Freud's earlier speculations, this understanding of the ego as incorporating a protective shield reveals it as literally post-traumatic due to the consequences of sustaining life under duress.
15. Ian Hacking, *Rewriting the Soul: Multiple Personality and the Sciences of Memory* (Princeton, NJ: Princeton University Press, 1995).
16. John Eric Erichsen, *On Railway and Other Injuries of the Nervous System* (Philadelphia: Henry C. Lea, 1867). See also: Paul Lerner and Mark S. Micale, "Trauma, Psychiatry, and History: A Conceptual and Historiographical Introduction," in *Traumatic Pasts: History, Psychiatry and Trauma in the Modern Age, 1860–1903*, eds. Mark S. Micale and Paul Lerner (Cambridge: Cambridge University Press, 2001), 1–27.
17. American Psychiatric Association, *Diagnostic and Statistical Manual of Mental Disorders: DSM-III* (Washington, DC: American Psychiatric Association, 1980), 236.
18. Allan Young, *The Harmony of Illusions: Inventing Post-traumatic Stress Disorder* (Princeton, NJ: Princeton University Press, 1995), 7.

19. Pierre Janet, *Psychological Healing: A Historical and Clinical Study*, Vol. 1, trans. Eden and Cesar Paul (London: G. Allen & Unwin, 1925), 660–698.
20. Hans Blumenberg, *Paradigms for a Metaphorology*, trans. Robert Savage (Ithaca, NY: Cornell University Press, 2010).
21. See Alan W. Scheflin, "Ground Lost: The False Memory/Recovered Memory Therapy Debate," *Psychiatric Times*, 16(11), 1999. http://www.psychiatrictimes.com/articles/ground-lost-false-memoryrecovered-memory-therapy-debate.
22. This is indeed Caruth's claim as to the inadequacy of history as a factual discourse to provide an account of trauma, since trauma remains tied to what she calls the "referential literality" of the original event (Caruth, *Unclaimed Experience*, 16). A history of trauma, according to her, is possible only indirectly, as a literary approach that treats historical texts symptomatically, as though containing inadvertent traces of unclaimed experiences. Following this reasoning, Caruth's literary account can be read as an attempt to give account of trauma as precisely what resists accounting for.
23. Young, *Harmony of Illusions*, 5.
24. Hacking, *Rewriting the Soul*, especially chapters 13 and 14.
25. Ruth Leys, *Trauma: A Genealogy* (Chicago: University of Chicago Press, 2000).
26. Elssaesser, "Postmodernism as Mourning Work," *Screen* 42(2), 2001, 198–199.
27. Andreas Huyssen, "Present Pasts: Media, Politics, Amnesia," *Public Culture* 12(1), 2000, 36.
28. Allen Meek, *Trauma and Media: Theories, Histories, and Images* (New York: Routledge, 2010), 13.
29. Elsaesser clearly rejects the possibility that media are active agents in the transformations he describes: "In the face of technological changes in our recording media and communication systems, forms of cultural memory and intersubjectivity are emerging (though they are by no means caused by them, unless the crises of the symbolic order mentioned earlier are regarded as technological in origin)" (Elssaesser, "Postmodernism as Mourning Work," 12).
30. Marianne Hirsch, *The Generation of Postmemory: Writing and Visual Culture after the Holocaust* (New York: Columbia University Press, 2012), 36.
31. Ibid., 122.
32. Alison Landsberg, *Prosthetic Memory: The Transformation of American Remembrance in the Age of Mass Culture* (New York: Columbia University Press, 2004), 113.
33. Joshua Hirsch, *Afterimage: Film, Trauma, and the Holocaust* (Philadelphia: Temple University Press, 2004), 7.
34. Bernhard Siegert, "Cultural Techniques: Or the End of the Intellectual Postwar Era in German Media Theory," *Theory, Culture & Society* 30(6), 2013, 60–61.
35. Walter Benjamin, *Illuminations: Essays and Reflections*, trans. Harry Zohn (New York: Schocken Books, 1969), 163.
36. Ibid., 175.
37. Ibid., 250.
38. Ibid., 84.
39. Marshall McLuhan, *Understanding Media: The Extensions of Man* (New York: McGraw Hill, 1964), 43.
40. Ibid., 67.

41. Friedrich A. Kittler, *Discourse Networks 1800/1900*, trans. Michael Metter with Chris Cullens (Stanford, CA: Stanford University Press, 1990), 369.
42. Friedrich A. Kittler, *Gramophone, Film, Typewriter*, trans. Geoffrey Winthrop-Young and Michael Wutz (Stanford, CA: Stanford University Press, 1999), 4.
43. Daniel Paul Schreber, *Memoirs of My Nervous Illness*, trans. Ida Macalpine and Richard A. Hunter (New York: New York Review Books, 2000), 123.
44. Kittler, *Discourse Networks*, 298–299.
45. Kittler, *Gramophone, Film, Typewriter*, 15–16.
46. Jacques Lacan, *The Seminars of Jacques Lacan: Book XI The Four Fundamental Concepts of Psychoanalysis*, trans. Alan Sheridan (New York: W. W. Norton, 1998), 55.
47. Kittler, *Gramophone, Film, Typewriter*, 15.
48. Friedrich Kittler, *Optical Media*, trans. Anthony Enns (Cambridge: Polity, 2010), 35.
49. See Fred H. Frankel, "The Concept of Flashback in Historical Perspective," *International Journal of Clinical and Experimental Hypnosis* 42(4), 1994, 321–336. For an extensive study of the term in the context of film, see Maureen Turim, *Flashback in Film: Memory and History* (New York: Routledge, 1995).
50. Hugo Münsterberg, *The Film: A Psychological Study: The Silent Photoplay in 1916* (New York: Dover, 1970), 41.
51. Marshall McLuhan, *Letters of Marshall McLuhan*, eds. Matie Molinaro, Corinne McLuhan, and William Toye (Oxford: Oxford University Press, 1987), 193.
52. Hacking, *Rewriting the Soul*, 252–253.
53. Kittler finds evidence of the cut-back or flashback in early twentieth century literature as an illustration of involuntary memory within written narrative. See Kittler, *Gramophone, Film, Typewriter*, 163–164.
54. Alan Sheridan in Lacan, *The Seminars of Jacques Lacan*, 280.
55. Geoffrey Winthrop-Young, *Kittler and the Media* (Cambridge: Polity, 2011), 137.

CHAPTER 1
1. Haim Gouri, *Facing the Glass Booth: The Jerusalem Trial of Adolf Eichmann*, trans. Michael Swirsky (Detroit, MI: Wayne State University Press, 2004), 22.
2. Tom Segev, *The Seventh Million: The Israelis and the Holocaust*, trans. Haim Watzman (London: Macmillan, 2000), 350.
3. Idith Zertal, *Israel's Holocaust and the Politics of Nationhood*, trans. Chaya Galai (Cambridge: Cambridge University Press, 2005), 92.
4. Shoshana Felman, *The Juridical Unconscious: Trials and Traumas in the Twentieth Century* (Cambridge, MA: Harvard University Press, 2002), 127.
5. Anita Shapira, "The Eichmann Trial: Changing Perspectives," *Journal of Israeli History* 23(1), 2004, 20.
6. Nor do others; see Omer Bartov, *Mirrors of Destruction: War, Genocide, and Modern Identity* (Oxford: Oxford University Press, 2000); Leora Bilsky, *Transformative Justice: Israeli Identity on Trial* (Ann Arbor: University of Michigan Press, 2004); Lawrence Douglas, *The Memory of Judgment: Making Law and History in the Trials of the Holocaust* (New Haven, CT: Yale University Press, 2001); Judith Stern, "The Eichmann Trial and Its Influence on Psychiatry and

Psychology," *Theoretical Inquiries in Law* 1(2), 2000, 1–36; Hanna Yablonka, *The State of Israel vs. Adolf Eichmann* (New York: Random House, 2004).
7. Amit Pinchevski, Tamar Liebes, and Ora Herman, "Eichmann on the Air: Radio and the Making of an Historic Trial," *Historical Journal of Film, Radio, and Television* 27(1), 2007, 1–25.
8. Hannah Arendt, *Eichmann in Jerusalem: A Report on the Banality of Evil* (New York: Viking, 1965).
9. See Tim Cole, *Selling the Holocaust: From Auschwitz to Schindler; How History Is Bought, Packaged, and Sold* (New York: Routledge, 1999); Zertal, *Israel's Holocaust*.
10. Felman, *The Juridical Unconscious*, 4.
11. Pierre Legendre, *Law and the Unconscious: A Legendre Reader*, trans. Peter Goodrich (New York: St. Martin's, 1997).
12. Peter Goodrich, *Oedipus Lex: Psychoanalysis, History, Law* (Berkeley: University of California Press, 1995).
13. Peter Goodrich and David G. Carlson (eds.), Introduction to *Law and the Postmodern Mind: Essays on Psychoanalysis and Jurisprudence* (Ann Arbor: University of Michigan Press, 1998).
14. Ibid., 127.
15. Ka-tzetnik (a Yiddish contraction for "concentration camp inmate") was the pseudonym of Yehiel Dinur (Feiner); his true name and identity were revealed for the first time during the trial, when he was asked to testify before the court.
16. Arendt, *Eichmann in Jerusalem*, 223–224.
17. Felman, *The Juridical Unconscious*, 164, 153.
18. Ibid., 7.
19. Ibid., 127.
20. Ibid.
21. Jeffrey C. Alexander, Ron Eyerman, Bernhard Giesen, Neil J. Smelser, and Piotr Sztompka, *Cultural Trauma and Collective Identity* (Berkeley: University of California Press, 2004), 8.
22. See Kai Erikson, "Notes on Trauma and Community," in *Trauma: Explorations in Memory*, ed. Cathy Caruth (Baltimore: Johns Hopkins University Press, 1995), 183–199; Ron Eyerman, *Cultural Trauma: Slavery and the Formation of African American Identity* (Cambridge, MA: Harvard University Press, 2001).
23. Eyerman, *Cultural Trauma*, 4.
24. Alexander, "Toward a Theory of Cultural Trauma," *Cultural Trauma and Collective Identity*, 1–31.
25. See Susan J. Douglas, *Listening In: Radio and the American Imagination* (New York: Times Books, 1999); John Ellis, *Seeing Things: Television in the Age of Uncertainty* (London: Tauris, 2000); Joshua Meyrowitz, *No Sense of Place: The Impact of Electronic Media on Social Behavior* (Oxford: Oxford University Press, 1985); John Durham Peters, *Speaking into the Air: A History of the Idea of Communication* (Chicago: University of Chicago Press, 1999); Paddy Scannell, *Radio, Television, and Modern Life: A Phenomenological Approach* (Oxford: Blackwell, 1996); Jo Tacchi, "Radio Texture: between Self and Others," in *Material Culture: Why Some Things Matter*, ed. Daniel Miller (Chicago: University of Chicago Press, 1998), 25–46; Allen S. Weiss, *Phantasmic Radio* (Durham, NC: Duke University Press, 1995).

26. Gregory Whitehead, "Out of the Dark: Notes on the Nobodies of Radio Art," in *Wireless Imagination: Sound, Radio, and the Avant-Garde*, eds. Douglas Kahn and Gregory Whitehead (Cambridge, MA: MIT Press, 1992), 253–263.
27. Weiss, *Phantasmic Radio*, 78.
28. Mladen Dolar, *A Voice and Nothing More* (Cambridge, MA: MIT Press, 2006), 60.
29. Edmund Carpenter and Marshall McLuhan, "Acoustic Space," in *Explorations in Communication*, eds. Edmund Carpenter and Marshall McLuhan (Boston: Beacon, 1960), 65–70. A famous example is Orson Welles's radio drama *War of the Worlds*, aired in October 1938, which reportedly caused panic among audiences who thought Martians were actually about to invade New Jersey; see Hadley Cantril, Hazel Gaudet, and Herta Herzog, *The Invasion from Mars: A Study in the Psychology of Panic* (Princeton, NJ: Princeton University Press, 1940). The panic, so it seems, was related not only to the imminent alien invasion but also to the (simulated) collapse of the broadcasting network itself; see Jeffrey Sconce, *Haunted Media: Electronic Presence from Telegraphy to Television* (Durham, NC: Duke University Press, 2000), 113–114.
30. Gaston Bachelard, "Reverie and Radio," in *Radiotext(e)*, eds. Neil Strauss and David Mandl (New York: Semiotext[e], 1993), 222.
31. McLuhan, *Understanding Media*, 299. He also associated the tribal ecological environment created by radio to trauma and paranoia. See Marshall and Eric McLuhan, *Laws of Media: The New Science* (Toronto: University of Toronto Press, 1992), 172.
32. Kittler, *Gramophone, Film, Typewriter*, 118.
33. Ibid., 16.
34. Daniel Dayan and Elihu Katz, *Media Events: The Live Broadcasting of History* (Cambridge, MA: Harvard University Press, 1992); Donald Horton and Richard R. Wohl, "Mass Communication and Para-social Interaction: Observations on Intimacy at a Distance," *Psychiatry* 19, 1956, 215–229; Meyrowitz, *No Sense of Place*; Scannell, *Radio, Television, and Modern Life*; Paddy Scannell, "For-Anyone-as-Someone Structures," *Media, Culture and Society* 22(1), 2000, 5–24.
35. Gregory Whitehead, "Who's There? Notes on the Materiality of Radio," *Art and Text* 31, 1989, 10–13.
36. Joe Milutis, "Radiophonic Ontologies and the Avant-Garde," *TDR: The Drama Review* 40 (3), 1996, 63–79; Weiss, *Phantasmic Radio*.
37. Roland Barthes, *Image-Music-Text*, trans. Stephen Heath (London: Fontana, 1977), 188.
38. Julia Kristeva, *Revolution in Poetic Language*, trans. Margaret Waller (New York: Columbia University Press, 1984), 25–30.
39. Five groups of Israelis between the ages of fifty-five and seventy-five were interviewed (nine to twelve members in each group) in 2006–2007. Groups were selected specifically to include members with previous acquaintances, preferably childhood friends. The rationale was that such groups would better approximate the social conditions of collective memory, with individuals reminding one another of certain occurrences and discussing together their memories. Each interview proceeded in two phases. First, individual questionnaires were distributed, asking each member to sketch briefly his or her first encounter with Holocaust survivors and to rank the following items

according to their importance in Israeli Holocaust memory: the Israel (Rudolf) Kastner trial, Anne Frank, Oskar Schindler's list, the Eichmann trial, and Yad Vashem. Although Eichmann's trial figured prominently in the replies, results were not conclusive. In the second phase, each group was interviewed collectively, first by presenting general questions about Holocaust memory in Israel without referring either to the Eichmann trial or to the radio. Only later were specific questions about radio listening during the trial introduced. Groups were from different cities representing different social backgrounds: Jerusalem (religious, orthodox); Binyamina (secular, rural); Kiryat Haim (northern Israel; secular, urban); Petach Tikva (Tel Aviv area, including B'nei Brak and Ramat Gan; religious, liberal); and Herzliya (secular, urban). Each group included both members of the second generation to the Holocaust and Israelis without any direct family connection to Holocaust survivors. Quotations were translated from Hebrew by the author.

40. Maurice Halbwachs, *The Collective Memory*, trans. Francis J. Ditter and Vida Yazdi Ditter (New York: Harper and Row, 1980).
41. Barry Schwartz and Howard Shuman, "History, Commemoration, and Belief: Abraham Lincoln in American Memory, 1945–2001," *American Sociological Review* 70, 2005, 183–203.
42. Bartov, *Mirrors of Destruction*; Felman, *The Juridical Unconscious*; Segev, *The Seventh Million*; Shapira, "The Eichmann Trial"; Yablonka, *The State of Israel vs. Adolf Eichmann*; Zertal, *Israel's Holocaust*.
43. See Sharon Geva, *To the Unknown Sister* (Tel Aviv: Hakibbutz Hameuchad, 2010) [in Hebrew]; Deborah E. Lipstadt, *The Eichmann Trial* (New York: Schocken Books, 2011).
44. Oz Almog, *The Sabra: The Creation of the New Jew* (Berkeley: University of California Press, 2000); Bartov, *Mirrors of Destruction*; Amit Pinchevski and Roy Brand, "Holocaust Perversions: The Stalags Pulp Fiction and the Eichmann Trial," *Critical Studies in Media Communication* 24, 2007, 387–407.
45. Segev, *The Seventh Million*; Hanna Yablonka, "The Formation of Holocaust Consciousness in Israel," in *Breaking Crystal: Writing and Memory after Auschwitz*, ed. Efraim Sicher (Urbana: University of Illinois Press, 1998), 119–136.
46. David Grossman, *See Under: Love*, trans. Betsy Rosenberg (New York: Picador, 2002), 4, 6.
47. Amos Oz, *My Michael*, trans. Nicholas de Lange (Orlando, FL: Harcourt, 1968), 197.
48. Yoram Kaniuk, *Adam Resurrected*, trans. Seymour Simckes (New York: Atheneum, 1971).
49. Yael S. Feldman, "Whose Story Is It, Anyway? Ideology and Psychology in the Representation of the Shoah in Israeli Literature," in *Probing the Limits of Representation: Nazism and the "Final Solution*,*"* ed. Saul Friedlander (Cambridge. MA: Harvard University Press, 1992), 223–239; see also Yosefa Loshitzky, *Identity Politics on the Israeli Screen* (Austin: University of Texas Press, 2003).
50. Radio program, *When Eichmann Entered My Home*, Galei Tzahal radio station, Israel. Broadcast May 2002.
51. Bilsky, *Transformative Justice*; Douglas, *The Memory of Judgment*; Felman, *The Juridical Unconscious*; Annette Wieviorka, *The Era of the Witness*, trans. Jared

Stark (Ithaca, NY: Cornell University Press, 2006); Yablonka, *The State of Israel vs. Adolf Eichmann*.

52. Ariana Melamed, "The Year When Silence Was Broken [in Hebrew]," *Ynet*, April 5, 2008. www.ynet.co.il/articles/0,7340,L-3527554,00.html.
53. Kristeva, *Revolution in Poetic Language*, 86–89.
54. See also Caruth, *Unclaimed Experience*; Geoffrey Hartman, *The Longest Shadow: In the Aftermath of the Holocaust* (Bloomington: Indiana University Press, 1996); Dominick LaCapra, *Writing History, Writing Trauma* (Baltimore: Johns Hopkins University Press, 2001).
55. See also Erikson, "Notes on Trauma and Community"; Eyerman, *Cultural Trauma*.
56. Felman, *The Juridical Unconscious*, 133.
57. For another example see: Jeffery C. Alexander, "On the Social Construction of Moral Universals: The 'Holocaust' from War Crime to Trauma Drama," *Cultural Trauma and Collective Identity*, 196–263. Alexander's analysis of the diary of Anne Frank as a dramatic universalization of the Holocaust is oblivious to the technological specificities of the different media through which Frank's story has been performed and disseminated over the years.
58. Jeffrey Shandler, *While America Watches: Televising the Holocaust* (New York: Oxford University Press, 1999), 129.
59. Ibid., 117.
60. Barthes, *Image-Music-Text*, 179–189; Roland Barthes, *Camera Lucida: Reflections on Photography*, trans. Richard Howard (New York: Hill and Wang, 1981), 15.
61. Jacques Derrida and Bernard Stiegler, *Echographies of Television: Filmed Interviews*, trans. Jennifer Bajorek (Cambridge: Polity, 2002), 117.
62. For more on this subject, see Anthony Enns, "Voices of the Dead: Transmission/Translation/Transgression," *Culture, Theory and Critique* 46, 2005, 11–27; Louis Kaplan, *The Strange Case of William Mumler, Spirit Photographer* (Minneapolis: University of Minnesota Press, 2008); Roger Luckhurst, *The Invention of Telepathy 1870–1901* (Oxford: Oxford University Press, 2002); Simone Natale, *Supernatural Entertainments: Victorian Spiritualism and the Rise of Modern Media Culture* (University Park: Pennsylvania State University Press, 2016); Peters, *Speaking into the Air*, 94–101; Sheri Weinstein, "Technologies of Vision: Spiritualism and Science in Nineteenth-Century America," in *Spectral America: Phantoms and the National Imagination*, ed. Jeffery Andrew Weinstock (Madison: University of Wisconsin Press, 2004), 124–140.
63. Freud's own speculations evoke themes of technological disembodiment: as Laurence A. Rickels notes, for Freud the superego is comparable to an internally received radio transmission; see *Aberrations of Mourning: Writing on German Crypts* (Detroit, MI: Wayne State University Press, 1988), 284–285. Also of note is Freud's interpretation in *Beyond the Pleasure Principle* of the story of Tancred, who is haunted by the voice of his dead beloved, whom he had accidentally killed; see Caruth, *Unclaimed Experience*, 1–10.
64. See Rickels, *Aberrations of Mourning*, 297.
65. Kittler, *Grammophone, Film, Typewriter*, 12–13.

66. Gideon Hausner, *Six Million Accusers: Israel's Case against Eichmann; The Opening Speech and Legal Argument of Mr. Gideon Hausner, Attorney-General* (Jerusalem: Jerusalem Post, 1961), 29.
67. Jacques Derrida, *Specters of Marx: The State of the Debt, the Work of Mourning, and the New International*, trans. Peggy Kamuf (New York: Routledge, 1994), 97.
68. Sconce, *Haunted Media*, 91. Recent studies report similar dynamics of mediated performance of trauma through acoustic media in the case of 9/11; see Elisia L. Cohen and Cynthia Willis, "One Nation under Radio: Digital and Public Memory after September 11," *New Media and Society* 6(5), 2004, 591–610; Joshua Gunn, "Mourning Speech: Haunting and the Spectral Voices of Nine-Eleven," *Text and Performance Quarterly* 24(2), 2004, 91–114. My contention, however, is that visual media were dominant in the mediation of trauma in that event; see Chapter 3.
69. LaCapra, *Writing History, Writing Trauma*; Segev, *The Seventh Million*; Idith Zertal, *From Catastrophe to Power: Holocaust Survivors and the Emergence of Israel* (Berkeley: University of California Press, 1998).
70. Dayan and Katz, *Media Events*.
71. Axel Honneth, *The Struggle for Recognition: The Moral Grammar of Social Conflicts* (Cambridge, MA: MIT Press, 1996).
72. In many respects, the Eichmann trial serves as the legal and historical precedent for later cases that conflate trial, trauma, and media: the Truth and Reconciliation Commissions (TRC) in South Africa, Sierra Leone, and Ghana; the National Commission on the Disappearance of Persons (CONADEP) in Argentina; the International Criminal Tribunal for the Former Yugoslavia (ICTY); see David A. Crocker, "Truth Commissions, Transitional Justice, and Civil Society," in *Truth v. Justice: The Morality of Truth Commissions*, eds. Robert I. Rotberg and Dennis Thompson (Princeton, NJ: Princeton University Press, 2000), 99–121; Branislav Jakovljevic, "From Mastermind to Body Artist: Political Performances of Slobodan Milosevic," *TDR: The Drama Review* 52(1), 2008, 51–74; Ron Krabil, "Symbiosis: Mass Media and the Truth and Reconciliation Commission of South Africa," *Media, Culture and Society* 23(5), 2001, 567–585. The case of the CONADEP hearings in Argentina constitutes what is perhaps the polar opposite of the Eichmann trial in terms of its media broadcasting. The 1985 public hearings were broadcast on television but, astonishingly, without sound, arguably so not to incite criticism against the military. The tapes were finally broadcast with the soundtrack in 1998. Thus if in the Eichmann trial the mediated summoning of the painful past involved sound without image, in the CONADEP it involved image without sound. I am indebted to Margaret Schwartz for bringing this case to my attention. See Antonius C. G. M. Robben, *Political Violence and Trauma in Argentina* (Philadelphia: University of Pennsylvania Press, 2005), 324; Claudia Feld, *Del Estrado A La Pantalla: Las Imágenes del Juicio A Los ex Comandantes en Argentina* (Madrid: Siglo XXI De España Editores, 2002), 33–38.
73. Pinchevski, Liebes, and Herman, "Eichmann on the Air."
74. Dan Lander, "Radiocasting: Musings on Radio and Art," 1999. http://econtact.ca/2_3/Radiocasting.htm.
75. Kittler, *Gramophone, Film, Typewriter*, 14.

76. John Durham Peters, "Witnessing," *Media, Culture and Society* 23, 2000, 707–723.
77. Roger Brown and James Kulik, "Flashbulb Memories," *Cognition* 5, 1977, 73–99. See also Andrew Hoskins, "Flashbulb Memories, Psychology and Media Studies: Fertile Ground for Interdisciplinary?" *Memory Studies* 2(2), 2009, 147–150.

CHAPTER 2
1. See Friedrich A. Kittler, *Discourse Networks, 1800/1900*, and *Gramophone, Film, Typewriter*. For a discussion of the term *Aufschreibesystem*, see John Johnston, "Friedrich Kittler: Media Theory after Poststructuralism," in Kittler, *Literature, Media, Information Systems*, 3–26.
2. Kittler, *Gramophone, Film Typewriter*, 4.
3. As Thomas Elsaesser notes, Kittler's logic can be extended to view Freud's "psychic apparatus" as consisting of two, mutually exclusive media functions: storage ("'system of the Unconscious'") and transmission ("'perception-consciousness system'"), see Elsaesser, "Freud as Media Theorist," 101.
4. Jacques Derrida offers a different configuration of the archival apparatus of psychoanalysis in the form of printing, handwritten correspondence, and the postal system. See Jacques Derrida, *Archive Fever: A Freudian Impression*, trans. Eric Prenowitz (Chicago: University of Chicago Press, 1996), 15–20.
5. See Simone Gigliotti, "Technology, Trauma, and Representation: Holocaust Testimony and Videotape," in *Temporalities, Autobiography, and Everyday Life*, eds. J. Campbell and J. Harbord (Manchester and New York: Manchester University Press, 2002), 204–218; Oren Baruch Stier, *Committed to Memory: Cultural Mediations of the Holocaust* (Amherst and Boston: University of Massachusetts Press, 2003), 67–109; Aleida Assmann, "History, Memory and the Genre of Testimony," *Poetics Today* 27(2), 2006, 261–273; and Meek, *Trauma and Media*, 133–170.
6. Hans Ulrich Gumbrecht, *Production of Presence: What Meaning Cannot Convey* (Stanford, CA: Stanford University Press, 2004), 8.
7. Laub mentions the American psychologist David P. Boder as pioneering the recording of Holocaust survivors. Boder traveled to Europe in 1946 equipped with a wire recorder, an audio recording device developed for the Armour Research Foundation during the war. He published the interviews in his *I Did Not Interview the Dead* (Champaign: University of Illinois Press, 1949). See also Alan Rosen, *The Wonder of Their Voices: The 1946 Holocaust Interviews of David Boder* (Oxford: Oxford University Press, 2010), especially chapter 5. See more on Boder in Chapter 4.
8. The original recording format was three-quarter-inch U-Matic videocassettes with a running time of one hour and seven minutes. Due to deterioration of the magnetic tape, the original videocassettes were stored in a temperature-controlled room in the Yale archives and over the last few years have been digitized. This development reasserts the tension between storage and dissemination at the base of this archive.

9. Mary Marshall Clark, "Holocaust Video Testimony, Oral History, and Narrative Medicine: The Struggle against Indifference," *Literature and Medicine* 24(2), 2006, 273. See also Dori Laub, "Testimonies in the Treatment of Genocidal Trauma," *Journal of Applied Psychoanalytic Studies* 4(1), 2002, 76–77.
10. Hartman, *The Longest Shadow*, 143.
11. Yale University Library: Fortunoff Video Archive for Holocaust Testimonies, "About the Archive: History," www.library.yale.edu/testimonies/about/history.html. Last accessed January 2018.
12. Ibid.
13. Hartman, *The Longest Shadow*, 144.
14. The film is available online at: https://www.youtube.com/watch?v=n91gS55QC9E; https://www.youtube.com/watch?v=_EtYO0oj8W8. Last accessed January 2018.
15. Siegfried Zielinski, *Audiovisions: Cinema and Television as Entr'actes in History*, trans. Gloria Custance (Amsterdam: Amsterdam University Press, 1999), 237–239.
16. Arjun Appadurai suggests that, with the advent of interactive technologies, the archive is becoming freed from the orbit of the state and its official networks, transforming instead into "a deliberate site for the production of anticipated memories by intentional communities"; see "Archive and Aspiration," in *Information Is Alive: Art and Theory on Archiving and Retrieving Data*, eds. J. Bower, A. Mulder, and S. Charlton (Rotterdam: V2/NAi, 2003), 17. In this sense, the Yale archive can be seen as a precursor to more recent archival formations based on interactive technologies that invite social participation and collaborative contributions.
17. Derrida, *Archive Fever*, 17.
18. Videography is to be understood here in the double sense: the writing of and writing about the videotape, the inscription and description of videotestimonies—or better in this case, the traumatogrphy of videography.
19. See Friedrich A. Kittler, "The City Is a Medium," *New Literary History* 27(4), 1996, 722.
20. Shoshana Felman and Dori Laub, *Testimony: Crises of Witnessing in Literature, Psychoanalysis, and History* (New York: Routledge, 1992), 15, 85.
21. Jennifer Ballengee and Geoffrey Hartman, "Witnessing Video Testimony: An Interview with Geoffrey Hartman," *Yale Journal of Criticism* 14(1), 2001, 220.
22. Felman and Laub, *Testimony*, 57.
23. See Wolfgang Ernst, *Chronopoetics: The Temporal Being and Operativity of Technological Media*, trans. Anthony Enns (London: Rowman & Littlefield, 2016), 113–117.
24. Andrea F. Bohlman and Peter McMurray, "Tape: Or, Rewinding the Phonographic Regime," *Twentieth-Century Music* 14(1), 2017, 7.
25. Felman and Laub, *Testimony*, 70.
26. Ibid., 57.
27. Kittler, *Gramophone, Film, Typewriter*, 141–142.
28. Hartman, *The Longest Shadow*, 139.

29. Geoffrey Hartman, "Tele-suffering and Testimony in the Dot Com Era," in *Visual Culture and the Holocaust*, ed. Barbie Zelizer (New Brunswick, NJ: Rutgers University Press, 2001), 116.
30. Ibid., 117.
31. Ibid. This antispecular aesthetics is reminiscent of Emmanuel Levinas's idea of a de-objectifying vision: "a 'vision' without image, bereft of the synoptic and totalizing virtues of vision"; see Emmanuel Levinas, *Totality and Infinity: An Essay on Exteriority*, trans. Alphonso Lingis (Dordrecht: Kluwer Academic, 1979), 23.
32. Felman and Laub, *Testimony*, 57.
33. Ibid., 60.
34. This testimony was at the center of a controversy in which Thomas Trezise charged Laub with misrepresenting the woman's testimony due to Laub's overidentification with her. In his response, Laub admits to some inaccuracies (including overdramatizing the above description) but criticizes Trezise for failing to understand the therapeutic testimonial process. This debate can be read as well in terms of media: Laub, who interviewed the woman, speaks as the immediate addressee of the testimony; Trezise speaks as a mediated addressee, as an audience, watching the tape years later. See Thomas Trezise, "Between History and Psychoanalysis: A Case Study in the Reception of Holocaust Survivor Testimony," *History and Memory* 20(1), 2008, 7–47; and Dori Laub, "On Holocaust Testimony and Its 'Reception' within Its Own Frame, as a Process in Its Own Right: A Response to 'Between History and Psychoanalysis' by Thomas Trezise," *History and Memory* 21(1), 2009, 127–150.
35. Baruch Greenwald, Dori Laub, Oshrit Ben-Ari, and Rael Strous, "Psychiatry, Testimony, and Shoah: Reconstructing the Narratives of the Muted," *International Social Health Care Policy, Programs, and Studies* 43(2–3), 2006, 200–203. The project of recording hospitalized survivors is presented and discussed extensively in Dori Laub and Andreas Hamburger eds., *Psychoanalysis and Holocaust Testimony: Unwanted Memories of Social Trauma* (London and New York: Routledge, 2017). See also my chapter in this collection, "Counter-Testimony, Counter-Archive," 242–254.
36. Kittler, *Gramophone, Film Typewriter*, 141–143; See also Kittler, *Discourse Networks*, 277; and Georges Didi-Huberman, *Invention of Hysteria: Charcot and the Photographic Iconography of the Salpêtrière*, trans. Alisa Hartz (Cambridge and London: MIT Press, 2003), chapters 1–3.
37. Milton M. Berger, "The Use of Videotape in Private Practice," in *Videotape Techniques in Psychiatric Training and Treatment*, ed. Milton M. Berger (New York: Brunner/Mazel, 1970), 144. See also, Carmine Grimaldi, "Televising Psyche: Therapy, Play, and the Seduction of Video," *Representations* 139, Summer, 2017, 95–117.
38. Laub, "Testimonies in the Treatment of Genocidal Trauma," 73.
39. Walter Benjamin, *Illuminations*, 263.
40. Kittler, *Discourse Networks*, 284.
41. Lawrence L. Langer, *Holocaust Testimonies: The Ruins of Memory* (New Haven, CT: Yale University Press, 1991), xi.
42. Langer, *Holocaust Testimonies*, 17.

43. Ibid., 58.
44. Ibid., 19.
45. Ibid., 41.
46. This double temporality marks each of Langer's five types of memory— deep, anguished, humiliated, tainted, and unheroic—which correspond respectively to five types of self: buried, divided, besieged, impromptu, and diminished.
47. Langer, *Holocaust Testimonies*, 6.
48. Ibid., 20.
49. Saul Friedlander, "Trauma, Memory, and Transference," in *Holocaust Remembrance: The Shapes of Memory*, ed. Geoffrey Hartman (Oxford: Blackwell, 1994), 254.
50. Kittler, *Gramophone, Film Typewriter*, 13.
51. Art Spiegelman, *The Complete Maus*, Vol. 2 (New York: Pantheon, 1997), 296. For further analysis of these last panels, see James E. Young, "The Holocaust as Vicarious Past: Art Spiegelman's *Maus* and the Afterimages of History," *Critical Inquiry* 24(3), 1998, 666–699.
52. This is also evident in Marianne Hirsch's concept of postmemory, another account for which *Maus* is the paradigmatic case. As a deeply mediated form of memory, postmemory is the second-generation Holocaust memory, typically as received and transmitted by novels, testimonies, photographs, and films. See Marianne Hirsch, *Family Frames: Photography, Narrative, and Postmemory* (Cambridge, MA: Harvard University Press, 1997), 12–40; and "Surviving Images: Holocaust Photographs and the Work of Postmemory," in *Visual Culture and the Holocaust*, 215–246.
53. James E. Young, *Writing and Rewriting the Holocaust: Narrative and the Consequences of Interpretation* (Bloomington and Indianapolis: Indiana University Press, 1988), 157.
54. For further discussion on time-axis manipulation, see Sybille Krämer, "The Cultural Techniques of Time-Axis Manipulation: On Friedrich Kittler's Conceptions of Media," *Theory, Culture, and Society* 23(7–8), 2006, 93–109; and Hartmut Winkler, "Geometry of Time: Media, Specialization, and Reversibility," http://homepages.uni-paderborn.de/winkler/hase_e.pdf. Last accessed June 2018.
55. See Harvey Sacks, *Lectures on Conversation*, Vol. 1 (Oxford: Blackwell, 1995). Gilles Deleuze and Félix Guattari make a related point with respect to the work of linguist William Labov; see Gilles Deleuze and Félix Guattari, *A Thousand Plateaus: Capitalism and Schizophrenia*, trans. Brain Massumi (London: Bloomsbury, 1988), 92–110.
56. Kittler, *Optical Media*, 221. According to Kittler, television cameras were similarly developed as surveillance mechanisms for missile experiments at Peenemünde; see Kittler, "Unconditional Surrender," in *Materialities of Communication*, 331.
57. Langer, *Holocaust Testimonies*, 67.
58. Here one might be reminded of Benjamin's idea of "*das optische Unbewusste*" (literally "the optical unconscious," but translated as "unconscious optics"). According to Benjamin, "the camera introduces us to unconscious optics as does psychoanalysis to unconscious impulses"; see Benjamin, *Illuminations*,

237. In Langer's case, however, Benjamin's optical unconscious is realized twice over: not only does the camera allow observing what would otherwise remain unseen, the camera and the accompanying videotape apparatus provide a glimpse into the unconscious itself.
59. Maurice Blanchot, *The Writing of the Disaster*, trans. Ann Smock (Lincoln: University of Nebraska Press, 1995), 51.
60. Langer, *Holocaust Testimonies*, 69.
61. Felman and Laub, *Testimony*, 7.
62. Ibid., 47.
63. Ibid., 52.
64. Ibid., 47.
65. Ibid., 55.
66. Claude Lanzmann, "Seminar with Claude Lanzmann 11 April 1990," *Yale French Studies* 79, 1991, 93.
67. Felman and Laub, *Testimony*, 224.
68. Ibid., 42.
69. Ibid., 50.
70. Here are some instructive Google trivia: According to Google Books, "transmission of trauma" has a physiological parallel in medicine as early as the 1940s; and according to Google Ngram, the term itself is virtually nonexistent before the 1980s, whereas its occurrence in English books increases almost a thousandfold by the end of the 1990s.
71. One of the first to use the term is James Herzog, "World beyond Metaphor: Thoughts on the Transmission of Trauma," in *Generations of the Holocaust*, eds. Martin S. Bergmann and Milton E. Jucovy (New York: Columbia University Press, 1982), 103–119. A precursor to this idea can be found in the work of Nicholas Abraham and Maria Torok, especially in their discussion on "the phantom effect"; see Nicholas Abraham and Maria Torok, *The Shell and the Kernel: Renewals of Psychoanalysis*, trans. Nicholas T. Rand (Chicago: University of Chicago Press, 1994), 165–176.
72. Natan P. F. Kellermann, "Transmission of Holocaust Trauma—An Integrative View," *Psychiatry* 64(3), 2001, 260.
73. American Psychiatric Association, *Diagnostic and Statistical Manual of Mental Disorders: DSM-V* (Washington, DC: American Psychiatric Association, 2013), 271.
74. The stakes in broadening PTSD criteria are ever so high in the wake of 9/11—the culmination of the transmission of trauma, if there ever was one—which is, as I argue in Chapter 3, the backstory behind the proposed revisions.
75. Felman, *The Juridical Unconscious*, 7.
76. Ibid., 133. Italics are in the original. Here is how Felman explains the rationale behind the trial (italics hers):
The reason he decided to add living witnesses to documents, the Israeli prosecutor Gideon Hausner in his turn explained, was that the Nuremberg trials had *failed to transmit*, or to impress on human memory and "on the hearts of men," the knowledge and the shock of what had happened. The Eichmann trial sought, in contrast, not only to establish facts but to transmit (transmit truth as event and as the shock of an *encounter* with events, transmit history as an experience). (Ibid.)

77. Ibid., 154.
78. Ibid., 127. In her essay on Shoshana Felman, Cathy Caruth states that "Originally, Felman was confronted with the Eichmann trial in its real-time historical occurrence through the daily broadcasts of the proceedings over Israeli radio. But she was very young then, and not terribly impressed by it." Cathy Caruth, "Trauma, Justice and the Political Unconscious—Arendt and Felman's Journey to Jerusalem," in *The Claims of Literature: A Shoshana Felman Reader*, eds. Emily Sun, Eyal Peretz, and Ulrich Baer (New York: Fordham University Press, 2007), 416. It is tempting to interpret Felman's omission of the radio along the lines she herself interprets, in a most insightful essay, Arendt's omission of her dead friend, Walter Benjamin, when using the term "storyteller" in her Eichmann trial report. Felman designates Benjamin as "a hidden presence" (*The Juridical Unconscious*, 131) in Arendt's text—a phrase that might also apply to the status of radio in Felman's own text on the Eichmann trial.
79. Régis Debray, *Media Manifestos: On the Technological Transmission of Cultural Forms*, trans. Eric Rauth (London and New York: Verso, 1996), 45.
80. Ibid., 48.
81. Derrida, *Archive Fever*, 91.
82. On Kittler's view of war, see Geoffrey Winthrop-Young, "Drill and Distraction in the Yellow Submarine: On the Dominance of War in Friedrich Kittler's Media Theory," *Critical Inquiry* 28(4), 2002, 825–854; and Winthrop-Young, *Kittler and the Media*, 120–146.
83. See Ellis, *Seeing Things*, 1–38; Paul Frosh and Amit Pinchevski, "Why Media Witnessing? Why Now?" in *Media Witnessing: Testimony in the Age of Mass Communication*, eds. Paul Frosh and Amit Pinchevski (Basingstoke, UK: Palgrave Macmillan, 2009), 1–19.
84. See Giorgio Agamben, *Remnants of Auschwitz: The Witness and the Archive*, trans. Daniel Heller-Roazen (New York: Zone Books, 1999), chapter 4.
85. Michel Foucault, *The Archeology of Knowledge and the Discourse on Language*, trans. A. M. Sheridan Smith (New York: Vintage Books, 1972), 129.
86. Agamben, *Remnants of Auschwitz*, 146.
87. Agamben ultimately argues that contingency is the primary modal category: "Contingency is not one modality among others, alongside possibility, impossibility, and necessity: it is the actual giving of a possibility, the way in which a potentiality exists as such" (ibid.).
88. Kittler, *Gramophone, Film Typewriter*, 5.
89. Claude E. Shannon and Warren Weaver, *The Mathematical Theory of Communication* (Urbana: University of Illinois Press, 1963).
90. Winthrop-Young, *Kittler and the Media*, 142.
91. In a recent (and probably recorded) interview, Kittler gives this brief autobiographical note: "it is perhaps important that your readers know that I was born in East Germany in 1943 and that I still have some dim memories of the Second World War and afterwards when the Red Army was all around. And, of course, in East Germany during the 1940s and 1950s, it was very difficult to obtain a university education under that particular government.... That is why my parents left East Germany in 1958." Someone such as Laub or Felman would probably make much of the omission (or blunder) in the fact that East Germany

was not established until 1949. John Armitage, "From Discourse Networks to Cultural Mathematics: An Interview with Friedrich A. Kittler," *Theory, Culture, and Society* 23(7–8), 2006, 17.

CHAPTER 3

1. Charles Pugh and Michael R. Trimble, "Psychiatric Injury after Hillsborough," *The British Journal of Psychiatry* 163, 1993, 427–428.
2. See Hacking, *Rewriting the Soul*; Ruth Leys, *Trauma: A Genealogy*; Micale and Lerner, *Traumatic Pasts*; Young, *The Harmony of Illusions*.
3. See James Herzog, "World beyond Metaphor: Thoughts on the Transmission of Trauma," in *Generations of the Holocaust*, 103–119.
4. It seems that psychiatry is now catching up with continuing discussions in the humanities that have long speculated about television as a medium prone to catastrophe and trauma. See Mary Ann Doane, "Information, Crisis, Catastrophe," in *Logics of Television: Essays in Cultural Criticism*, ed. Patricia Mellencamp (Bloomington: Indiana University Press, 1990), 222–239; Avital Ronell, "Trauma TV: Twelve Steps beyond the Pleasure Principle," in *Finitude's Score: Essays for the End of the Millennium* (Lincoln: University of Nebraska Press, 1994), 305–328.
5. Robert Sklar, *Movie-Made America: A Cultural History of American Movies* (New York: Vintage Books, 1994), 122–140.
6. Cantril, Gaudet, and Herzog, *The Invasion from Mars*.
7. George Gerbner and Larry Gross, "Living with Television: The Violence Profile," *Journal of Communication* 26(2), 1976, 188.
8. For a small sample, see Craig A. Anderson et al., "The Influence of Media Violence on Youth," *Psychological Science in the Public Interest* 4(3), 2003, 81–110; Haejung Paik and George Comstock, "The Effects of Television Violence on Antisocial Behavior: A Meta-analysis," *Communication Research* 21(4), 1994, 516–546; Susan Villani, "Impact of Media on Children and Adolescents: A 10-Year Review of the Research," *Journal of the American Academy of Child & Adolescent Psychiatry* 40(4), 2001, 392–401.
9. Leys, *Trauma: A Genealogy*, 229–265. Her critique is directed at Bessel van der Kolk, *Post-Traumatic Stress Disorder: Psychological and Biological Sequelae* (Washington, DC: American Psychiatric Press, 1984); and Caruth, *Unclaimed Experience*.
10. Young, *The Harmony of Illusions*, 5.
11. Ian Hacking, "The Looping Effect of Human Kinds," in *Casual Cognition: A Multidisciplinary Debate*, eds. Dan Sperber, David Premack, and Ann J. Premack (Oxford: Oxford University Press, 1995), 368–370.
12. American Psychiatric Association, *Diagnostic and Statistical Manual of Mental Disorders: DSM-V*, 271.
13. Ian Hacking, "Lost in the Forest. Review of DSM-5: Diagnostic and Statistical Manual of Mental Disorders, Fifth Edition by the American Psychiatric Association," *London Review of Books* 35(15), 2013, 7–8.
14. American Psychiatric Association, *Diagnostic and Statistical Manual of Mental Disorders: DSM-III* (Washington, DC: American Psychiatric Association, 1980).

See, Wilbur J. Scott, "PTSD in DSM-III: A Case in the Politics of Diagnosis and Disease," *Social Problems* 37(3), 1990, 294–310.
15. Leys, *Trauma: A Genealogy*, 15.
16. American Psychiatric Association, *DSM-III*, 236.
17. American Psychiatric Association, *Diagnostic and Statistical Manual of Mental Disorders: DSM III-R* (Washington, DC: American Psychiatric Association, 1987), 247–248.
18. American Psychiatric Association, *Diagnostic and Statistical Manual of Mental Disorders: DSM-IV* (Washington, DC: American Psychiatric Association, 1994), 426.
19. Emily A. Holmes and Corin Bourne, "Inducing and Modulating Intrusive Emotional Memories: A Review of the Trauma Film Paradigm," *Acta Psychologica* 127(3), 2008, 553.
20. Richard S. Lazarus et al., "A Laboratory Study of Psychological Stress Produced by a Motion Picture Film," *Psychological Monographs: General and Applied* 76(34), 1962, 3.
21. Richard S. Lazarus, "A Laboratory Approach to the Dynamics of Psychological Stress," *Administrative Science Quarterly* 8(2), 1963, 192–213.
22. For more on the *Subincision* film, see Catarina Albano, *Memory, Forgetting and the Moving Image* (Basingstoke: Palgrave Macmillan, 2016), 86–94. Joshua Hirsch discusses the film in the context of filmic traumatic memory of the Holocaust; see in *Afterimage*, 16–17.
23. Lazarus et al., "Motion Picture Film," 27.
24. Lazarus, "Dynamics of Psychological Stress," 211–212.
25. Bassant Puri and Ian Treasaden, *Psychiatry: An Evidence-Based Text* (Boca Raton, FL: CRC Press, 2009), 175.
26. Lazarus, "Dynamics of Psychological Stress," 194.
27. Lazarus et al., "Motion Picture Film," 3.
28. Kittler, *Gramophone, Film, Typewriter*, 160.
29. Mardi J. Horowitz, "Psychic Trauma: Return of Images after a Stress Film," *Archives of General Psychiatry* 20(5), 1969, 552.
30. Mardi J. Horowitz, *Stress Response Syndromes* (New York: Aronson, 1976), 62–63.
31. Horowitz, "Psychic Trauma," 558.
32. Mardi J. Horowitz, *Image Formation and Cognition* (New York: Appleton-Century-Crofts, 1978), 199.
33. Ibid., 215.
34. See Elizabeth A. Brett and Robert Ostroff, "Imagery and Posttraumatic Stress Disorder: An Overview," *American Journal of Psychiatry* 142(4), 1985, 417–424.
35. Scott, "PTSD in DSM-III," 306; Young, *The Harmony of Illusions*, 110.
36. Mardi J. Horowitz, John E. Adams, and Burton B. Rutkin, "Visual Imagery on Brain Stimulation," *Archives of General Psychiatry* 19(4), 1969, 470.
37. Mardi J. Horowitz, "Flashbacks: Recurrent Intrusive Images after the Use of LSD," *American Journal of Psychiatry* 126(4), 1969, 565.
38. See Frankel, "The Concept of Flashback in Historical Perspective," 332. For an extensive study of the term in the context of film, see Turim, *Flashback in Film*.

39. Edgar Jones et al., "Flashbacks and Post-traumatic Stress Disorder: The Genesis of a 20th-Century Diagnosis," *The British Journal of Psychiatry* 182(2), 2003, 158–163.
40. Ibid., 162.
41. Ruth Leys, *From Guilt to Shame: Auschwitz and After* (Princeton, NJ: Princeton University Press, 2007), 15.
42. Ibid., 115–117.
43. Allan Young, "Posttraumatic Stress Disorder of the Virtual Kind: Trauma and Resilience in Post 9/11 America" in *Trauma and Memory: Reading, Healing, and Making Law*, eds. Austin Sarat, Nadav Davidovitch, and Michal Alberstein (Stanford, CA: Stanford University Press, 2007), 27–28. For accounts on the trauma of 9/11 from a critical cultural approach, see Meek, *Trauma and Media*, 171–195; Marc Redfield, "Virtual Trauma: The Idiom of 9/11," *Diacritics* 37(1), 2007, 55–80; Kaplan, *Trauma Culture*, 1–23.
44. Kathleen O. Nader et al., "A Preliminary Study of PTSD and Grief among the Children of Kuwait following the Gulf Crisis," *British Journal of Clinical Psychology* 32(4), 1993, 407.
45. Lenore C. Terr et al., "Children's Symptoms in the Wake of Challenger: A Field Study of Distant-Traumatic Effects and an Outline of Related Conditions," *American Journal of Psychiatry* 156(10), 1999, 1542.
46. Ibid., 1543.
47. Betty Pfefferbaum et al., "Clinical Needs Assessment of Middle and High School Students following the 1995 Oklahoma City Bombing," *American Journal of Psychiatry* 156(7), 1999, 1073.
48. Betty Pfefferbaum et al., "Posttraumatic Stress Two Years after the Oklahoma City Bombing in Youths Geographically Distant from the Explosion," *Psychiatry* 63(4), 2000, 367.
49. Betty Pfefferbaum et al., "Television Exposure in Children after a Terrorist Incident," *Psychiatry: Interpersonal and Biological Processes* 64(3), 2001, 209.
50. Mark A. Schuster et al., "A National Survey of Stress Reactions after the September 11, 2001, Terrorist Attacks," *New England Journal of Medicine* 345(20), 2001, 1507.
51. Ibid., 1511.
52. Jennifer Ahern et al., "Television Images and Psychological Symptoms after the September 11 Terrorist Attacks," *Psychiatry: Interpersonal and Biological Processes* 65(4), 2002, 299.
53. Jennifer Ahern et al., "Television Images and Probable Posttraumatic Stress Disorder after September 11: The Role of Background Characteristics, Event Exposures, and Perievent Panic," *The Journal of Nervous and Mental Disease* 192(3), 2004, 224.
54. Gerry Fairbrother et al., "Posttraumatic Stress Reactions in New York City Children after the September 11, 2001, Terrorist Attacks," *Ambulatory Pediatrics* 3(6), 2003, 304–311.
55. William E. Schlenger et al., "Psychological Reactions to Terrorist Attacks: Findings from the National Study of Americans' Reactions to September 11," *JAMA* 288(5), 2002, 581–588.

56. Ruth E. Propper et al., "Is Television Traumatic?: Dreams, Stress, and Media Exposure in the Aftermath of September 11, 2001," *Psychological Science* 18(4), 2007, 340.
57. Michael W. Otto et al., "Posttraumatic Stress Disorder Symptoms following Media Exposure to Tragic Events: Impact of 9/11 on Children at Risk for Anxiety Disorders," *Journal of Anxiety Disorders* 21(7), 2007, 888–902.
58. Betty Pfefferbaum et al., "Does Television Viewing Satisfy Criteria for Exposure in Posttraumatic Stress Disorder?," *Psychiatry: Interpersonal and Biological Processes* 65(4), 2002, 306–307.
59. Arieh Y. Shalev, "Further Lessons from 9/11: Does Stress Equal Trauma?," *Psychiatry: Interpersonal and Biological Processes* 67(2), 2004, 175.
60. Frank W. Putnam, "Televised Trauma and Viewer PTSD: Implications for Prevention," *Psychiatry: Interpersonal and Biological Processes* 65(4), 2002, 312.
61. Didier Fassin and Richard Rechtman, *The Empire of Trauma: An Inquiry into the Condition of Victimhood*, trans. Rachel Gomme (Princeton, NJ: Princeton University Press, 2009), 163–164.
62. Alison E. Holman et al., "Media's Role in Broadcasting Acute Stress following the Boston Marathon Bombings," *Proceedings of the National Academy of Sciences* 111(1), 2014, 93–98.
63. See American Psychology Association advice on "Building resilience to manage indirect exposure to terror" at http://www.apa.org/helpcenter/terror-exposure.aspx. See Dr. Phil's webpage on life strategies in a time of war at http://drphil.com/articles/article/1. Last accessed January 2018.
64. Carrie Rentschler, "From Danger to Trauma: Affective Labour and the Journalistic Discourse of Witnessing," in *Media Witnessing*, 151–181.
65. Anthony Feinstein, John Owenand, and Nancy Blair, "A Hazardous Profession: War, Journalists, and Psychopathology," *American Journal of Psychiatry* 159(9), 2002, 1570–1575.
66. Anke Weidmann and Jenny Papsdorf, "Witnessing Trauma in the Newsroom: Posttraumatic Symptoms in Television Journalists Exposed to Violent News Clips," *The Journal of Nervous and Mental Disease* 198(4), 2010, 269.
67. American Psychiatric Association, *DSM-V*, 273.
68. Elisabeth Bumiller, "Air Force Drone Operators Report High Levels of Stress," *New York Times*, December 18, 2011. http://www.nytimes.com/2011/12/19/world/asia/air-force-drone-operators-show-high-levels-of-stress.html; Scott Lindlaw, "UAV Operators Suffer War Stress," *Air Force Times*, August 7, 2008. http://archive.airforcetimes.com/article/20080807/NEWS/808070315/UAV-operators-suffer-war-stress; David Zucchino, "Stress of Combat Reaches Drone Crews," *The Los Angelas Times*, March 18, 2012. http://articles.latimes.com/2012/mar/18/nation/la-na-drone-stress-20120318.
69. Quoted in Peter Warren Singer, *Wired for War: The Robotics Revolution and Conflict in the Twenty-First Century* (New York: Penguin, 2009), 347.
70. Peter M. Asaro, "The Labor of Surveillance and Bureaucratized Killing: New Subjectivities of Military Drone Operators," *Social Semiotics* 23(2), 2013, 197.
71. Derek Gregory, "From a View to a Kill: Drones and Late Modern War," *Theory, Culture and Society* 28(7–8), 2011, 200–201.
72. Quoted in Zucchino, "Stress of Combat Reaches Drone Crews."

73. Caroline Holmqvist, "Undoing War: War Ontologies and the Materiality of Drone Warfare," *Millennium: Journal of International Studies* 41(3), 2013, 542.
74. Gregory, "From a View to a Kill," 197.
75. Rachel Martin, "Report: High Levels of 'Burnout' in U.S. Drone Pilots," *National Public Radio*, December 18, 2011. http://www.npr.org/2011/12/19/143926857/report-high-levels-of-burnout-in-u-s-drone-pilots; John Sifton, "A Brief History of Drones," *The Nation*, 27, 2012. http://www.thenation.com/article/166124/brief-history-drones.
76. Joseph A. Ouma, Wayne L. Chappelle, and Amber Salinas, "Facets of Occupational Burnout among US Air Force Active Duty and National Guard/Reserve MQ-1 Predator and MQ-9 Reaper Operators," Air Force Research Labs Technical Report. http://www.dtic.mil/cgi-bin/GetTRDoc?AD=ADA548103. Last accessed January 2018.
77. Quoted in Matthew Power, "Confessions of a Drone Warrior," *GQ Magazine*, October 22, 2013. http://www.gq.com/news-politics/big-issues/201311/drone-uav-pilot-assassination.
78. Heather Linebaugh, "I Worked on the US Drone Program," *The Guardian Online*, December 29, 2013. http://www.theguardian.com/commentisfree/2013/dec/29/drones-us-military.
79. Omer Fast, *5000 Feet Is the Best*, 2011. http://www.gbagency.fr/en/42/Omer-Fast/#!/5-000-Feet-is-the-Best/site_video_listes/88.
80. Zygmunt Bauman, "Effacing the Face: On the Social Management of Moral Proximity," *Theory, Culture and Society* 7(1), 1990, 31.
81. Stanley Milgram, *Obedience to Authority, an Experimental View* (London: Tavistock, 1974).
82. Rachel MacNair, *Perpetration-Induced Traumatic Stress: The Psychological Consequences of Killing* (Westport, CT: Praeger, 2002).
83. American Psychiatric Association, *DSM-V*, 278.
84. Young, *The Harmony of Illusions*, 80.
85. Dave Grossman, *On Killing: The Psychological Cost of Learning to Kill in War and Society* (New York: Back Bay Books, 1996), 31.
86. Ibid., 108–109.
87. Jean Baudrillard, *Selected Writings*, trans. Paul Patton (Stanford, CA: Stanford University Press, 2001), 243.
88. Scott Fitzsimmons and Karina Sangha, "Killing in High Definition: Combat Stress among Operators of Remotely Piloted Aircraft" (paper presented at the *Canadian Political Science Association*, 2010), http://www.cpsa-acsp.ca/papers-2013/fitzsimmons.pdf.
89. Fast, *5000 Feet*.
90. Shira Maguen and Brett Litz, "Moral Injury in Veterans of War," *PTSD Research Quarterly* 23(1), 2012, 1–6.
91. Jean-Jacques Rousseau, *Discourse on the Origin of Inequality*, trans. Donald A. Cress (Indianapolis/Cambridge: Hackett, 1992), 36–38.
92. Luc Boltanski, *Distant Suffering: Morality, Media and Politics*, trans. Graham Burchell (Cambridge: Cambridge University Press, 1999); Susan Sontag, *Regarding the Pain of Others* (New York: Penguin, 2004); Ellis, *Seeing Things*.

93. Jennifer Medina, "Warning: The Literary Canon Could Make Students Squirm," *The New York Times*, May 17, 2014. http://www.nytimes.com/2014/05/18/us/warning-the-literary-canon-could-make-students-squirm.html?_r=0.
94. Lilie Chouliaraki, *The Ironic Spectator: Solidarity in the Age of Post-humanitarianism* (Oxford: Polity, 2013), 3.
95. Leys, *Trauma: A Geneology*, 229–265.

CHAPTER 4

1. The wire recorder served various functions prior to and during World War II: it was used in submarine detection research, language classes, pilot training, and also to record battle sounds that would then be played back, amplified, so as to deceive the German military. See "Wire Recording," in *Encyclopedia of Radio*, Vol. 3, eds. Christopher H. Sterling and Michael S. Keit (New York and London: Fitzroy Dearborn, 2004), 2531–2534.
2. Boder, *I Did Not Interview the Dead*, xi. The principal source on Boder and his project is Alan Rosen's *The Wonder of Their Voices*.
3. Boder, *I Did Not Interview the Dead*, xviii.
4. Some 120 recorded interviews were digitized by the Voices of the Holocaust project at the Illinois Institute of Technology and can be accessed at http://voices.iit.edu.
5. Hartman, *The Longest Shadow*, 137.
6. "New Dimensions in Testimony," http://ict.usc.edu/prototypes/new-dimensions-in-testimony/. Last accessed January 2018.
7. Ron Artstein et al., "Time-Offset Interaction with a Holocaust Survivor," in *IUI '14: Proceedings of the 19th International Conference on Intelligent User Interfaces*, 163 http://dl.acm.org/citation.cfm?id=2557540&preflayout=tabs. Last accessed January 2018.
8. Lev Manovich, *The Language of New Media* (Cambridge, MA: The MIT Press, 2001), 194–205. Manovich mentions in passing the digitization of videotaped interviews with Holocaust survivors created by Steven Spielberg's project with the Shoah Foundation, which at the time had collected material that "would take one person forty years to watch." Manovich, *Language of New Media*, 198.
9. David Traum et al., "New Dimensions in Testimony: Digitally Preserving a Holocaust Survivor's Interactive Storytelling," in *Interactive Storytelling—8th International Conference on Interactive Digital Storytelling*, eds. Henrik Schoenau-Fog et al. (Heidelberg: Springer, 2015), 269–270.
10. Heather Maio et al., "New Dimensions in Testimony: How New Technologies—and Interview Questions—Will Contribute to the Dialogue between Students and Survivors," *PastForward*, Summer 2012, 24. https://sfi.usc.edu/sites/default/files/docfiles/PastForward_Summer2012_0.pdf.
11. Traum et al., "New Dimensions in Testimony," 270.
12. Stephen D. Smith, "Testimony & Technology: A Basic Truth about Technology: Its Power Depends on Its Purpose," *PastForward*, Summer 2012, 5.
13. These and other facts about the project can be seen online at: https://www.youtube.com/watch?v=xd7pcdceUQE.
14. Ron Artstein et al., "Time-Offset Interaction with a Holocaust Survivor," *Proceedings of the 19th International Conference on Intelligent User Interfaces*,

163–168. http://people.ict.usc.edu/~leuski/publications/papers/2014-iui-holocaust-survivor.pdf. Last accessed January 2018.

15. Ron Artstein et al., "How Many Utterances Are Needed to Support Time-Offset Interaction?," *Proceedings of the 28th International Florida Artificial Intelligence Research Society Conference*, 2015, 144. http://people.ict.usc.edu/~leuski/publications/papers/2015-ndt-wizard.pdf
16. Traum et al., "New Dimensions in Testimony," 275.
17. Artstein et al., "Time-Offset Interaction with a Holocaust Survivor," 166.
18. The technology itself is featured in Ari Folman's 2013 science fiction film *The Congress*. For more on the technology, see http://gl.ict.usc.edu/LightStages/.
19. http://www.today.com/series/are-we-there-yet/holograms-add-new-dimension-holocaust-survivors-story-t20511.
20. https://www.youtube.com/watch?v=AnF630tCiEk.
21. Margaret Talbot, "Pixel Perfect," *The New Yorker*, April 28, 2014, http://www.newyorker.com/magazine/2014/04/28/pixel-perfect-2.
22. Wendy Hui Kyong Chun, *Programmed Visions: Software and Memory* (Cambridge, MA: The MIT Press, 2011), xii.
23. Britta Lokting, "Meet the World's First 3-D Interactive Holocaust Survivor," *Forward*, November 24, 2015. http://forward.com/culture/324989/meet-the-worlds-first-3-d-interactive-holocaust-survivor/.
24. Hartman, *The Longest Shadow*, 144.
25. Wolfgang Ernst, "From History to Zeitkritik," *Theory, Culture and Society* 30(6), 2013, 141.
26. Ernst, *Chronopoetics*, 3–14. See also Anthony Enns's excellent Forward to the book, xiii–xxx.
27. Jacques Lacan, *Écrits*, trans. Bruce Fink (New York: Norton, 2002), 324.
28. Kittler, *Literature, Media, Information Systems*, 79.
29. Wolfgang Ernst, *Digital Memory and the Archive* (Minneapolis: Minnesota University Press, 2013), 191.
30. For more on the logic of algorithms, see Alexander R. Galloway, *Gaming: Essays on Algorithmic Culture* (Minneapolis: University of Minnesota Press, 2006); Ted Striphas, "What Is an Algorithm?" *Culture Digitally* http://culturedigitally.org/2012/02/what-is-an-algorithm/. Last accessed January 2018.
31. Florian Sprenger, *The Politics of Micro-decisions: Edward Snowden, Net Neutrality, and the Architectures of the Internet*, trans. Valentine A. Pakis (Lüneburg, Germany: Meson Press, 2015).
32. Ernst, *Digital Memory and the Archive*, 191.
33. Masahiro Mori, "The Uncanny Valley," *IEEE Robotics & Automation Magazine*, trans. Karl F. MacDorman and Norri Kageki 19(2), 2012, 98–100 http://macdorman.com/kfm/writings/pubs/Mori1970-2012UncannyValleyIEEER&A.pdf. See also Lydia H. Liu, *The Freudian Robot: Digital Media and the Future of the Unconscious* (Chicago: The University of Chicago Press, 2010), 224–230; Eleanor Sandry, *Robots and Communication* (Basingstoke, UK: Palgrave Macmillan, 2015), 22–23.
34. Sigmund Freud, *The Uncanny*, trans. David McLintock (London: Penguin Books, 2003), 148.

35. Freud relates the uncanny to unconscious compulsion to repeat, which he associates with the death drive: "anything that can remind us of this inner compulsion to repeat is perceived as uncanny," ibid., 145.
36. See Sconce, *Haunted Media*; Peters, *Speaking into the Air*, especially chapter 4.
37. Amanda Lagerkvist, "Existential Media: Toward a Theorization of Digital Throwness," *New Media and Society* 19(1), 2017, 104.
38. Thomas Trezise, *Witnessing Witnessing: On the Reception of Holocaust Survivor Testimony* (New York: Fordham University Press, 2013).
39. Traum et al. "New Dimensions in Testimony," 2.
40. Gumbrecht, *Production of Presence*, 15–20.
41. Quoted from USC Shoah Foundation clip: https://www.youtube.com/watch?v=xd7pcdceUQE. Last accessed January 2018.
42. Felman and Laub, *Testimony*, 60.
43. Ibid., 224, 241.
44. Felman, *The Juridical Unconscious*, 153, 165.
45. Mark Andrejevic, "'Framelessness,' or the Cultural Logic of Big Data" in *Mobile and Ubiquitous Media: Critical and International Perspectives*, eds. Michael S. Daubs and Vincent R. Manzerolle (New York: Peter Lang, 2018), 254.
46. Langer, *Holocaust Testimonies*, 16–17.
47. Trezise, *Witnessing Witnessing*, 223–225. Indeed even the founding father of the testimony enterprise is not exempt from such a predicament, as Trezise contends with respect to Dori Laub; see especially chapter 1: "Frames of Reception."
48. Alison Landsberg, "America, the Holocasut, and the Mass Culture of Memory: Toward a Radical Politics of Empathy" *New German Critique* 71, 1997, 63–86.
49. Marita Struken, *Tangled Memories: The Vietnam War, the AIDS Epidemic, and the Politics of Remembering* (Berkeley: University of California Press, 1997).
50. Marianne Hirsch, "The Generation of Postmemory," *Poetics Today* 29(1), 2008, 103–128.
51. José van Dyke, *Mediated Memories in the Digital Age* (Stanford, CA: Stanford University Press, 2007), 2–8.
52. N. Katherine Hayles, *How We Became Posthuman: Virtual Bodies in Cybernetics, Literature and Informatics* (Chicago: Chicago University Press, 1999), 196.
53. Ibid., 198.
54. Scott Lindenbaum, "Testimony on Location," *PastForward*, Summer, 2012, 10–11.
55. "Extreme Campaign for Holocaust Remembrance Day: "Tattooing" Adolescents' Arms," Walla News, February 27, 2013. http://news.walla.co.il/item/2620319.
56. Chouliaraki, *The Ironic Spectator*.
57. Todd Presner, "The Ethics of the Algorithm: Close and Distant Listening to the Shoah Foundation Visual History Archive" in *Probing the Ethics of Holocaust Culture*, eds. Claudio Fogu, Wulf Kansteiner, and Todd Presner (Cambridge, MA: Harvard University Press, 2016), 198. Presner also makes an interesting case for the digital humanities in relation to Holocaust testimonies; see in Anne Burdick et al. *Digital Humanities* (Cambridge, MA: The MIT Press, 2012), 37–39.
58. Presner, "The Ethics of the Algorithm," 200.
59. Paul Frosh, "The Mouse, the Screen, and the Holocaust Witness: Interface Aesthetics and Moral Response," *New Media and Society*, 20(1), 2018, 351–368.

60. On the notion of the punctum in photography, see Barthes, *Camera Lucida: Reflections of Photography*.
61. Felman and Laub, *Testimony*, 49.
62. David J. Bolter and Richard Grusin, *Remediation: Understanding New Media* (Cambridge, MA: The MIT Press, 2000), 45–47.
63. Friedlander, "Trauma, Memory and Transference," 254.
64. Emmanuel Levinas, *Otherwise than Being; Or, Beyond Essence*, trans. Alphonso Lingis (Pittsburgh: Duquesne University Press, 1998), 47.
65. See more in Amit Pinchevski, *By Way of Interruption: Levinas and the Ethics of Communication* (Pittsburgh: Duquesne University Press, 2005), especially chapter 2.
66. For more on the question of ethics and mediation, see Amit Pinchevski, "Levinas as Media Theorist: Toward an Ethics of Mediation," *Philosophy and Rhetoric* 47(1), 2014, 48–72.
67. Huyssen, "Present Pasts: Media, Politics, Amnesia," 30.
68. LaCapra, *Writing History, Writing Trauma*, 43–85.
69. Ibid., 141–153.
70. Derrida and Steigler, *Echographies of Television*, 117.
71. Barthes, *Camera Lucida,* 106.

CHAPTER 5

1. Hacking, *Rewriting the Soul*, especially chapters 3 and 13; Leys, *Trauma: A Genealogy*; Young, *The Harmony of Illusions*.
2. http://ict.usc.edu/prototypes/pts/.
3. Harun Farocki, "Serious Games," *NECSUS: European Journal of Media Studies*, 3(2), 2014, 94.
4. Pasi Väliaho, "Affectivity, Biopolitics, and the Virtual Reality of War," *Theory, Culture and Society* 29(2), 63–83.
5. Kathrin Friedrich, "Therapeutic Media: Treating PTSD with Virtual Reality Exposure Therapy," *MediaTropes* 6(1), 2016, 86–113.
6. Elizabeth Losh, *Virtualpolitik: An Electronic History of Government Media-Making in a Time of War, Scandal, Disaster, Miscommunication, and Mistakes* (Cambridge, MA: The MIT Press, 2009), 97–136.
7. Marissa Renee Brandt, "War, Trauma, and Technologies of the Self: The Making of Virtual Reality Exposure Therapy" (PhD diss., University of California, San Diego, 2013).
8. See Kittler, *Optical Media*, 174–178; Winthrop-Young, *Kittler and the Media*, 60.
9. Kittler, *Gramophone, Film, Typewriter*, 160.
10. This is a much-simplified description of Kittler's argument in the second part of *Discourse Networks*.
11. Giuliana Bruno, "Film, Aesthetics, Science: Hugo Münsterberg's Laboratory of Moving Images," *Grey Room* 36, Summer, 2009, 90.
12. A. A. Roback, *History of American Psychology* (New York: Library, 1952), 203.
13. Hugo Münsterberg, *Psychology General and Applied* (New York: D. Appleton, 1914), 354, 357.
14. Hugo Münsterberg, *The Film*, 40, 41.
15. Ibid., 46.

16. Kittler, *Literature, Media, Information Systems*, 100.
17. Kittler, *Optical Media*, 35.
18. Kittler, *Literature, Media, Information Systems*, 45, 140–141.
19. Myron W. Krueger, *Artificial Reality II* (Reading, MA: Addison-Wesley, 1991), 199, 198, 204, 84.
20. See Howard Rheingold, *Virtual Reality* (New York: Touchstone, 1991), 76–81; Tim Lenior, "All but War Is Simulation: The Military-Entertainment Complex," *Configurations* 8(3), 2000, 289–335; Brenda K. Wiederhold and Mark K. Wiederhold, *Virtual Reality Therapy for Anxiety Disorders: Advances in Evaluation and Treatment* (Washington DC: American Psychological Association, 2005), 11; Losh, *Virtualpolitik*, 100–108.
21. Mark B. N. Hansen, *Bodies in Code: Interfaces with Digital Media* (New York: Routledge, 2006), 1–22.
22. Michael Heim, *Virtual Realism* (Oxford: Oxford University Press, 1998), 7.
23. Rheingold, *Virtual Reality*, 55. See also Morton Heilig, "The Future of Cinema" in *Technology and Culture, The Film Reader*, ed. Andrew Utterson (London and New York: Routledge, 2005), 17–25.
24. Thomas P. Hughes, ed. *Funding a Revolution: Government Support for Computing Research* (Washington, DC: National Academy Press, 1999), 236.
25. Ivan E. Sutherland, "A Head-Mounted Three Dimensional Display," *Proceedings of the AFIPS Fall Joint Computer Conference* (Washington DC: Thompson Books, 1968), 757–764.
26. Jonathan Steuer, "Defining Virtual Reality: Dimensions Determining Telepresence," *Journal of Communication* 42(4), 1992, 73–93.
27. Jean Baudriallard, *Simulation and Simulacra*, trans. Sheila Faria Glaser (Ann Arbor: The University of Michigan Press, 1994), 1.
28. Max M. North, Sarah M. North, and Joseph R. Coble, *Virtual Reality Therapy: An Innovative Paradigm* (Colorado Springs, CO: IPI Press, 1996).
29. Much of the information related here on the early stages of VR therapy relies on Marissa Brandt's excellent ethnographic work in her PhD dissertation *War, Trauma, and Technologies of the Self: The Making of Virtual Reality Exposure Therapy*.
30. Max M. North Sarah M. North, and Joseph R. Coble, "Virtual Reality Therapy: An Effective Treatment for Psychological Disorders" in *Virtual Reality in Neuro-Psycho-Physiology: Cognitive, Clinical and Methodological Issues in Assessment and Rehabilitation*, ed. Giuseppe Riva (Amsterdam: IOS Press, 1997), 66.
31. North and his colleagues were not the only ones to recognize the potential of virtual therapy. Around the same time Ralph Lamson developed his own version of VR therapy for acrophobia, and others proposed the treatment for specific phobias such as social phobia and agoraphobia. See Ralph J. Lamson, *Virtual Therapy: Prevention and Treatment of Psychiatric Conditions by Immersion in Virtual Reality Environments* (Montreal, Canada: Polytechnic International Press, 1997); Wiederhold and Wiederhold, *Virtual Reality Therapy for Anxiety Disorders*, 14. According to Brandt, Lamson's contribution is under-recognized in the history of virtual therapy; see in *War, Trauma, and Technologies of the Self*, 188–194.
32. See B. O. Rothbaum et al., "Effectiveness of Computer-Generated (Virtual Reality) Graded Exposure in the Treatment of Acrophobia," *American Journal of Psychiatry* 152(4), 1995, 626–628.

33. Here, too, I summarize Brandt's account in *War, Trauma, and Technologies of the Self*, 171–195.
34. Rothbaum et al. "Virtual Reality Exposure Therapy for PTSD Vietnam Veterans: A Case Study," *Journal of Traumatic Stress* 12(2), 1999, 266.
35. Ibid., 264.
36. Nick Turse, *The Complex: How the Military Invades Our Everyday Lives* (New York: Metropolitan Books, 2008), 120. Fittingly, a new Xbox One ad depicts a gamer experiencing a PTSD flashback of a Roman battlefield after playing an immersive videogame: http://www.recode.net/2014/1/13/11622274/video-new-xbox-one-ad-promises-to-give-you-ancient-roman-ptsd. Last accessed January 2018.
37. Albert Rizzo et al., "Development of a VR Therapy Application for Iraq War Veterans with PTSD," *USC Institute for Creative Technologies, White Paper*, 2005, 1–6. Available at: http://ict.usc.edu/pubs/Development%20of%20a%20VR%20Therapy%20Application%20for%20Iraq%20War%20Veterans%20with%20PTSD.pdf.
38. Ibid., 3.
39. Corey Mean, *War Play: Video Games and the Future of Armed Conflict* (Boston and New York: Houghton, Mifflin, Harcourt, 2013), 161.
40. Statistics published by U.S. Department of Veterans Affairs: http://www.ptsd.va.gov/public/PTSD-overview/basics/how-common-is-ptsd.asp. Last accessed January 2018.
41. For more on this point, see Marcus Power, "Digitized Virtuosity: Video War Games and Post-9/11 Cyber-Deterence," *Security Dialogue* 38(2), 2007), 271–288; see also Losh, *Virtualpolitik*, especially chapter 3.
42. Andrejevic, "'Framelessness,' or the Cultural Logic of Big Data," 259.
43. "Bravemind: Virtual Reality Exposure Therapy," available at http://ict.usc.edu/prototypes/pts/.
44. Here is a selection of clips (last accessed January 2018): https://www.youtube.com/watch?v=Oe_3uL4JxEc; https://www.youtube.com/watch?v=M1orx97sFGc; https://www.youtube.com/watch?v=Z56PE8SpFR8; https://www.youtube.com/watch?v=nU-Cd7k9rY8; https://www.youtube.com/watch?v=4F4i6vEZ-H4&t=7s; https://www.youtube.com/watch?v=QCCWH_CNjM0; https://www.youtube.com/watch?v=6p7FM-mBsNk; https://www.youtube.com/watch?v=lNpmaKcf6PI.
45. See http://gracepointwellness.org/109-post-traumatic-stress-disorder/article/28895-an-interview-with-edna-foa-phd-on-the-nature-and-treatment-of-post-traumatic-stress-disorder-ptsd. Last accessed January 2018.
46. Bessel A. van der Kolk, *The Body Keeps the Score: Brain, Mind and Body in the Healing of Trauma* (New York: Penguin Books, 2014), 176.
47. See also in Bessel A. van der Kolk, "The Body Keeps the Score: Memory and the Evolving Psychobiology of Posttraumatic Stress," *Harvard Review of Psychiatry* 1(5), 1994, 253–265.
48. van der Kolk, *The Body Keeps the Score*, 180.
49. Ibid., 47, 207.
50. Edna B. Foa and Michael J. Kozak, "Emotional Processing of Fear: Exposure to Corrective Information," *Psychological Bulletin* 99(1), 1986, 21.

51. Ibid., 22.
52. A good place to start such an investigation is Jean Pierre Dupuy, *The Mechanization of the Mind: On the Origins of Cognitive Science*, trans. M. B. DeBevoise (Princeton and Oxford: Princeton University Press, 2000).
53. Foa and Kozak, "Emotional Processing of Fear," 25, 26.
54. Edna B. Foa and Barbara Olasov Rothbaum, *Treating the Trauma of Rape: Cognitive-Behavioral Therapy for PTSD* (New York: The Guilford Press, 1998), 99–109.
55. Edna B. Foa and Reid Wilson, *Stop Obsessing: How to Overcome Your Obsessions and Compulsions* (New York: Bantam Books, 2001), 90–94.
56. Rothbaum et al., "Virtual Reality Exposure Therapy for PTSD Vietnam Veterans," 264.
57. van der Kolk, *The Body Keeps the Score*, 221.
58. Maryrose Gerardi et al., "Virtual Reality Exposure Therapy Using a Virtual Iraq: Case Report," *Journal of Traumatic Stress* 21(2), 2009, 211.
59. Manovich, *The Language of New Media*, 229–232.
60. Bernard Stiegler, "Memory" in *Critical Terms for Media Studies*, eds. W. J. T. Mitchell and Mark B. N. Hansen (Chicago: Chicago University Press, 2010), 71.
61. Ibid.
62. For discussion on Freud's implicit media logic, see Derrida, *The Postcard*, 259–386; and "Freud and the Scene of Writing" in *Writing and Difference*, trans. Alan Bass (Chicago: The University of Chicago Press, 1978), 196–231. See also Thomas Elsaesser's excellent discussion in "Freud as a Media Theorist."
63. Benjamin, *Illuminations*, 194. See also Meek, *Trauma and Media*, 91–96.
64. Stiegler's argument on the matter is fully developed in *Taking Care of Youth and the Generations*, trans. Stephen Barker (Stanford, CA: Stanford University Press, 2010).
65. STRIVE: Stress Resilience in Virtual Environments: http://ict.usc.edu/wp-content/uploads/overviews/STRIVE_Overview.pdf. Last accessed January 2018.
66. https://www.youtube.com/watch?v=bIj26r4VPaA&t=10s. Last accessed January 2018.
67. And the same could be said were Alex to undergo psychoanalysis, which is a form of literal grammatization in Stiegler's terms.
68. Brandt, *War, Trauma, and Technologies of the Self*, chapter 4.
69. Ari Hollander, "Playing Games with Painful Memories: Designing VR Exposure Therapy Simulations for PTSD" (paper presented at the Game Developers Conference, San Jose, California, March 2006), 5, 6.
70. Leys, *Trauma: A Genealogy*, 1–17.
71. N. Katherine Hayles, "Traumas of Code," *Critical Inquiry* 33(1), 2005, 141.
72. Brandt, *War, Trauma, and Technologies of the Self*, 270.
73. Simon Critchley, "The Original Traumatism: Levinas and Psychoanalysis" in *Questioning Ethics: Contemporary Debates in Philosophy*, eds. Richard Kerany and Mark Dooly (London and New York: Routledge, 1999), 220–242.
74. Francine Shapiro, *Eye Movement Desensitization and Reprocessing: Basic Principles, Protocols, and Procedures* (New York: The Guilford Press, 2001).
75. http://www.pbs.org/wgbh/pages/frontline/digitalnation/virtual-worlds/health-healing/a-new-therapy-for-a-new-generation.html?play. Last accessed January 2018.

76. Väliaho, "Affectivity, Biopolitics, and the Virtual Reality of War," 76.
77. Judith Butler, *Precarious Life: The Powers of Mourning and Violence* (London and New York: Verso, 2004), 130.
78. Benjamin, *Illuminations*, 84.

CONCLUSION

1. Shannon and Weaver, *The Mathematical Model of Communication*.
2. Michelle R. Ancharoff, James F. Munroe, and Lisa Fisher, "The Legacy of Combat Trauma: Clinical Implications of Intergenerational Transmission," in *International Handbook of Multigenerational Legacies of Trauma*, ed. Yael Danieli (New York: Plenum Press, 1998), 265.
3. I owe this observation to Katie Trumpener.
4. Sybille Krämer, *Medium, Messenger, Transmission: An Approach to Media Philosophy*, trans. Anthony Enns (Amsterdam: Amsterdam University Press, 2015), 31.
5. Ibid., 185.
6. Alexander R. Galloway, "Love of the Middle" in *Excommunications: Three Inquiries in Media and Mediations*, by Alexander R. Galloway, Eugene Thacker, and McKenzie Wark (Chicago: The University of Chicago Press, 2014), 43.
7. Frantz Kafka, *The Metamorphosis, In the Penal Colony, and Other Stories*, trans. Joachim Neugrochel (New York: Simon & Schuster, 2000), 205.
8. Steven Connor, "Mortification," in *Thinking through the Skin*, eds. Sarah Ahmed and Jackie Stacey (London: Routledge, 2001), 40.
9. See Stanley Corngold and Benno Wagner, *Franz Kafka: The Ghosts in the Machine* (Evanston, IL: Northwestern University Press, 2011), 75–91. According to Corngold and Wagner, Kafka may have heard about the Hollerith machine when attending a course in 1905 given by the leading Austrian statistician, Heinrich Rauchberg.
10. Kittler, *Discourse Networks*, 316.
11. Barthes, *Camera Lucida*, 51.
12. For more on this point, see Geoffrey Winthrop-Young, "Krautrock, Heidegger, Bogeyman: Kittler in the Anglosphere," *Thesis Eleven* 107(1), 2011, 11–13.

INDEX

Figures are indicated by an italic *f,* following the page number.

9/11, televised images, 6, 19, 68, 75–78, 140, 142
5000 Feet is the Best (Fast), 81–82

absence
  definition, 110
  with presence, videotestimony, 111
  presencing, 100–104
  testimony, 111
absence-as-presence, 111
access, 88
acrophobia, VR therapy for, 171n31
Adam Resurrected (Kaniuk), 33
after-death communication, 100
Agamben, Giorgio, 62, 161n87
agenda, 18
Alexander, Jeffrey, 27, 37
algorithmic-holographic testimony, 91
algorithmic processing, 106
analogue, 71–72
analogy, 71
anamnesis, 131
Andrejevic, Mark, 102, 123
Anne Frank diary, Holocaust memory, 154n57
antimimetic strand, trauma theory, 74, 135
antispecular aesthetic, 158n31
Appadurai, Arjun, 157n16
archeology, Foucault on, 62

archive, 45–48, 46*f*, 62, 157nn16, 18
Arendt, Hannah, 23, 26, 60
Artaud, Antonin, 29, 30
Artificial Reality II (Krueger), 117–118
Artzi, Shlomo, 32
Aufschreibesystem, 14–15, 43
auratic effect, digitalization, 109
availability, 88

Bachelard, Gaston, 29
Barthes, Roland, 10, 30, 107, 110, 111, 144
Baudrillard, Jean, 83, 119
Bauman, Zygmunt, 82
bearing witness, 140
  Eichmann trial, 40
  media, 21, 40
  narrative failure, 62
  New Dimensions in Testimony, 91–92, 97–98, 101, 104, 109, 111
  processing, 53
  radio broadcast, live, 42
  traumatic memory, 88–89
  video archive, 91
  videotestimony, 20, 47, 48–49, 50, 52, 63
Beckett, Samuel, 49
Beilin, Yossi, 33
Ben-Gurion, David, 23, 35

Benjamin, Walter, 12–13, 14, 109, 131, 137–138, 159–160n58
Beyond the Pleasure Principle (Freud), 4
bias, in metaphors, 7
Blanchot, Maurice, 57
Blumenberg, Hans, 7
Boder, David, 87–88, 88f, 156n7, 167n1
Boltanski, Luc, 84
Boston marathon bombing, 78
Brandt, Marisa, 114, 134, 135
BRAVEMIND, 121–124, 122f, 137
Bryant, Brandon, 81
Butler, Judith, 137

Camras, Marvin, 87
Carpenter, Edmund, 29
Caruth, Cathy, 4–5, 149n22, 161n78
Challenger space shuttle explosion, televised, 76
Charcot, Jean-Martin, 52, 66
Chouliaraki, Lilie, 85, 106
Chun, Wendy, 95
cinematic traumatography, 75
cinematography
  cut-back (Münsterberg), 116
  psychotechnology, 114
Closed Circuit TV (CCTV), 56
code, trauma and, 135, 140
cognitive technologies, 132
cognitivization, 131
collective memory, Holocaust survivors, 29–30, 152–153n33
collective silence, 31–32
communication
  after-death, 100
  dwindling of, due to mechanized warfare, 13
  materialities, 45
  vs. transmission, 60–61
  trauma, difficulties, 7–8
conditioning, pre-trauma, 132–133, 137
confession, law and psychoanalysis, 25–26
Connor, Steven, 144
counter-irritants, 13
cut-back (Münsterberg), 116

database, 130
  as materialized paradigm, 91
  as operational logic, 90–91, 150
Dayan, Daniel, 40
Debevec, Paul, 93, 101, 102–103
Debray, Régis, 60–61
deep memory, 54–55, 57, 108, 159n52
Delbo, Charlotte, 54
de-objectifying vision, 158n31
Derrida, Jacques, 40, 45, 47, 61, 110, 157n18
Diagnostic and Statistical Manual of Mental Disorders 5 (DSM-5), 69–71
  drone stress, 82
  trauma through media, 79–80, 140
Diaspora, old Jew of, 31–32
digital future of traumatic past
  virtual testimony, 87–111, 141 (*see also* virtual testimony, digital future of traumatic past)
  virtual therapy, 112–138 (*see also* VR therapy)
digital humanities, 169n57
digital PTSD, 129–135
Dinur, Yehiel (Ka-tzetnik), 26–27, 35, 151n15
discourse networks, 14–15, 43
  1900, 114
  1900 *vs.* 2000, 18
  2000, 91, 111
disembodied speech
  Eichmann trial radio broadcasts, 28–31
  speechless body to, 31–37
distant trauma, 65, 68, 75–80
drone stress, 68, 80–84
DSM-V, 69–71
  drone stress, 82
  trauma through media, 79–80, 140

Edison, Thomas, 43–44
Eichmann trial, 18, 22–42, 140. *See also* radiocasting trauma, Eichmann trial
  collective silence before, 31
  daily diary, 24, 24f, 41
  intergenerational drama, 35–36

Ka-tzetnik's testimony, 26–27, 35, 36–37, 60, 102, 151n15
living witnesses, rationale, 60, 160n76
as mediation, 39–40
radiocast on public perception, 24–25
scholarly attention, recent, 22–23
as transmission of trauma, 59
trauma, 25–28
trauma conflation, 40, 155n72
Eigenzeit, 96
Ellis, John, 84
Elsaesser, Thomas, 9, 149n29, 156n3
Embodiment, 105
emotional brain, 125
emotional processing, 127
epistemological architectonics, 115, 115f
Erichsen, John Eric, 6
Ernst, Wolfgang, 96, 98
ethics, mediation and, 107, 170n66
ethics of kinaesthetics, 107
evocative media, 127
exposure, 78
exposure media, VR therapy, 124–129
exposure therapy, 113, 120, 124–129
extra-subjective referencing, 8–9
Eye Movement Desensitization and Reprocessing (EMDR), 136

Farocki, Harun, 113
Fassin, Didier, 78
Fast, Omer, 81–82
fear structure, 117, 127
feedback loops, psychotechnology, 114
Felman, Shoshana, 48
  breaking the frame, 102–103
  Caruth on, 161n78
  class crisis, after Yale testimony viewing, 107, 142
  crises of testimony, 48
  crisis of narrative, 17
  psychoanalytic approach, 37
  on *Shoah,* 102
  Testimony: Crises of Witnessing in Literature, Psychoanalysis and History, 57–58
  transmission, 57–61

trauma and testimony, 44, 89
trial and trauma, 25–27
film. *See also* videography
  trauma, 3, 17, 71–75
flashbacks, 74
  McLuhan, 16–17
  media concepts and logic, 14
  as media mediating trauma, 11
  term, history of, 16–17
  traumatic memory, 126
  traumatic symptoms and visual media, 3
  traumatographical metaphors, 16
  Wilkomirski's, 7
flashbulb memory, 42
Foa, Edna, 124, 126–128
Forever Yesterday (Vlock), 47
Fortunoff Video Archive for Holocaust Testimonies, Yale, 19, 45–46, 46f, 53, 89, 140
Foucault, Michel, 62
Fragments: Memories of a Wartime Childhood (Wilkomirski), 1
framelessness, 102–103, 123
Frankel, Fred, 74
Freud, Sigmund, 4, 43–44, 148n14
  Beyond the Pleasure Principle, 4
  mystic writing pad, 4, 132
  protective shield, 4, 148n14
  psychoanalysis, speech–vision separation, 50
  superego, 25, 154n63
  Totem and Taboo, 71
  traumatic neurosis, 66
  uncanny, 169n35
  Unheimlich, 100
Friedlander, Saul, 55, 108
Friedrich, Kathrin, 113
Frosh, Paul, 106
Full Spectrum Command, 121
Full Spectrum Warrior, 121, 172n36
future proof testimony, 92–96, 94f

Galloway, Alexander, 143
generic realism, 134
genotex, 37
Gouri, Haim, 22

grammatization
  analog, 131, 132, 133
  digital, 131, 132, 135
  literal, 131, 132, 173n67
  memory, 131, 173n67
Grosjean, Bruno, 1
Grossman, David, 32–33
Grossman, Dave, 82–83
gross stress reaction, 66
Gulf War conflict, 83
Gumbrecht, Hans Ulrich, 3, 45, 101, 103, 140
Gutter, Pinchas, 92–93, 94f, 97

habituation instruments, media as, 12
Hacking, Ian, 6, 8, 17, 67, 112
Halbwachs, Maurice, 31, 49
Hansen, Mark, 118
Hartman, Geoffrey, 45–47, 49, 50, 89, 95
Hausner, Gideon, 26, 35–36, 39–40, 160n76
Hayles, N. Katharine, 105, 135
Heilig, Morton, 118
Heim, Michael, 118
Hermes, 143
Hirsch, Joshua, 10–11
Hirsch, Marianne, 10, 104
Hodges, Larry, 120–121
Hollerith Tabulating Machine, 144, 174n9
Holocaust, 45
Holocaust memory, 1, 10
  Anne Frank diary, 154n57
  Eichmann trial, 34
  media construction, 38, 154n57
Holocaust survivors
  collective memory, 29–30, 152–153n33
  collective silence, 31–32
  at Eichmann trial, 36
  Eichmann trial radiocast on, 25
  Ka-tzetnik's testimony, 26–27, 35, 36–37, 60, 102, 151n15
  legitimization and validation, 26, 28, 34–35
  mental illness, 32–34
  narratives, 53
  publicly bearing witness, 25
  Holocaust Survivors Film Project, Yale, 45, 89, 156n8
Holocaust Testimonies (Langer), 53–54
Holocaust testimony. *See also* Eichmann trial; radiocasting trauma, Eichmann trial; *specific topics*
  as physical effects of the Real, 17
  trauma theory, 44
holographic testimony. *See* New Dimensions in Testimony (NDT)
Honneth, Axel, 40
Horowitz, Mardi, 17, 73–74
Huyssen, Andreas, 9, 109
hyperreal, 119
hypomnemata, 132
hypomnesis, 131, 132

I Did Not Interview the Dead (Boder), 87–88, 88f
Imaginary, 15–16, 29
immediacy, 142–143
  mediated, 145
immersion, immediacy and, 142–143
immersive fill, 134
incorporating practices, 105
indexical power, 7
  of media to historical Real, 9–10
  indexing the non-indexical, 108–109
Institute for Creative Technologies
  New Dimensions in Testimony, 93–95, 94f (*see also* New Dimensions in Testimony (NDT))
  Virtual Reality Exposure Therapy, 113 (*see also* VR therapy)
"In the Penal Colony" (Kafka), 143–144, 174n9
Invasion from Mars, The, 66
inverted remediation, 61–62
irony, paradigm of (Chouliaraki), 85
Israeli, native, 31

James, William, 114
Janet, Pierre, 7, 9, 125

Kafka, Franz, 143–144, 174n9
Kaniuk, Yoram, 33
Kaplan, Ann, 3, 4, 147n6
Katz, Elihu, 40
Ka-tzetnik (Yehiel Dinur), 26–27, 35, 36–37, 60, 102, 151n15
Keren, Nili, 32
kinaesthetics, ethics of, 107
Kittler, Friedrich
  Aufschreibesystem, 14–15, 43
  autobiography, 161–162n91
  on Foucault's archeology, 62
  on Freud and psychoanalysis, 50
  Lacan's Symbolic, Imaginary, and Real, 8, 15–16, 17, 18
  media and psychoanalysis, 43–44, 61–66
  media and trauma, 14–16, 63–64
  media infiltrating mind, 12, 18
  media specters, 39
  psychotechnology, 20, 21, 73, 114, 116
  Real, 15–17, 18, 29, 97, 117
  recording thresholds, 53
  selective *vs.* nonselective inscription, 126
  technology and physiology, 144
  testimony and trauma, as inverted remediation, 61–62
  on war, 21
Kol Yisrael radio station, 23–24, 24*f*
Kozak, Michael, 126–128
Krämer, Sybille, 142
Krapp's Last Tape (Beckett), 49
Kristeva, Julia, 30–31, 37
Krueger, Myron, 117–118

Lacan, Jacques, 8, 15–16, 17, 29, 97
LaCapra, Dominick, 110
Lagerkvist, Amanda, 100
Lamson, Ralph, 171n31
Landsberg, Alison, 10, 104
Langer, Lawrence, 44, 53–56, 95, 103
Lanier, Jaron, 119
Lanzmann, Claude, 58, 60, 102
Lappin, Elena, 2
latency, 14

latent content, 109
Laub, Dori, 44
  on Auschwitz uprising, women recounting, 51
  on Boder's recordings, 156n7
  breaking the frame, 102–103
  crises of testimony, 62
  Holocaust videotaping idea, 45
  Trezise controversy, 158n34
  video camera as listener, 48–49
  videotaping in therapy, 51–53
  Yale archive for Holocaust testimonies, 48–49, 89
law
  confession and testimony, 25–26
  vs. psychoanalysis, 26
Lazarus, Richard, 71–72
Levinas, Emmanuel, 109, 136, 158n31
Leys, Ruth, 8, 9, 16, 67, 70, 74, 86, 112, 135
Light Stage technology, 93–95, 94*f*
limbic system therapy, 126–127
Lindenbaum, Scott, 105
Linebaugh, Heather, 81
literal impact, trauma, 8–9, 16
looping effects, 67
Losh, Elisabeth, 113
loss, 110

male hysteria, 66
Manovich, Lev, 90, 130, 167n8.
  See also New Dimensions in Testimony (NDT)
Maus (Spiegelman), 55, 159nn51–52
McLuhan, Marshall, 12, 13–14, 16–17, 29
media
  as counter-irritants, 13
  definition, 3
  as extension of man, 13
  as habituation instruments, 12
  historical experience depictions, 9
  inside mind, 12
  latency, 14
  memory, new forms, 9
  in memory transformation, 149n29
  numbness from, 13–14

media (*cont.*)
  sensory overload, 12
  on social life of trauma, 140
  trauma, war, and, 61–66
  trauma through, DSM-V, 80, 140
  traumatic representational operation, 11
mediation. *See also specific topics*
  Eichmann trial as, 39–40
  ethics, 107, 170n66
  of failed mediation, 1–21 (*see also specific topics*)
  representation to, 3–6
  of trauma, radio as, 39–40
  trauma as outside gone inside without, 4–5
Meek, Allen, 9–10
Memoirs of My Nervous Illness (Schreber), 15
memory, 4
  aids, 132
  anamnesis, 131
  common, 54, 159n52
  deep, 54–55, 57, 108, 159n52
  external-technical *vs.* internal-living, 131
  extra-subjective referencing, 8–9
  flashback (*see* flashbacks)
  flashbulb, 42
  grammatization, 131, 132, 133, 135, 173n67
  hypomnesis, 131, 132
  narrative and non-narrative, 7, 9
  pathology, PTSD, 112
  personal cultural, 104
  postmemory, 104, 159n52
  prosthetic, 10–11
  recovery, recording, 49
  somatic, 125
  therapy of, 112 (*see also* VR therapy)
  traumatic (*see* traumatic memory)
mental wounds, media predicating, 4
message over medium, 13–14
metaphor
  bias in, 7
  as precursor to thought, 7
  technological, 7
  traumatographical, 16
Milgram, Stanley, 82
mimetic model, trauma, 8–9
mimetic streak, trauma theory, 135
mind, reception and memory functions, 4
morality
  from afar, 84–86
  basis, vulnerability, 145
Mori, Masahiro, 99–100, 99f, 134
Münsterberg, Hugo, 16, 20, 73, 114–116, 124
My Michael (Oz), 33
mystic writing pad, 4, 132

narrative memory, 7, 9
New Dimensions in Testimony (NDT), 89–111
  bearing witness, 91–92, 97–98, 101, 104, 109, 111
  database, as materialized paradigm, 91
  database, as operational logic, 90–91, 150
  discourse network (2000), 91, 111
  future proof testimony, 92–96, 94f
  human-computer interface, 93
  Institute for Creative Technologies, 93–95, 94f
  Light Stage technology, 93, 94f
  media temporality, 96–100, 98f, 99f
  novel features, 90
  origins and overview, 89–90
  presencing absence, 100–104
  remediating traumatic memory, 107–111
  syntagm and paradigm, 90
  system architecture, 97, 98f
  time-offset interaction, 92, 101
  from witness to witnessee, 104–107
newsroom workers, PTSD, 79
9/11, televised images, 6, 19, 68, 75–78, 140, 142
non-indexical
  content, 106, 107–108
  indexing, 108–109

[180] Index

non-narrative memory, 7, 9
North, Max, 119–120, 171n31
numbness, 13–14

Oklahoma City bombing, televised images, 76
Ophüls, Marcel, 45
Oppenheim, Herman, 66
Oz, Amos, 33

paradigm, syntagm and, 90, 97, 130–131
Payne Fund Studies (1930s), 66
Peirce, Charles Sanders, 7
perpetration-induced traumatic stress (PITS), 82–83
Peters, John Durham, 3
Pfefferbaum, Betty, 76, 78
phenotext, 37
phonography, psychotechnology, 114
photographs, as postmemory, 10
Photoplay: A Psychological Study, The (Münsterberg), 115–116
pity, paradigm of (Chouliaraki), 85
postmemory, 10, 104, 159n52
presencing absence, 100–104
preservation, 87
Presner, Todd, 106, 107–108, 169n57
pre-trauma conditioning, 132–133, 137
processing
  bearing witness, 53
  videography and testimony, 53–57, 159nn46, 52, 55, 56
Prolonged Exposure (PE) therapy, 124
prosthetic memory, 10–11
protective shield
  Benjamin, 12
  Freud, 4, 148n14
psychoanalysis
  confession and testimony, 25–26
  Felman, 37
  vs. law, 25–26
  media, 43–44, 156nn3–4
  speech–vision separation, 50
psychotechnology, 20, 73, 115, 115f, 127
  cinematography, 114
  feedback loops, 114
  phonography, 114
  PTSD as, 21
  VR therapy, 114–117
PTSD, 6, 66
  9/11 televised images, 6, 19, 68, 75–78, 140, 142
  Boston marathon bombing, 78
  as contemporary pathology, 67
  criteria, broadening, 59, 160n74
  digital, 129–135
  drone stress, 68, 80–84
  DSM, 69–71, 79–80
  exposure effects, 78
  flashbacks, 74
  as historically specific pathology, 8
  limbic system therapy, 126–127
  media exposure, 75
  mediated images, 67 (*see also* screen trauma)
  memory pathology, 112
  newsroom workers, 79
  perpetration-induced traumatic stress, 82–83
  as psychotechnology, 21
  theory, current, 67
  trigger warnings, 85
  virtual kind, 75
  VR therapy, 113, 129, 141 (*see also* VR therapy)
  VR therapy, Virtual Iraq (BRAVEMIND), 113, 121–124, 122f, 130, 137
  VR therapy, Virtual Vietnam, 120–121
  war correspondents, 79
punctum, 10, 107, 144, 170n60

radio, 140
  body–voice separation, 28–31
  double return of repressed, 18
  embodiment and disembodiment, 18
  Hitler and Nazi use, 29
  Real, 29–30, 152–153n33
  social space, paradoxes, 28
  sound, power, 29, 151n29
  as trauma mediation, 39–40 (*see also* radiocasting trauma, Eichmann trial)

Index [181]

radiocasting trauma, Eichmann trial, 18, 22–42, 60
  on Holocaust survivors, 25
  live broadcasts, 22–23, 24f, 35, 41
  live broadcasts, on Israelis, 23–24
  media and publicity strategy, 23
  on public perception, 24–25
  radio, body, voice, 28–31
  radiophonic Real, 37–42, 41f
  speechless body to disembodied speech, 31–37
  trial and trauma, 25–28
  trial diary, daily Israeli, 24, 24f, 41
radiophonic Real, 37–42, 41f
railway spine, 66
Real, 15–16, 17, 29, 97, 140
  audiovisual effects, 57
  Holocaust testimony, 17
  meaning, 117
  radio(phonic), 29–30, 37–42, 41f, 152–153n33
  traumatic, instantiation of mediation of, 18
reception, 4
Rechtman, Richard, 78
recognition, 40
recording
  Boder's wire recorder, 87–88, 88f, 156n7, 167n1
  memory recovery, 49
  stories, 87
  tape, 87
  thresholds, 53
  videographic testimony, 48–53
referential literality, 8, 149n22
remediation, testimony as inverted, 61–62
  traumatic memory, 107–111
remote-controlled warfare, 80
  drone stress, 68, 80–84
Rentschler, Carrie, 79
representation. *See also specific types*
  to mediation, 3–6
  traumatic, 11
Rheingold, Howard, 119
Rizzo, Albert, 113, 121, 123, 129–130, 132, 136

Róheim, Géza, 71, 163n22
Rothbaum, Barbara Olasov, 120–121, 128, 129
Rousseau, Jean Jacques, 84
Rudof, Joanne, 95

Sabra, 31
Sacks, Harvey, 56
Said, 109
Saying, 109
Schreber, Daniel Paul, 15
screen trauma, 65–86
  distant trauma, 65, 68, 75–80
  drone stress, 68, 80–84
  DSM, 69–71, 79–80
  Hillsborough Stadium disaster (England), 65
  history, 68
  key moments, 68
  live broadcast, traumatic, 65
  morality from afar, 84–86
  technologically mediated trauma, psychiatric recognition, 66–67
  television, trauma and violence, 66
  trauma film paradigm, 17, 68, 71–75
  trauma terminology, history, 66
  trauma through media, 66, 162n4
  vicarious traumatization, 65
See Under: Love (Grossman), 32–33
Sensorama Simulator, 118–119
sensory overload, 12
September 11, 2001, televised images, 6, 19, 68, 75–78, 140, 142
Serious Games (Farocki), 113
Shandler, Jeffrey, 38
Shannon, Claude, 62, 139
shell shock, 6, 66. *See also* PTSD
Shoah (Lanzmann), 58, 60, 102
shock, from media, 12
  deep effects, 12–13
Siegert, Bernhard, 11
silence, collective, 31–32
smart bomb, 83
Smith, Stephen, 92
social space
  experience of, 30
  radio, Eichmann trial, 28, 30

sociolinguistics, 56
somatic memory, 125
spectral logic, media technologies, 39
speech, disembodied
   Eichmann trial radio broadcasts, 28–31
   speechless body to, 31–37
Spiegelman, Art, 55
Stiegler, Bernard, 131–133, 173n67
Stop Obsessing (Foa), 128
stories. *See also* testimony; videography, testimony
   recording and preserving, 87
   stressful (trauma) film, 17, 68, 71–75
STRIVE, 132, 137
Sturken, Marita, 104
Subincision Rites of the Arunta (Róheim), 71, 73, 163n22
superego, 25, 154n63
Sutherland, Ivan, 119
"Sword of Damocles," 119
Symbolic, 15–16, 29, 108
symbolic channel, collapse, 17
syntagm, paradigm and, 90, 97, 130–131

talk therapy, 128
   for traumatic memory, failure, 126
   VR therapy *vs.*, 123, 135–138
tape recording, 87
technology. *See also* psychotechnology
   cognitive, 132
   Light Stage, 93–95, 94f
   metaphor, 7
   transmission, 139
   trauma mediation, 16
   trauma mediation, psychiatric recognition, 66–67
   traumatography, 12–17
television
   9/11 images, 6, 19, 68, 75–78, 140, 142
   Challenger space shuttle explosion, 76
   flashbacks, 74
   Oklahoma City bombing, 76
   trauma through, 66, 162n4 (*see also* screen trauma)
   violence on, 66
television cameras
   Closed Circuit TV, 56
   surveillance, 56, 159n56
testimony. *See also* videography, testimony; *specific topics*
   absence, 111
   algorithmic-holographic, 91 (*see also* New Dimensions in Testimony (NDT))
   algorithmic processing, 106
   audience interpellation, 88
   broadcasting, 141
   connections and dialogue, 88
   conversational model, 92
   future proof, 92–96, 94f
   holographic (*see* New Dimensions in Testimony (NDT))
   lapses and parapraxes, 98
   law and psychoanalysis, 25–26
   media temporality, 96–100, 98f, 99f
   from narrative to database, 106
   performative aspect, 51
   as remediation, inverted, 61–62
   as remediation, of traumatic memory, 107–111
   videotaping, 141
Testimony: Crises of Witnessing in Literature, Psychoanalysis and History (Felman and Laub), 57–58
The Photoplay: A Psychological Study (Münsterberg), 115–116
The Sorrow and the Pity (Ophüls), 45
"The Sword of Damocles," 119
Those Who Were There, 45, 46f
time-axis manipulation, 56–57, 96
time-critical media, 96
time-offset interaction, 101
To Have Done with the Judgment of God (Artaud), 30
Totem and Taboo (Freud), 71
transmission. *See also specific topics*
   communication *vs.*, 60–61
   definition, 139
   non-symbolic inscription of temporality, 145
   psychological, 139
   radiophonic, 18

transmission (*cont.*)
   technological, 139
   of trauma, 59–60, 160nn70–71, 74
   of trauma, potential, 11
   of trauma, private into collective, 37–38
   videotestimony, 57–61, 160n76, 161n78
   wounding, 139–145
trauma
   bearing witness, 48–49
   body to mind transfer, 6
   carrier groups, 28
   code and, 135, 140
   collective, 27
   collective, transmission of private trauma into, 37–38
   communication difficulties, 7–8
   conflation, via trials, 40, 155n72
   cultural, 27–28
   cultural, narrativization, 27–28, 39
   distant, 65, 75–80
   Eichmann trial narration, 26
   genealogy, 8, 67
   image, 74
   intergenerational transfer, 10
   literal impact, 8–9, 16
   literalistic view, 86
   meaning, 6
   media, 4
   media, war, and, 61–66
   media construction, 38, 154n57
   media memory, 9
   mediated performance, 40, 155n68
   as mental wound, media and, 16
   mimetic model, 8–9
   mind and media, 4
   as modern malaise, 8
   as outside gone inside without mediation, 4–5
   as privileged recollection, 17
   as protective shield breaking, 4, 148n14
   recounting, historic or literary, 8, 149n22
   referential literality, 8, 149n22

   representational operation, 11
   screen, 65–86 (*see also* screen trauma)
   social, 27–28
   social and moral reckoning, 136
   social construction, 28
   technologically mediated, psychiatric recognition, 66–67 (*see also* screen trauma)
   through media, DSM-V, 79–80, 140
   transmission, 59–60, 160nn70–71, 74
   transmission, potential, 11
   trials, 25–28
   vicarious, 65, 107, 142
   work-related, through media, 59
trauma film (paradigm), 17, 68, 71–75
trauma theory, 56
   antimimetic strand, 74, 135
   Holocaust testimony, 44
   media theory, 4
   Meek's critique, 9–10
   mimetic streak, 135
   proliferation, 3
   seminal studies, 44
traumatic index (Boder), 87, 97, 108
traumatic memory
   discretization, 130–131
   emotional brain, 125
   film-like, 1–2
   flashback, 126
   impact and bearing witness, 88–89
   indeterminable data, 108
   looping effects, 67
   mind and media, 2
   modern developments, 112
   neurobiology, 125
   as non-declarative, 125–126
   photography, 10
   remediating, 107–111
   structural disassembling and reassembling, 130
   talk therapy failure, 126
   time element, 6–7
   understanding, changed, 130
   unresolved past, 6–7
   as unresolved past, 6–7
   Wilkomirski Holocaust, false, 1–2

traumatic neurosis, 6, 66. *See also* PTSD
traumatography, 6–11, 132, 149nn20, 22
   analog, 132
   cinematic, 75
   definition, 140
   digital, 132
   technology, 12–17
   videographic, 45 (*see also* videography, testimony)
Trezise, Thomas, 101, 104, 158n34, 169n47
trials
   Eichmann (*see* Eichmann trial; radiocasting trauma, Eichmann trial)
   trauma and, 25–28
   trauma conflation via, 40, 155n72
trigger warnings, 84

unbidden image, 73
uncanny valley, 99–100, 99*f*, 134, 169n35
Unclaimed Experience (Caruth), 4–5
unconscious mnemic systems, 4
Understanding Media (McLuhan), 14
Unheimlich (unhomely), 100

Väliaho, Pasi, 113, 137
van der Kolk, Bessel, 125–127, 129
van Dyke, José, 104
vicarious traumatization, 65, 107, 142
videography, 140
   meaning, 157n18
   traumatic material, 3
videography, testimony, 43–64
   absence and presence, 111
   archive, media, and trauma, 45–48, 46*f*, 157nn16, 18
   bearing witness, 20, 47, 48–49, 50, 52, 63
   as celluloid *megilla,* 53
   historical context, 43–44
   Holocaust Survivors Film Project, Yale, 45–48, 46*f*, 89, 140, 156n8
   Holocaust testimony and trauma theory, 44

materialities of communication, 45
media, trauma, war, 61–66
non-synchronicity, testimony and viewing, 103
processing, 53–57, 159nn46, 52, 55, 56
psychoanalysis and media, 43–44, 156nn3–4
recording, 48–53
reversible continuity, 54
as therapeutic, 51–52
transmission, 57–61, 160n76, 161n78
vs. virtual testimony, 103, 141
VIDEOPLACE, 117–118
virtual environment desensitization, 120
Virtual Iraq (BRAVEMIND), 113, 121–124, 122*f*, 130, 137
Virtual Reality (Rheingold), 119
virtual reality, term origins, 119
Virtual Reality Exposure Therapy (VRET), 84, 113. *See also* VR therapy
virtual reality therapy. *See* VR therapy
Virtual Reality Therapy: An Innovative Paradigm (North), 119
virtual testimony, 141
   vs. videotestimony, 103, 141
virtual testimony, digital future of traumatic past, 87–111, 141
   Boder's wire recordings, 87–88, 88*f*, 156n7, 167n1
   David Boder, 87–88, 88*f*
   New Dimensions in Testimony, 89–111 (*see also* New Dimensions in Testimony (NDT))
   recording and preserving stories, 87
virtual therapy, digital future of traumatic past, 112–138. *See also* VR therapy
Virtual Vietnam, 120–121
vision, de-objectifying, 158n31
Visual History Archive, 106–107
Vlock, Laurel, 45, 47, 89
VR therapy, 112–138
   for acrophobia, 171n31
   code and trauma, 135, 140
   definition, 118, 120

VR therapy (*cont.*)
  development, 113
  digital PTSD, 129–135
  effectiveness, 113
  experience, 113
  exposure media, 124–129
  Full Spectrum Command, 121
  history of, short, 117–124, 122*f*
  limbic system therapy, 126–127
  pre-trauma conditioning, 132–133, 137
  psyche and techne, 120
  psychotechnology, 114–117, 115*f*
  PTSD, 113, 129, 141
  PTSD, memory pathology, 112
  PTSD, Virtual Iraq (BRAVEMIND), 113, 121–124, 122*f*, 130, 137
  PTSD, Virtual Vietnam, 120–121
  STRIVE, 132
  studies, 113–114
  suggestive content, 134
  talk beyond therapy, 135–138
  as talk therapy alternative, 123
  VIDEOPLACE, 117–118
  Virtual Vietnam, 120–121

Walker, Janet, 3, 4
war
  Gulf War conflict, 83
  Kittler on, 21
  media, trauma and, 61–66
  modern mechanized warfare, on communication, 13
war correspondents, PTSD, 79
war neurosis, 66. *See also* PTSD
War of the Worlds, 152n129
Weaver, Warren, 139
Weiss, Allen S., 29
Welles, *War of the Worlds*, 152n129
When Eichmann Entered My Home, 32, 33
Whitehead, Gregory, 29, 30
Wilkomirski, Binjamin, 1
Winthrop-Young, Geoffrey, 21, 62
wire recorder, 87–88, 88*f*, 167n1
witnessee, 104–105
witnessing witnessing, 101, 104
witness to witnessee, 104–107
wounding transmissions, 139–145
writing-down system, 14–15, 43
writing machines, 114
Writing of Disaster, The (Blanchot), 57

Yale archive, Holocaust Survivors Film Project, 45–48, 46*f*, 89, 140, 156n8
Yoman Ha'mishpat, 24, 24*f*
Young, Allan, 6, 8, 67, 112
Young, James, 53, 55

www.ingramcontent.com/pod-product-compliance
Lightning Source LLC
LaVergne TN
LVHW021713060526
838200LV00050B/2647